Bike Touring

"Probably the best bicycle-touring handbook currently available . . . highly recommended."

American Library Association Booklist

"Detailed, in-depth information on all aspects of touring."

Bicycle Journal

"Should prove particularly useful to those for whom bike touring is a novel venture."

Publishers Weekly

"What you need to know to make touring on wheels a happy experience: technical information on bicycles, equipment, tour-planning, living on the road, camping, lists of organizations and suppliers."

Country Journal

Bike Touring

The Sierra Club Guide to Outings on Wheels

Raymond Bridge

Illustrated by John Lencicki

The Sierra Club, founded in 1892 by John Muir, has devoted itself to the study and protection of the earth's scenic and ecological resources—mountains, wetlands, woodlands, wild shores and rivers, deserts and plains. The publishing program of the Sierra Club offers books to the public as a nonprofit educational service in the hope that they may enlarge the public's understanding of the Club's basic concerns. The point of view expressed in each book, however, does not necessarily represent that of the Club. The Sierra Club has some fifty chapters coast to coast, in Canada, Hawaii, and Alaska. For information about how you may participate in its programs to preserve wilderness and the quality of life, please address inquiries to Sierra Club, 530 Bush Street, San Francisco, California 94108.

Library of Congress Cataloging in Publication Data

Bridge, Raymond.
    Bike touring.

    Bibliography: p.
    Includes index.
1. Bicycles and tricycles.   2. Cycling.
3. Camping.   I. Sierra Club.   II. Title.
GV1041.B73   796.6   79–474
ISBN 0–87156–250–2

Cover design by Jon Goodchild
Book design by Jill Casty

Printed in the United States of America
10 9 8 7 6

To the memory of
Shirli Voigt,
whose spirit endures
with the mountains she loved
and with her friends.

The Sierra Club Outdoor Activities Guides

Simple Foods for the Pack, by Vikki Kinmont and Claudia Axcell

Walking Softly in the Wilderness: The Sierra Club Guide to Backpacking, by John Hart

Wildwater: The Sierra Club Guide to Kayaking and Whitewater Boating, by Lito Tejada-Flores

Bike Touring: The Sierra Club Guide to Outings on Wheels, by Raymond Bridge

Starting Small in the Wilderness: The Sierra Club Outdoors Guide for Families, by Marlyn Doan

Exploring Underwater: The Sierra Club Guide to Scuba and Snorkeling, by John L. Culliney and Edward S. Crockett

Weathering the Wilderness: The Sierra Club Guide to Practical Meteorology, by William E. Reifsnyder

Backcountry Skiing: The Sierra Club Guide to Skiing Off the Beaten Track, by Lito Tejada-Flores

Caving: The Sierra Club Guide to Spelunking, by Lane Larson and Peggy Larson

The Complete Bicycle Commuter: The Sierra Club Guide to Wheeling to Work, by Hal Zina Bennett

Land Navigation Handbook: The Sierra Club Guide to Map and Compass, by W. S. Kals

Contents

Introduction

BICYCLE TOURING HAS much in common with backpacking, kayaking, canoeing, ski touring, and mountaineering. All are forms of self-propelled travel and bring the participant into close contact with the natural world, in both its gentle and harsh moods. There is a special appeal to bicycle touring, however, that makes it unique among the various types of self-propelled travel. The bicycle is a practical means of transportation as well as a recreational vehicle, and this fact has important implications.

In terms of convenience, bicycle touring is an extremely attractive outdoor activity, particularly for those who live in densely populated regions a long way from large tracts of public land. When the closest good backpacking trail is a couple of hundred miles away, a weekend backpacking trip involves a tiresome amount of driving, a considerable investment of time and money before and after the trip, and a lot of pressure and fatigue because of the tight scheduling needed to mesh the normal work week with the weekend's recreation. Especially for those with busy schedules, the logistics of driving from San Francisco to the High Sierra or from Boston to northern New Hampshire are likely to limit the number of trips that can be taken to just a few each season.

In contrast, pleasant bicycle tours can begin from most people's front doors or, at worst, a few miles from home. The enjoyable part of the trip thus can be had without hours of driving time at each end. Instead of having to be ready for your trip before the weekend arrives, taking off directly from work on Friday afternoon, and getting to the trailhead late that night, you can make leisurely preparations Friday evening, get a good night's rest, and start from home on Saturday morning.

In our world of limited resources, cycling also offers important advantages to those who are concerned about the consumption of non-renewable energy sources. Many of us who consider ourselves environmentalists and conservationists are quite pious about the fossil fuels wasted in daily commuting. We are irate about people who drive their cars to work every day without passengers rather than using public transportation, car-pooling, or riding a bike. However, we often are quite complacent about our own use of fuel for recreation. A commuter who drives 15 miles to his job travels 150 miles in a normal work week. Thus a wilderness lover who drives 200 miles to the mountains and back every other weekend is using more gasoline, all other things being equal. A single vacation drive to Alaska may require more fuel than a commuter consumes in an entire year.

One should not belabor this comparison, but for those concerned with fuel conservation there is clearly a good case for taking some bicycle tours that start close to home in preference to wilderness treks that require long drives. Even bike trips that start some distance from home often are easier to manage by public transportation than are backpacking, ski touring, kayaking, mountaineering, or canoeing trips. Wilderness jaunts generally begin far from heavily traveled transportation corridors, while bicycle tours often start at the nearest freeway interchange, wherever an interesting side road winds away from the main thoroughfare.

For these reasons and others, it seems particularly appropriate that the Sierra Club should publish a book on bicycle touring, a means of travel that brings the outdoors enthusiast close to his or her natural surroundings while having little damaging effect on them. Besides its attraction as a challenging recreational activity, bicycle touring enables us to enjoy the open country with less negative impact on the earth.

The Rediscovery of the Bicycle

Our culture is dominated by the automobile, and few Americans today are aware of how popular the bicycle was in the United States at the beginning of the century. Bikes were a major form of both transportation and recreation at that time. Bicycling clubs were tremendously popular everywhere; the bicycle-built-for-two was one of the standard vehicles for courtship; and bicycle racing was one of the major spectator sports in the country. The roads were paved for bicyclists, not for automobiles. It is ironic that in the United States, which was once the home of innovative bicycle design and manufacture, bikes were reduced for many years to being just children's toys. Even now, there is only one major manufacturer of high-quality bicycles in the United States, and most of the accessory components on today's American-made bikes are imported from Europe or Japan.

The bicycling renaissance which began a few years ago is almost certain to continue to flourish as more people begin to discover the bike's advantages as a practical form of transportation and as a satisfying and healthful recreational activity. Consider the advantages of a bicycle as a means of getting around: it is relatively cheap and very economical of resources; it does not consume fossil fuels, except for the relatively small amounts of fuel needed to build it and to manufacture replacement parts, such as tires and brake blocks; it is compact to store, can be easily picked up and carried into a house or other building, and is readily taken along on any well-designed means of public transportation; it is a personal vehicle, like a car, so that it is ready to go when and where you are; and it is fast enough and efficient enough to cover considerable distances in reasonable time periods, with speeds of ten to twenty miles per hour being typical, depending on circumstances. If we removed the current incentives for sprawl in our major population centers and introduced a few minor reforms, within a few years the bicycle again could become one of our major forms of everyday transportation. For many of us it can be that today.

Many people who buy touring bicycles as recreational vehicles soon find that their bikes are the best way to get around the rest of the time too. For traveling reasonably short distances, a bike often is faster than a car and a lot less frustrating. Riding to work or school can help you stay in shape for longer weekend rides, while providing a welcome form of relaxation at the beginning and end of each day. In contrast with automobile commuting, which often leaves the driver tense and out of sorts, riding a bike to and from work usually is pleasant. Finally, because of its practical uses, the purchase of a rather costly, good-quality bike actually may save you money in the long run, unlike most other purchases of recreational equipment.

Styles of Bicycle Touring

Bicycle touring covers a lot of ground, both literally and figuratively. Tours range from fifteen-mile Sunday-morning jaunts down the road to cross-country trips covering thousands of miles. Riders who tour include casual cyclists who never cover more than ten or twenty miles a day and dedicated athletes who regularly ride several hundred miles a week. For multi-day touring, camping cyclists carry everything they need on their bikes while other riders prefer to stop at hotels every night. Some large group tours are followed by a car known as a "sag-wagon," which hauls the group's luggage and picks up any riders having trouble.

Bicycle touring refers to any traveling by bicycle simply for the pleasure of riding the roads, as distinct from using a bike as a commuting vehicle or for the sport of bicycle racing. A lot of touring consists of one-day rides on the weekend that cover a circuit fairly close to the cyclist's home, perhaps with longer trips on full weekends or on vacations. The varieties of touring that can be enjoyed even near home are amazing. Since good cyclists are quite likely to cover a hundred miles or so on a day's trip, there is a wide range of possibilities starting from your own doorstep, and if some sort of public transportation or shuttle is used to get to or from the ride itself, the choice of routes becomes enormous. From my house, a day's ride can take me well out onto the Great Plains, along rolling foothills country, or into the mountains, across the Continental Divide and back. As you tour more and more, you are likely to discover more interesting country seamed with delightful back roads near your home than you ever imagined.

Cycling Equipment

Any how-to book of this sort devotes a great deal of space to equipment, because questions about gear naturally preoccupy anyone starting out in a sport. Mistakes in choosing equipment can be disheartening as well as expensive. Bicyclists in general probably are even more equipment-oriented than are other self-propelled travelers because of the nature of the sport. The touring bicycle is a precision machine that is highly sophisticated in design, and the cyclist is quite dependent on its proper functioning. Hence, much of this book consists of information about bikes and accessory equipment.

The cyclist's concern with equipment is not frivolous. In contrast to the bicycle tourer, the backpacker's ability to travel is not really affected by the design of the pack carried, providing it doesn't fall apart completely. One pack may make load carrying somewhat easier than another, particularly for an out-of-shape novice, but an experienced backpacker will not double the mileage he or she covers by trading in an old Trapper Nelson frame for the newest frame design on the market.

The cyclist is far more dependent on equipment. You can have a lot of fun riding around on an old clunker, but you cannot make long tours on it. Good equipment does not make you a good cyclist, but even the best cyclist cannot ride well without equipment that meets certain minimum standards. Light weight is even more important to the cyclist than it is to the backpacker, simply because far more ground is covered; the additional work required to carry a few extra pounds is quite significant. Safety considerations also are important. Making a fast downhill run can be suicidal on a bike that is weak or that has bad brakes.

While concentrating on equipment, however, it is important to keep your main goals in sight. Equipment provides a means of having a good time, of directly experiencing the world around you, and of enjoying the companionship of friends, all in a way that does not waste valuable resources. It is these goals that make bicycle touring worthwhile; don't lose sight of them among the shiny bicycle parts and fancy touring bags. I hope that the information included in this book on technique, conditioning, and equipment helps you to plan interesting tours, get out on the road with a minimum of fuss, and enjoy some good riding and touring.

Part One

Touring Styles and Skills

Chapter 1

The Varieties of Cycle Touring

A BICYCLE IS the ideal vehicle from which to see the country. It allows you to travel fast enough to move from one place to another at a reasonable rate, but slow enough to permit you to enjoy the scenery along the way. It is quiet, so you can hear the songs of the birds and the wind in the trees. The touring cyclist isn't cut off from his or her surroundings by walls of glass, metal, and noise. Other means of transportation are sometimes more efficient to get from one place to another or to negotiate rugged wilderness, but for *touring*—traveling along the back roads, and seeing what a region is like—the bicycle is unsurpassed. The interstate highway system enables automobile passengers to travel from the Atlantic to the Pacific without seeing much except gas stations and motels. It is impossible to do that on a bike.

The bicycle is suited for a wide variety in styles of travel. You can go first class or steerage, eat beans or filet mignon, putter along at your leisure or ride at a pace that would challenge a trained athlete, stay in luxury hotels or make do with improvised campgrounds. You can carry huge quantities of gear and supplies (none of it superfluous), as those who tour primitive roads do, or take only your water bottle, repair kit, and a mid-morning snack. Aside from costs, there are many logistical and aesthetic differences among the various approaches to cycling, and some of these are discussed in this chapter to better acquaint the beginner with the variety of touring styles possible.

Day Trips

Going out for rides ranging from a few hours to a full day naturally is the most common sort of touring because it is fun, convenient, and the best training for longer trips. Even with a busy schedule, it nearly always is possible to get up early one morning each weekend to go out and ride. Expert riders who push hard can put in fifty or a hundred miles this way and be home by ten in the morning with practically a full day ahead of them.

Some people prefer to cycle alone, at least on many of their day trips, but the great majority tour with a few friends or with a regular group of riders. Group touring enjoys great popularity because riding with others is a pleasant social activity and because it is easier. Much of the energy expended by a cyclist is used to overcome wind resistance, particularly in fast riding, and several riders sharing the effort of breaking the wind can move a lot faster than one person riding alone. If you do not have friends who ride, try to find a bike club in your community with some riders near your level of experience and interest. Local bike shops are a good place to ask about clubs. If you can't find a club, try putting up notices at the bike shops, describe the kinds of rides you like to take, and indicate that you'd like company.

Some recommendations for conditioning and preparation for longer tours are given in Chapter 2, but the prescription for the novice is simple—get out and ride. The more day trips you take, the more accustomed your body will become to riding and the more you will learn about the sport. As your physical condition and ability improve, your speed will pick up and you will gain in endurance.

One important rule to observe at the beginning is to start your trip back at a reasonable point. Clearly, if you ride down the nearest road until you are sore and tired, the return journey is likely to turn into an experience you will not soon want to repeat, particularly if a head wind comes up that you have to fight all the way home. Physical discomfort is likely to be more acute for the beginning cyclist than for the novice in almost any other sport because of the unaccustomed and unnatural pressure between the bicycle's seat and your own. Work up to longer distances gradually.

The variety of day trips is astonishing; there is something for every taste and every ability. Try a morning ride to a nearby town, starting early and arriving at a pleasant cafe in time for breakfast. Hedonists who haven't yet experienced the joys of early-morning riding can go for brunch instead. Spartan types can strive to emulate riders who take early morning trips to the mountains covering seventy-five miles, including thousands of feet of climbing, and then return home in time for breakfast.

The key to enjoying bicycle touring from the beginning is to find your own mood, pace, and pleasure. Don't let someone else convince you of what you should like. If you start out with a group that is far more experienced or stronger than you are, you are likely to learn to hate cycling, unless you are quite athletically inclined. The difference between highly conditioned riders and neophytes is incredible. Start at your own level and have a good time, even if your long-term goal is to ride much more extensively. Couples should be wary of riding together all the time if they have widely disparate abilities. It is a good idea to ride with people at your own level of competence at least some of the time, so that you feel neither held back nor pushed too much by your companions. One positive aspect of riding with a larger group is that it can split into smaller groups of roughly equal ability, with the better riders moving faster on a longer circuit, perhaps with the groups getting together at a predetermined spot along the way.

Longer Tours

Any tour lasting several days or longer is bound to entail logistical problems that don't exist on day trips. You have to have a place to sleep and a way to secure your bike while doing so, and you need to plan both the overall tour and distance you intend to cover each day. The day tourist simply rides in one direction for a time and then turns around and comes back. On a long trip, you should consider the consequences of mechanical breakdown or bad weather more carefully. Getting soaking wet in an afternoon rainstorm may be of no real importance when you are out on a ride near home and can simply take a hot shower, change, and put a pan of soup on the stove. If you are camping outdoors, however, it may be a lot harder to warm up and dry your clothes.

There are several basic approaches to making longer tours, each with many variations. The most important distinction is the way you plan to spend your nights. You can stay in conventional public accommodations—hotels and motels if you're traveling in the United States. This style of touring requires the least extra equipment, so you can travel very lightly burdened. The investment required is fairly low unless you buy special clothing to meet the sometimes contradictory requirements of bicycling and dining in hotel restaurants. The daily cost of this type of touring can be quite high, however, so it generally is the most expensive style of long-distance cycling.

The bicycle tourist who relies on public accommodations also is dependent on their location, schedules, and routines. There may not be any motels along the road you want to ride. Automobile drivers, to whom such establishments cater, tend to stay up late and sleep late; so, if you are trying to get to bed early and start riding early in the day, you may find that noise levels make early sleep impossible and that the restaurant doesn't start to serve breakfast nor the desk open until two hours after you want to leave. You may need to make advance reservations that lock you into a particular schedule. Finally, depending on your own tastes and ingenuity, you may find yourself taking enough dress clothing to make up for the weight you hoped to save by not camping.

At the other extreme is the bicycle camper, who carries all the necessities on the bike except for food and water, which can be picked up at stores along the way. Bicycle camping typically requires the

1. Typical luggage arrangement using front and rear panniers.

highest initial investment, since camping supplies and appropriate packs for carrying them have to be purchased or made; however, daily expenses are minimal or non-existent, so that over the long run this is the cheapest sort of touring. The camper has to carry more weight on the bike than any other tourist, but he or she is the most free from external constraints. Except in cities and a few areas with severe restrictions, like Hawaii, it is nearly always possible to find a place to camp, so reservations do not have to be made and daily schedules can be revised at will. The camper also is free to spend an occasional night at a motel or hotel during a spell of nasty weather or because the mood strikes, while the cyclist without any camping equipment along cannot suddenly decide to camp for a couple of nights.

In between the extremes of conventional lodging and camping is the possibility of staying at the inexpensive accommodations operated by American

Youth Hostels or one of its worldwide affiliates. Hostels originated in Europe to provide places to stay for self-propelled travelers. They usually were dormitory-style accommodations, often in people's homes or barns, with lots of camaraderie and a minimum of frills. Guests were expected to do their share of the chores and to bring their own sheet-type sleeping bags to go between the mattresses and blankets provided. The lodging was very inexpensive, meals often were available, and no one was allowed to use the hostels who did not arrive under his or her own power. Things have changed in some hostels, but these conditions generally still apply. Except in a couple of European countries, there are no age limits for staying in hostels. (Additional information on hosteling is included in Appendix III.)

Hostelers need to carry only an uninsulated sleeping bag made from old sheets or nylon fabric, along with personal clothing and toilet items, so they travel with virtually the same weight as those using public accommodations but stay more cheaply. Planning details may be much more cumbersome and the itinerary more limited, however. There are a lot fewer hostels than hotels, especially in the United States. Space at a hostel often has to be reserved well in advance and the hours are limited, so that you may arrive in a city with plans to leave your bike and equipment in the hostel only to find it closed until five in the evening. Hours and locations change, too, and it is not always possible to keep track of the changes.

Obviously, it is quite possible to stay at hostels part of the time to add a little convenience to a camping trip or to reduce the overall expenses of a tour that relies mainly on hotels and motels. You can work out many other variations in lodging to meet your needs.

Large groups of bicycle tourists, whether camping or using public accommodations, sometimes arrange to have a car, known as the "sag-wagon," follow the group at a distance. The sag-wagon carries the group's luggage, provides assistance in case of mechanical breakdowns, and aids riders having physical problems. The sag-wagon may be driven by a non-rider willing to follow at the slow pace set by the bicyclists, or the task of driving may be shared by members of the group. With a large number of riders, each person needs to spend only a short time driving. The sag-wagon enables the cyclists to ride at a faster pace by reducing the weight carried and to enjoy the pleasantly responsive feel of their bikes that comes with light loads. Riding is more pleasant this way, although many cyclists find the technique less aesthetically pleasing and more complicated logistically.

The Importance of Weight

The real key to freedom on the open road is light weight—both in your bike and in the gear you carry. You can have a good time pedaling around on a heavy three-speed or even on an old balloon-tire monster, but you won't be able to go nearly as far. Your range is more limited and so is the length of time that you can comfortably pedal. Those wide mattress seats that look so comfortable don't feel that way after ten or twenty miles. The reduction of weight, therefore, is probably the most important art in long-distance bicycle touring. If you are a casual cyclist, it means that the weight of the bike will be low enough to permit enjoyable riding for moderate distances. If you are a serious rider, it will enable you to cover many miles each day for as long and as far as you want to tour.

Oddly, quite a few experienced cyclists who realize the importance of a lightweight bicycle don't apply the same logic to the gear they take with them while touring. It is common to see someone spend a hundred dollars to shave a few ounces off a bike and then carry along a ten-pound sleeping bag designed for car camping. Your equipment and touring style always should be thought out to keep weight to a minimum. Riding will be far more enjoyable and you will see much more if you plan your gear carefully, whether you are visiting museums in Italy or camping in national parks.

Even without sag-wagons, it is quite possible to make extended tours with your bike and still avoid heavy loads. By choosing your equipment carefully, you can reduce your luggage to twenty-five pounds or less, even on a camping trip. A good touring bike with traveling and camping gear thus can be set up to weigh between forty and sixty pounds. On a tour where you are staying at houses, hotels, or hostels, the load can be reduced still further. With this sort of weight you can travel quickly and with reasonable effort, touring the continent or the world. Your bike will be lively and responsive, and you won't feel as though you are pedaling a Mack truck.

Many of the chapters that follow are focused on reducing weight, especially in accessory equipment. Lightweight equipment does not have to be less comfortable or less effective, just as a lightweight bicycle is rarely inferior in performance to a heavier one. The cyclist simply has to put a premium on efficiency, whether in sleeping bags or dress clothes.

The reward for this attention to equipment and weight is comfortable, relaxed cycling and the freedom of the roads that goes with it. You can take off on your bike and ride for a week or a month without polluting the air or draining your pocketbook too quickly. The bicycle can become an incomparable instrument of freedom for the footloose traveler. With it you can cross North America or tour Europe, climb over mountain passes or meander through New England woods, ride highways or explore back roads. You can pack your trusty bike in a carton, take a bus or a plane to the start of your ride, and be an hour into your tour while your fellow passengers are still getting to their cars.

Chapter 2

Riding Techniques, Safety, and Training

PEOPLE INTERESTED IN touring by bicycle start from very different levels of skill, ranging from those who have never ridden a bicycle to regular commuters and racers. Any discussion of riding technique is bound to be too elementary for some, while assuming too much background knowledge for others. For rank beginners who do not know how to ride a bike and for those unfamiliar with the basic workings of the standard ten-speed bicycle, an appendix on basic skills has been included at the end of the book (see Appendix I). This chapter assumes that you know how to ride a ten-speed, work the gears, operate the brakes, and so on. It concentrates on improving your basic riding technique and developing some of the special skills that are useful for bicycle touring.

Fitting and adjusting a bicycle are discussed in the following few chapters, and it is important to make sure your bike is correctly set up for you before you do much touring on it. A bike that is too large for you or improperly adjusted may be dangerous, particularly in traffic. It certainly makes it impossible for you to ride efficiently or comfortably, so it is worth paying a good deal of attention to the fit of the frame, height of the seat, handlebar stem length, and so on.

Cyclists who use their bikes primarily for commuting on city streets may pick up a good deal of conditioning, but they tend to develop an inefficient cycling style. Though a ten-speed bike works well for commuting, the design is far from ideal for that purpose. Rapid shifting comes only with a good deal of practice, and you can't shift after stopping at a light unless you lift the rear wheel off the pavement so that you can spin it. Most commuters and casual cyclists pedal too slowly in too high a gear. This habit is not just inefficient; on long tours it can cause injuries. It may be difficult to learn to use toe clips when you do a lot of stop-and-go riding in traffic. Toe clips also may be hard on dress shoes and can be dangerous in some commuting situations. (Toe clips are metal springs with straps attached that are used to hold the feet in position on the pedals.)

Efficient Pedaling

One of the most important habits to learn in the early stages of cycling is pedaling effectively with as little effort as possible. It is easiest to learn good pedaling technique on the open road rather than in traffic. Find a place where you can do a little uninterrupted riding to learn to use toe clips, practice pedaling, and work on your technique. It also is worth trying some of the exercises suggested in Appendix I for improving your control; they can be useful for almost any cyclist. Cycling shoes, toe clips, and cleats (see Chapter 12) allow much more efficient pedaling and are helpful in preventing some types of injury.

Like most bad habits, poor pedaling style becomes ingrained, so it is much easier to learn to pedal well in the first place than to improve later on. The biggest mistake that most beginners make is to pedal slowly in a high gear, putting a lot of effort into each stroke. This is inefficient because the body can do far more work if the legs move quickly, making less effort with each individual revolution.

When you start out, before you have learned to turn the pedals quickly and to move your feet in circles, fast pedaling seems unnatural and ineffective. Persevere! If you watch racers or accomplished touring cyclists on the road, you will see them spinning the pedals at what appears to be a very fast rate. Racers typically spin in the vicinity of 90 to 100 revolutions per minute, while strong touring cyclists usually turn the cranks at 70 to 90 rpm. You should rarely drop much below 60 rpm. The brisk tempo will be inefficient at first, because it takes time to learn to turn your feet in little circles, but once you have learned, you will be able to maintain such speeds for long periods without tiring. The steady rate at which you turn the pedals and cranks is known as *cadence.*

Another important reason you should learn to cycle at relatively fast cadences is that pushing higher gears at slower speeds is very hard on the legs, especially the knees. Sore knees rarely bother cyclists who pedal at relatively fast cadences, even when they are riding day after day over long distances. Even strong, experienced cyclists often have knee trouble from cycling in high gears at slower cadences, however.

The most effective cadence varies from person to person, but it is largely a function of training. Simply try to concentrate on pedaling at the maximum comfortable speed for a while, shifting down and pedaling faster rather than pushing harder at a slower cadence as the wind comes up or as you start up a hill. Once you have had a reasonable amount of practice at fast rates, you will be able to determine the best cadence and develop a feel for it.

Beginning cyclists tend to exert pressure on the pedals only when they are pushing straight down. In fact, you probably will find that when you push down with one leg, you actually are resting the other leg completely on its pedal, so that your working leg is not only pushing the bike forward, but lifting the weight of your other leg at the same time. Try to pedal all the way around the circle. Start pushing forward when the pedal reaches the top of its path and continue pushing back at the bottom. Most importantly, lift the leg that is on the upstroke rather than allowing it to hang like a dead weight on the pedal. This action of pedaling all the way around the circle made by your feet takes a number of forms. When you angle your feet to push backward at the bottom of a stroke and forward at the top, so that the muscles and flexing of the ankles play a significant part, the action is known as *ankling*. Generally, ankling is done at fairly slow cadences and disappears at higher rpm's. Racers who are sprinting or standing up on the pedals to climb hills (see below) may pull up on the rear pedal as well as pushing on the forward one. (Toe clips are necessary for this and for efficient pedaling generally.)

The important thing to concentrate on is not ankling, nor trying to power the bicycle with your rear leg, but simply moving both feet in circles rather than just up and down. You can feel the greater efficiency immediately whenever you do this, and eventually it will become habitual. By pulling your back leg up instead of letting the pedal push it up, you do not eliminate the relaxation period for the working muscles. An entirely different muscle group is used to lift the leg than to extend it. By sharing the load of powering the bicycle between muscle groups, you can ride much more effectively and will tire less quickly.

The only way to develop good cadence is to practice. One or two days' riding can give you the idea, but it is not sufficient to ingrain the motions in your muscles and nervous system so that you can pedal for hours at a fast cadence, moving your feet in those efficient circles that eat up miles and hills. When you are riding for fun, check your cadence occasionally and concentrate on it. Try riding for ten minutes at a faster cadence, but not at a faster speed. Drop down a gear and pedal faster. Relax your legs and attempt to spin fast without having them tense up. The cadence at which you can pedal efficiently will improve gradually with practice.

When you are riding up a hill and your legs begin to tire, you almost always will find that you are letting your back leg be pushed up by the pedal. Lift it during the upstroke, even if you only pull up hard enough to lift the weight of the leg. You'll find that the grade suddenly becomes easier since the load on the muscles at the front of your thighs has been reduced. The same trick works if you feel the soles of your feet becoming numb during a long ride. The reason for the numbness is that you have weight on your soles all the time. By pulling up slightly on each upstroke, you can take pressure off the balls of your feet during part of each rotation of the cranks. This almost always relieves the numbness.

Shifting Gears

The basic method of shifting gears on a touring bike is simple enough. The gear-shift levers simply tighten or loosen the cables attached to the front and rear *derailleurs,* which are devices designed to push the chain from one gear to the next. If you don't completely understand the shifting mechanism, you can either turn the bike upside down or hang it from a line attached to the seat so that you can operate the pedals with one hand and shift the gears while you watch.

There is some finesse involved in using gears well, however. Their function is to allow you to pedal at the most efficient cadence, regardless of wind resistance or the steepness of a hill. Though this ideal cannot always be met, well-chosen touring gears allow you to approach it. Once you have learned your gear pattern well, you should be able to shift smoothly and quickly to the correct combination as the gradient of the road changes or as you come around a corner into the wind. The touring cyclist does not have to be as quick at shifting as the racer, but it is a real help to know your gears well so that you don't have to fumble or use trial and error to get into the right configuration. It is essential to learn to shift when you need to, rather than pushing too high a gear as beginners often tend to do. Straining too hard at the pedals results in rapid muscle fatigue.

The ease with which you can turn the pedals

and the distance that the bike travels for each revolution the pedals make depend on the ratio of the number of teeth on the front gear to the number on the rear one, as well as on the size of your wheels. The different ratios that result depend on the number of teeth on each cog, and the pattern of shifting in order from the lowest to the highest gear depends on the particular combination on your bike.

Once you have a basic feel for your bicycle, it is worth spending some time learning the exact shifting sequence. Then, when you are riding along into the wind and feel yourself straining just a bit to keep up a good cadence, you can shift into the next lower gear easily without breaking your rhythm. To facilitate learning the sequence, you may want to make a chart of your gears similar to the ones illustrated in Chapter 5 and tape it to your stem or handlebars. Once you've learned the sequence well, you can dispense with the chart. In the process of learning, you may find that you have a lot of duplication of ratios or some jumps that are too large. If you want to redesign the ratios, refer to the discussion in Chapter 5.

Climbing Hills

For the beginner, the most frequent mistake in riding up hills is to try to stay in a relatively high gear too long, allowing the legs to tire and perhaps even grinding to a halt in the middle of a belated effort to shift into a lower gear. Shift down early and save your energy until you have built up the conditioning and ability to budget your strength that are necessary to ride up hills at a faster pace. This is particularly important on long, hilly tours. You may burn up the first few hills only to find your stamina ebbing before you are even halfway through the trip.

Weaker riders may occasionally encounter hills that are simply too long and steep for them to pedal up. It is no sin to get off your bike and walk. Be careful to stop before your legs give up the effort completely, so that you don't take a tumble. A bike loaded with touring gear slows to a halt quickly on an uphill grade, and you might find yourself struggling to remove your foot from the toe clip as the bike starts to fall.

The two alternatives to getting off and walking the steepest hills are to install a "granny gear" or to improve your conditioning. Methods to devise low gear ratios are discussed in Chapter 5, but the best approach usually is to add a third chainwheel to the crankset and turn the bike into a fifteen-speed. If the third chainwheel is the same size as the largest rear cog, the rear wheel will turn only once for each revolution of the pedals, enabling the cyclist with modest abilities to ride up nearly any slope the tires will stick to. This is an especially attractive solution for the older rider gradually working back into good physical shape who doesn't want to destroy his or her knees trying to push a gear that is not low enough on a long, hilly tour.

On the other hand, if you are in good shape and keep the load on your bike reasonable, you won't need to introduce the problems of a fifteen-speed system in order to get up any hill you are likely to encounter. You should be able to train your muscles to push you and your luggage through the mountains at just about the same speed that you can ride on the flats, because you can make up enough time on the downhill runs to recoup the little that you lose on the climbs.

Concentrate on your pedaling technique when you are climbing. When you are working hard on a hill, you tend to revert to sloppy pedaling, pushing down hard on the downstroke and neglecting either to move your legs in circles or to lift the rear leg. When climbing hills, you need all the help you can get, and it is amazing how much difference it makes when you suddenly remember to clean up your pedaling technique.

Strong riders can climb hills either in the normal sitting position or by *honking,* standing up and moving the body forward over the pedals, with the hands gripping the hoods of the brake levers (see Figure 2). Honking can be a very efficient way to climb hills, but only if you practice it a lot. It is very tiring at first, until you have developed the technique well and have conditioned the muscles that are used. A rider who is proficient at this technique can honk for long periods without tiring, however, and the method can be extremely useful on extended climbs. A touring cyclist may honk for an entire climb or may do so for only part of the time to make use of a different muscle group. Short desperate spurts are inadvisable, however. They are fatiguing and require awkward gear changes.

2. Honking up a grade, a technique common among racers, also is an effective touring method.

For the tourist, honking should not be an all-out effort. The idea is to get into a rhythm, almost like walking, using a considerably higher gear than you would riding in the seat, with a much slower cadence to match. Honking in a low gear forces you to move fast because you are using your body weight to push the pedals down. With a low gear you pedal fast and hard, and you tire rather quickly. With a properly chosen gear, your body weight drives the pedals down, but the pace is slow enough so that you don't begin to pant.

Don't try to learn to honk up hills until you are already in fairly good cycling condition. It is a vigorous method of pedaling even though it gets easier with training. Practice honking for progressively longer periods on short rides, starting out by honking up only the last part of a hill. Just shift into a higher gear as you near the top, stand up on the pedals, and try to keep up a slow rhythm without losing speed. You will soon get a feel for the proper gears to use when riding up hills in the seat and when honking, so that you can shift back and forth easily.

One of the bonuses of the honking technique is that when you reach a hill too steep to ride in your lowest gear while sitting, you can still honk up the grade. An additional advantage is that your rear end gets a rest. I like to ride out of the saddle for a little while once or twice an hour just to give my bottom a rest. On a hilly course it's easy to do this just by honking up some of the grades.

Descents

On steep descents with a lot of curves, it usually is best to ride with your hands "on the drops," or "hooks," the lowest position on the handlebars. This is the most stable position because your center of gravity is low. Be ready to brake at any time and be conservative about speed. A high-speed descent can be a lot of fun, but avoid riding at the limits of control. You have to allow for the possibility that a car may come around a corner on the wrong side or that you may come upon a chuckhole or patch of sand just around a bend.

Practice both normal braking and panic stops with and without touring equipment on your bike. Don't ride the brakes since overheated pads and rims can cause fading of the brakes or tire blowouts. To slow down, brake regularly for short intervals. For panic stops, the trick is to learn just how hard you can brake without having the bike skid out from under you. Use both brakes, but be cautious about applying maximum force to the rear brake. As you brake hard, your center of gravity tries to move forward, and most of the force is applied to the front wheel, which therefore has more traction. Panic squeezing of the rear brake will lock the back wheel and cause a skid. Be particularly careful when braking on curves, sand, and gravel. Brake and turn before you hit a patch of sand, straightening out and letting up on the brakes as you cross it. Whenever you are braking hard, it is best to sit as low and as far back as possible in order to minimize the tendency of the rear wheel to lose traction.

Riding in Traffic

Unfortunately, no matter how well you plan your tours, learning to ride safely in traffic is an essential skill. You may succeed in avoiding heavy automobile traffic most of the time and mitigate the contacts you have by riding with groups of cyclists, but the gas-burning behemoths cannot always be escaped. Knowing how to cope with cars can be a matter of survival; it also helps keep your anxieties at a reasonable level when you do have to share the road with a lot of automobiles, so that your tour will not be spoiled and you can ride with a clear head.

The matter of dealing with cars is so important that it is going to come up again and again in this book. Cars weigh at least ten times what you do and often are traveling at much higher rates of speed. Whether you are in the right or not, if you have too close an encounter with an automobile, you lose. The car is unlikely to sustain any damage worse than a few dents and the driver a few legal hassles, while you almost certainly will receive some nasty injuries.

Since your life is on the line in traffic, it behooves you to become as skillful as possible, to make your judgments conservatively, and to control the situation as best you can. This last point is particularly important. *The cyclist should be careful and courteous in traffic but should never be timid.* There are many traffic situations in which you must be reasonably aggressive to ensure your own safety. An overly nervous rider will be pushed into dangerous situations again and again by the drivers of cars, out of a combination of ignorance and in some cases even hostility. Remember that when you are riding a bicycle, you have the most to lose in an accident. Take the initiative and don't allow yourself to be placed in jeopardy.

A good example is the situation in which you are riding at the right side of a narrow, four-lane street with frequent hazards along your side of the road. If you pull to the far right edge of the road, the flow of traffic will continue in the right lane, passing by you with very little clearance. If there are parked cars, large pavement breaks, grates with openings parallel to the direction of the road, debris, or other obstacles in your path, you are likely to find yourself forced again and again to make emergency stops or to swerve into traffic on short notice. Even if cars can pass you with room to spare, drivers of larger vehicles often feel compelled to squeeze by, too, though there may not be enough room. Furthermore, drivers of cars often shy away from other large vehicles out of fear or nervousness and may pull into your path as a result. They know that they will be damaged more by another car than by you.

In such a situation you should either get onto another route or, if that choice is not open, ride in the *middle* of the right-hand lane. Take the space you need and hold it. The drivers behind may hate you, but they won't hit you. Remember, you pay tax money to maintain the roads, and you have a perfect right to use them. You are doing the public a service by riding your bike and not polluting the air we all have to breathe, so if your safety demands that you ride in the lane, do it!

This assertive attitude is important in many traffic situations. Don't be a lout and don't deliberately obstruct traffic. Wherever there is reasonable room to ride outside the flow of traffic, be courteous, but make sure that you have enough space to ride safely at all times. Anticipate trouble ahead, and when you see that you need to take a lane to maintain a safe amount of space on the road ahead, use the first opportunity to move out into the lane far enough so that the next car won't be tempted to squeeze by. This way you clearly establish your position in the lane, rather than leaving the driver with the impression that there may be enough room to pass.

Another common problem occurs at intersections. If you are riding along the right-hand edge of the road, it often is advisable to pull into the center of the right-hand lane at a stop light to avoid the possibility of a driver who wants to make a right turn accelerating right into you as you start up. In states where a right turn is permitted on a red light, I often move to the space between the far right lane and the next lane over, in order to allow drivers turning right to proceed. This also saves me from being trapped if a driver fails to signal or suddenly changes his mind and turns right as I am starting through the intersection.

One of the reasons that you need to be assertive in traffic is that many drivers are not really used to bicycles and do not take account of them. A driver of a car simply may not see you because his or her eyes are not trained to register bicyclists. Highly visible clothing helps, but sometimes it also is necessary to ride in a spot where you cannot be missed. The degree to which motorists are aware of cyclists varies a good deal with the locale. In some areas drivers are quite used to sharing the road with bicycle riders, while in other regions you must assume that drivers either will not be aware of you or will fail to yield the right-of-way to you.

It is important to realize that nearly all motorists regard bicycles as essentially stationary objects. Thus, one of the most common accidents and one of the hardest to avoid occurs when a driver accelerates past you and makes a hard right turn into a side street, running directly over you. Since the car approaches from the rear and may cross your path suddenly, it may be impossible for you to brake in time to avoid either hitting the car or being run down. The main reason that automobile drivers do this so frequently is that they do not allow for the bike's speed. Even though you may be moving at more than twenty miles per hour, drivers are likely to see you in the same way as they see a lamppost and ignore your existence once they have passed you, automatically assuming that you are not going fast enough for your speed to be significant to their actions.

You must remain constantly aware of this problem whenever you ride in traffic along a road with side streets; keep an eye on each car that passes you as you approach intersections and driveways. Cars making left-hand turns and those coming out of side streets and driveways also must be watched carefully, but they are generally less hazardous to the alert bicyclist because they can be seen from a distance and watched. Be careful of cars accelerating through a changing light to make a left-hand turn, however.

There are a host of other traffic hazards that a cyclist must learn to watch for, and not all of them involve moving vehicles. Beware of people in parked cars when you are riding at the edge of the traveled portion of the street. A car door opened suddenly in front of you can make for an unpleasantly rapid stop.

Learning to ride well in traffic takes time. Various aspects of riding in traffic are discussed later in this book, but much information is included here, too, since a lot of people just starting to tour have to begin in town and don't get out on the open road until they are in better condition. If you are really nervous about in-town traffic, then do your touring out in the country with a group of cyclists large enough to effectively claim a portion of the road. If necessary, drive out to a reasonable starting point in your car.

On the other hand, if you do ride in traffic daily, you have to develop an odd combination of attitudes and talents. You have to learn to be both considerate and assertive. Keep your own survival uppermost in your mind. Don't block a motorist's way if you can avoid it, but control your road space. Let drivers know what you are doing, even if they don't want to notice. Ride in a straight line and stay aware of what is going on in front of and behind you. Learn to take quick glances to the rear with a small rearview mirror that attaches to your glasses, sunglasses, or helmet (see Figure 3), or take glances backward by ducking your head. Be ready to brake quickly at any time.

Whenever you change lanes or make turns, signal your intentions clearly or make eye contact with the driver who will be affected. When making left turns at intersections, it often is best to let a car run interference for you. Ride defensively, always assuming that the cars around you may create a hazard for you at any time, and be ready to take appropriate action. Assume that pedestrians and

3. Rearview mirrors are helpful in traffic to keep track of dangerous situations developing behind you. One type attaches to glasses or sunglasses; other models clip to helmets.

other cyclists will do stupid things or will appear suddenly from behind parked trucks or blind corners. Watch out for turning buses and trucks. On a sharp turn, the side of a long vehicle passes a lot closer to the corner than the front wheels do; drivers frequently don't allow for this fact and thus may wipe you out if you happen to be waiting at the corner around which they are turning.

Make a strong distinction between streets on which traffic moves slowly, with many stops, and those routes that have coordinated lights or few signals so that the traffic moves at high speeds. On streets with stop-and-go traffic, a strong cyclist can ride with the traffic, generally matching speeds. If you are used to city riding, you can handle such streets reasonably safely. On the other hand, a street that carries high-speed traffic and has many side streets but no shoulder or bike lane is inherently dangerous. Avoid this type of street if you possibly can. The irritation suffered by drivers forced to slow down for a cyclist on such routes is considerable, and you are likely to cause an accident. If you must ride on such streets, however, don't cringe at the side. Drivers will experience dangerous moments of indecision trying to decide whether to pass or slow down. If there isn't room for cars to pass, ride in the middle of the right lane so that motorists realize they must wait for spaces in the far lane to pass you.

Obey traffic laws whenever possible, even though these laws in the United States are not designed with the cyclist in mind. The bicycle generally is defined as a vehicle and has the same rights and obligations as other users of roads, though the bicycle often is legally required to stay as far to the right as reasonably possible—an unfortunately vague guideline. Remember that you have to look out for yourself, however, and that it is occasionally safer to ignore traffic rules. If you have no choice but to travel on a heavily used street with no room for a car to pass, and the right-hand road edge has a wheel-trapping rain grate at every corner, ride out in the street where you are safe. It is a lot saner to argue your right to use the roads in court than to get yourself injured or killed obeying an ordinance passed and enforced by those who ply the roads in automobiles.

If you begin to encounter traffic after riding for some distance on a road, be sure to loosen the straps on your toe clips immediately. It frequently is necessary to make quick stops in traffic, and tight straps are a real hazard, particularly if you are wearing cleats. Helmets, lights, and reflectors are discussed in Chapters 11 and 12; they are more important in traffic than anywhere else. If you ride in a city at night, you are in dangerous territory. Even if you have the best lighting systems, many motorists won't see you; so if you have to ride at night, be aware that you are virtually invisible to drivers. Pay attention also to the road hazards discussed below, since they become doubly dangerous in traffic, where you often have little advance warning of a chuckhole or oil slick and where your escape routes frequently are blocked.

Road Hazards

There are many obstructions on public roadways that pose hazards to you or to your bike. Holes in pavement can be large enough to badly damage a wheel or to swallow it so deeply that you and the bike are pitched forward into the road ahead. Gratings and expansion joints in bridges frequently have slits running parallel to the roadway that are wide enough for your wheel to disappear into, though an automobile tire can pass over them easily.

It is important to remain constantly watchful for these and other hazards and to be ready to stop or take evasive action in time.

When crossing bumps that are not large enough to require you to stop, you should slow down, stand up on the pedals, and hold the handlebars loosely between your fingers and thumbs. The two ends of the bike then rise up separately, each pivoting on the other wheel. As the front wheel hits the bump, instead of having a third of your weight pressing down on the handlebars, which are pushed up rapidly, your weight rests on the pedals and cranks, so your mass is lifted a lesser distance around the pivot of the rear wheel. (The frame of the bike acts as a lever, lifting your body on the fulcrum of the rear axle. Weight on the pedals is closer to the fulcrum and does not have to be moved as far.) The same thing happens when the rear wheel hits the bump. Rising up from the seat and holding the bike loosely as it crosses a bump thus eliminates the impact on your hands and posterior and reduces the stress on the bike.

Railroad and streetcar tracks crossing a road always are hazards to cyclists, particularly when they come in at an angle to your bike's path or weave back and forth. These tracks are slippery, and they can trap your wheels as well as creating jarring breaks in the pavement. Always try to cross tracks at a right angle, especially with the front wheel. The wheel may be turned momentarily as it crosses the tracks, as long as the angle is not too acute. Metal surfaces are particularly hazardous when they get wet because they become very slippery.

Grate openings and bridge expansion joints can be killers, especially if you come on them suddenly at high speed. If you find yourself on a collision course with this kind of obstacle and it is too late to stop, swerve as you brake. This usually results in a skidding fall that does a lot less damage to you and the bike than the sudden stop and header caused by allowing the wheels to fall into a grating slit. If you are aware of such hazards in your community, point them out to the appropriate officials, noting that they could be sued for any injuries resulting from such dangerous conditions. If you receive no response, you may want to document your warnings ostentatiously, perhaps by sending a new batch of letters via certified mail and keeping copies, so that it is aparent that you are building a good legal case for the first cyclist who gets hurt due to these dangerous conditions. It is remarkable how many county commissioners and city officials suddenly take notice when they receive such warnings.

Oil patches are found frequently at intersections, where cars drip oil as they wait at lights. The oil can be quite slippery, so you should be very careful when making a turn. Metal manhole covers also are fairly slippery. They are worse when they get wet, as are fallen leaves. A light rain causes streets to become very slick, worse than they are after a downpour. This is especially true following a long dry period. The water forms a suspension with the oil that has gradually collected on the street, making an extremely slippery combination until enough rain has fallen to wash the oil away. Take extra care in all of these situations, especially with wet leaves, cobblestones, and diagonal crossings of railroad tracks.

One technique you may want to practice once you have become a fairly proficient cyclist is jumping your bike, which can prove useful in dealing with chuckholes and similar obstacles that you encounter unexpectedly. It also may be used as a planned crossing method under safe conditions. As you approach a bump or chuckhole, simply jump up lightly and then pull the bike up to you with the handlebars and toe clips. Keep the bike on a perfectly straight course until the tires have regained traction. Usually it is not necessary to actually lift the wheels from the ground, but simply to unweight them for a moment. The bike actually can be jumped into the air when necessary. This technique is most easily applicable to unloaded and lightly loaded bikes, though it also works with a fairly heavily loaded machine when the weight on the front and rear wheels is well balanced (see Chapter 13). Don't try this technique on the road unless you have practiced it in advance. The main difficulty is to learn the timing of the anticipatory jump. An easier tactic for dealing with obstacles is to pull only the handlebars up, which at least prevents loss of control and damage to the front wheel.

As with traffic problems, the most important habit to develop in avoiding road hazards is to be alert to what is going on around you and to what is ahead on the road. If you remain constantly aware of what is behind you, then you know at all times whether it is safe to swing out into the main roadway to dodge obstacles. By the time a hazard appears, it is often too late to check behind you.

Hazards frequently can be anticipated even before they are seen. At railroad crossings it is reasonable to assume that there may be bad pavement breaks. Storm drains generally are placed at corners. Exhaust coming from the tailpipe of a curbside auto should warn you that a driver may be pulling out, and a head visible in the window or a rearview mirror of a parked car is a warning to watch out for an opening door. A large piece of glass typically is surrounded by many smaller bits, and so on. It is easy to go into a trance-like state while humming along a highway, but a bike travels too fast for this attitude to be safe. Stay alert.

Trucks and Other Open-road Problems

Trucks are the major threat cyclists have to contend with on the open road (see Figure 4). This is particularly true on highways that provide direct routes between towns or attract commercial traffic for some other reason. It is always best to tour on roads that have little or no truck traffic. The next best alternative is to choose highways with wide lanes and large shoulders. Even though legislators and highway patrol officers have a difficult time understanding the fact, a modern superhighway is

4. *Trucks pose the greatest threat to the long-distance touring cyclist. In addition to being a direct physical threat, trucks create dangerous air blasts and often cause other motorists to ignore the bicyclist.*

sometimes far safer for cyclists than an old U.S. highway. When the older roads carry heavy truck traffic they can be extremely dangerous. Superhighways that have wide shoulders and few exits often are fairly safe, if not very aesthetic. Traffic speed is about the same, and modern trucks leave no room at all on older, narrow roads.

Trucks pose several distinct dangers. The direct one is obvious, particularly after your first experience of riding along the side of a narrow, two-lane highway with a big double-trailer semi approaching from each direction at seventy miles an hour. Sometimes the only alternative is to dump into a ditch. The second problem is the air blast from a truck. Combined with wind, this blast sometimes can be very hazardous, blowing the cyclist into the path of traffic or causing him or her to lose control of the bike. Finally, trucks often cause the drivers of other vehicles to threaten your safety. The driver of a car instinctively shies away from a truck, whether there is a bike in the way or not. A motorist who might normally give you a wide berth and drive around you carefully will often do something dangerous because of a truck. Expect it.

Dealing with the air blasts from trucks is largely a matter of anticipation. You have to realize how the truck's wave and any existing wind are going to combine. If you are riding along the right side of a two-lane road, for example, with the wind blowing from the left, the initial air blast from a truck passing either way will add to the wind and tend to blow you off the road. Immediately after this first blast, however, as the truck goes past, you will be sucked into the roadway, particularly if you have just made a correcting swerve to try to keep from being blown off. Finally, there are likely to be several less forceful, bumpy waves following the truck. The faster the truck is traveling and the more wind there is, the stronger all of these effects will be.

Loosen your toe clips in advance if you anticipate trouble, and be ready to dismount if necessary. Usually you can handle all these effects without difficulty once you are used to them, but the blast sometimes can be quite dangerous. One of the worst situations occurs when there is a wind already blowing from the right, tending to push you into the road. A fast truck passing close by you can cause a very strong blast just after it passes that may blow you into the roadway in front of any traffic following the truck.

The most important habit in dealing with any traffic on the open road is to be predictable. Make it an absolute rule never to pull out to the left without looking behind you first, either with a rearview mirror (see Figure 3) or directly. Always ride in a straight line. Bicyclists who weave along the road are a menace, particularly to themselves. You should be able to ride along a line without deviating more than a couple of inches in either direction. Indecisive or wavering movement is always dangerous on the road because drivers start paying attention to it, rather than to their driving. A motorist who is trying to figure out whether you will suddenly pull out is likely to become so fixed on you that he doesn't notice a vehicle coming in the opposite direction until the last minute, at which point he may swerve.

You are least likely to be clipped if you ride in a straight line and appear decisive. If you look as though you will get out of a car's or truck's way, the driver may keep to the right, expecting you to get out of the way, rather than moving out to pass. Hold your section of the road. Always be aware of what is going on in front of and behind you, however, so that you can get out of the way if a dangerous situation develops. If, for example, a driver sees one truck passing another a short distance ahead, the driver is likely to react to that situation without even noticing you. The big guys get the attention, and you have to take care of yourself. Learn to use your ears as well as your eyes. With practice you can gauge a vehicle's size, speed, and location fairly well with your ears.

If you are riding two abreast along a road, you should have an understanding at all times of which rider is to pull ahead when a car approaches. If you both sprint for the front at the same time, the outside cyclist won't be able to pull in. Usually the rider to the left pulls ahead and right, with the rider to the right slowing down if necessary.

All these problems are not the everyday fare of the touring cyclist. It is surprising how many pleasant roads there are with little traffic. Drivers normally are courteous, including the drivers of trucks. Usually the worst difficulty you have to deal with are the honks of well-meaning motorists, a startling irritant that can't be avoided. Once in a while, though, you are bound to be caught on a bad section of highway with a lot of truck traffic and poor shoulders. Be prepared to deal with the situation.

Overcoming Wind Resistance

Much of the energy expended by a cyclist is used in overcoming wind resistance, even when the air is still. The drag exerted by the air becomes more significant the faster you travel, particularly when you are carrying touring gear that projects from the bike. This is why a far greater effort is required to increase your speed from twenty to twenty-five miles per hour than from fifteen to twenty miles per hour. Somewhere around ten miles per hour the wind

resistance begins to consume more than half the
energy produced by the rider. The faster you ride,
the greater the energy required to overcome air
drag. Amazing speeds can be reached by a rider
sheltered by a wind screen pulled ahead of the bike
by a motorized vehicle, simply because the wind
resistance is eliminated.

There are two ways in which a cyclist can reduce
the energy expended to overcome air drag. One is to
use a streamlined riding position. Ride with your
hands in the lowest position on the handlebars some
of the time, particularly when you are trying to
make good time. It takes practice to get used to this
lower position, but it is worth learning to do it
comfortably. Riding on the drops is particularly
valuable on a long day's ride when a head wind
comes up.

A group of cyclists riding together also can
provide wind shelter for one another. By riding
behind another cyclist, you can greatly reduce the
pedaling effort required. This technique is known as
drafting (see Figure 5). The closer you follow, the
more effective the technique is, particularly when
you are riding fast. Trade off the lead frequently so
that the work of breaking the wind is shared.

Drafting effectively requires some practice
because you have to ride with your front wheel close
to the rear wheel of the cyclist ahead of you. This
means that your control and attention have to be
good and that the rider ahead has to be used to
riding in a straight line. Watch a group of racing
cyclists train sometime. You'll notice that they keep
a steady, fast pace, something they can do because of
long training and because they share the work of
breaking the wind. The technique can be just as
valuable for touring, though you naturally will not
want to use it all the time. It often is more fun to ride

5. Drafting, a technique that enables two or more riders to ride considerably faster, yet with less effort, than the solo tourist. One rider breaks the wind, and each succeeding cyclist follows closely behind.

side by side and chat. On a day when you want to cover a lot of miles, however, or in the afternoon when a head wind is sapping your strength, drafting provides valuable assistance.

When there is a wind coming partly from one side, drafting is done by fanning out diagonally so that each cyclist is in the wind shadow of the one ahead. Be careful of traffic whenever you are riding abreast or in a diagonal formation.

Riding in the Wind

Neophyte cyclists are unnerved by hills; experienced ones are rattled by winds. Every hill has a top that can be reached in a reasonably short period, usually with an effortless descent on the other side. Winds can blow against you for hundreds of miles, however. A steady head wind can easily cut your progress in half, and one lasting for several days can either destroy your carefully planned schedule or exhaust you if you manage to stick to your plans. When there also is heavy truck traffic, the combined effects of the wind and the air blasts from passing trucks can have terrifying effects on your control of the bike.

Many winds are fairly predictable, and it makes sense to take them into account when planning your tours. Pay attention to the normal wind patterns during different seasons in areas where you tour a lot, and try to use them to your advantage. The most common pattern is that the air tends to be calmest in the early morning and breeziest in the late afternoon. It makes sense, therefore, to get out early and stop early, since this greatly reduces your encounters with winds.

On a day tour that consists of a circuit, you may be able to pick a direction which will sometimes give you an advantage in wind direction. Along the coast, for example, in the absence of a passing weather system, the summer pattern usually is fairly predictable. On sunny days there is an onshore wind during the warmer parts of the day, when the sun is heating the land and causing the air there to expand and rise while cool air is sucked in from the water. During the evening and night the pattern is likely to be reversed, because the air over the land cools, becomes denser, and spills out toward the sea. In the mountains a similar pattern causes winds to blow up the warmed hillsides in the afternoons and cool air to blow down into the valleys in the evenings and nights.

Larger patterns are just as important. Cross-country bicycle tours usually are made from west to east because that is the direction of the prevailing winds. If you ride in the opposite direction, you must expect to fight head winds more often, particularly when crossing the Great Plains. Maps and charts that show prevailing winds for various locations during each month of the year can be obtained from the U.S. Weather Bureau. (See Appendix V for addresses.)

Besides drafting and adjusting the time of day in which you ride, there is not a lot you can do about the wind. Be sure to gear down and ride more slowly so that you don't waste more energy in fighting it than you can afford. Slowing down is inevitable when you are riding against a head wind, and it is better to do so voluntarily. Riding on the drops is far more efficient when you are riding against the wind, so it is important to be comfortable in this position. By adjusting your expectations, you can enjoy riding in the wind. Winds provide a challenge, giving you the feeling of being immersed in the elements, but it is important to realize that you won't be able to go nearly as fast or as far.

Training for Day Tours

Tours lasting a day or less naturally make up the bulk of the touring cyclist's fare. Day trips provide the necessary fund of experience for the beginning tourist, conditioning for the experienced bike tripper getting ready for a long tour, and are attractive activities in their own right on the many occasions when you don't have time for a longer trip. Day tours vary greatly from one another, both in terrain and difficulty. Experienced cyclists often make very long day tours, extending their physical abilities a good deal more than they would on a long tour because they know the next day will not make heavy physical demands on them.

Day trips require a minimum of luggage. You don't have to worry about changes of clothing or overnight gear. Since you normally pick good weather to ride far from home, less preparation has to be made for bad conditions—just enough to ensure a safe return ride, with a hot shower and warm change of clothes waiting at home. Repair kits can be kept to a minimum since routine maintenance is handled at home and a major breakdown can be dealt with by hitchhiking home or having someone pick you up.

Day tours range from easy jaunts lasting a few hours to endurance runs starting before dawn and ending after dark. Beginners are well advised to keep distances and duration at a moderate level. It takes time to build stamina, toughen parts of the body that are abraded during long rides, and develop an understanding of the limits of one's own body. All these elements are important on long rides. It is an unpleasant experience to be many miles from home, riding against a cold head wind, and have the body crash from depletion of glycogen reserves, suddenly cutting the rider's speed to a half or a third of what it was.

Start out by riding on tours lasting a few hours, perhaps with friends near your own level of ability. Then try longer tours at a more leisurely pace, gradually building up your endurance and experience. Try to keep up a steady rhythm, cutting rests short so that your muscles don't get cold and stiffen up. Maintain a good cadence and don't push too hard early in the ride, using up your strength too soon. Some groups like to picnic in a park or by a stream, some prefer to stop at a pleasant restaurant near the turnaround point, while others would rather snack along the ride, making no long stops at all.

It is worth carrying liquids and snacks on any ride of more than a couple of hours. It is quite possible to digest moderate amounts of food while cycling, even at a fairly hard pace. Drink and eat small quantities as you ride, anticipating your needs rather than waiting until you are hungry or thirsty. One tends to put off eating and drinking until the body is already suffering from reduced reserves.

Training for Longer Tours

Riding bicycles is fun, so that training normally is a pleasant experience. If you ride a lot throughout the year, you rarely need to think about training as such, unlike a racer who aims to peak for particular races. Many touring cyclists, however, plan long vacation tours on which they do a lot more riding than is normal for them, and training is important for enjoyment of these longer tours. This is especially true if winter riding is impractical where you live and you plan a spring vacation trip. Your enjoyment of the tour will be severely curtailed if you spend most of the trip exhausted and nursing saddle sores. The alternatives are either to plan very easy trips or to make sure you are in condition when you go.

Unless you are planning to do some very hard riding, you don't have to worry about the elaborate training routines of racers. The tourist's training formula is simply a scaled-down version of the one expounded by the great Belgian champion, Eddy Merxx: "Ride a lot!" It is best to get out at least a few times a week for a month before your tour, with a long ride every weekend that approximates the distance you plan to cover each day on the tour after the warm-up period. (Any long tour should begin with shorter, slower riding days to allow the body and mind to get into the rhythm of the trip.) This amount of riding is an absolute minimum for those who are *already* in good condition. Its purpose is to reaccustom your posterior to the bicycle seat and to tune up your legs. Anyone who is out of condition and intends to ride on a hard tour should plan to spend months getting in shape for it. If you are in this situation, either start very early or plan a series of easier tours and day rides that lead up during the season to your dream trip.

Since the primary goal of bicycle touring is to have fun rather than to endure pain, be sure you plan tours that are commensurate with your own strength and conditioning. You'll have more fun, and you'll keep cycling instead of quitting. If you dream about doing 150-mile-per-day tours, work up to them gradually and enjoy yourself along the way. Trying to do it all at once will merely break down your body and destroy your pleasure in cycling.

One specific training device that can be useful if you want to stay in shape during the winter, improve your technique, or get ready for a long trip early in the season is a set of rollers. Although rollers are used frequently by racers, they are rarely utilized by tourists. Personally, I prefer to stay in shape during inclement weather by running, but I have to go through the bother of toughening my bottom when the good weather arrives. Rollers eliminate this problem. They also provide an excellent way to improve your cadence and the smoothness of your pedaling action, as well as helping you to stay in shape.

Rollers consist of a frame with three rollers mounted on ball bearings. You ride your bike atop the rollers, balancing in the normal manner, even though you are riding in place. The rear wheel of the bike sits between two rollers and drives them, while the single roller under the front wheel is driven by a belt connected to the rear rollers. The effort involved in pedaling in any gear is similar to that expended on the road, except that there is no wind resistance; this makes it easy to practice spinning the pedals fast. Many cycling shops and mail-order companies sell rollers. There is a wide range in price between comparable sets, so shop around.

If you decide to try roller training, spend a little time carefully learning how to get on. I suggest that you work without toe clips until you have the knack. Set up the rollers in an area far from any sharp corners in case you should fall off. Rollers are easy to ride once you get the hang of it, but the feeling is a little weird at first. Rollers equipped with side platforms for mounting and dismounting are a bit safer. Once you have the knack, you can ride to your heart's content, as long as you don't go into a trance and steer the bike off the end of the device.

Part Two

The Touring Machine

Chapter 3

Touring Bicycles

BICYCLES USED FOR touring come in a great variety of designs, ranging from balloon-tire tanks to skittish racing machines. Touring can be interpreted in the broad sense to mean any traveling by bike simply for the pleasure of riding the roads, and you can have a good time on virtually any bike that doesn't break down in the middle of your ride. For a person who does a lot of riding, however, a bicycle that is designed specifically for touring can make the experience far more enjoyable. It is a lot more fun riding over a mountain pass on a bike that pedals smoothly and safely through sharp, steep corners, rather than requiring you to inch your way down or to risk your neck because the frame may not be strong enough to stand the stresses involved.

Touring normally is done on a derailleur-equipped lightweight bicycle, commonly known as a ten-speed or racing bicycle. Most touring bikes are ten-speeds, though there are a number of variations, including twelve- and fifteen-speed machines.

Bicycles designed for touring are subtly different from their racing cousins, although they look the same to the unpracticed eye. The nomenclature is further confused because the romance of the racing machine often is used as a selling point by bicycle manufacturers, whether the bike being described actually is designed for racing or touring.

Older-style English touring bicycles made for slower travel over rough roads are quite rare in the United States today, although you can still buy three-speed utility bikes that are similar. These bicycles are not discussed in this book because they are not suited to the style of touring advocated here. A faster, lighter bike is more suited to the conditions usually found in the United States and Canada. Our roads generally are good. In heavily populated areas, it may be necessary to travel a long way to get to the country, and it is more pleasant to be able to do this quickly. Once you are out on the open road, particularly in the West, it often is a long way between towns, or even gas stations. Sedate pedaling in an upright position on a heavy utility bicycle with limited gearing options requires a long time to cross such distances. As a consequence, the tourist would have to carry more water, food, and other supplies, making the bike still heavier. Touring is possible on any bike, but it is a lot more enjoyable for most of us on a fast, lightweight bicycle specifically designed for the purpose.

Until the last few years, nearly all derailleur-equipped bicycles available in the United States were made for serious bicyclists. Other adult-sized bikes were either heavy utility bikes or "English" three- or five-speed machines of medium weight. Now that ten-speeds have become popular, there is a glut of low-quality, mass-produced models on the market. It is important to understand the differences between high-quality ten-speeds with sophisticated designs and expensive components and the superficially similar bicycles designed for children or for casual neighborhood commuting. A department-store ten-speed is likely to be built from heavy, seamed tubing of high-carbon steel, which is much weaker than the seamless tubing made of high-strength alloys used in high-quality bikes. The tips of the fork on a department-store bike usually are formed by simply squeezing the tubing together and cutting out a pair of slots, while the pieces holding the axle in the rear are crimped into the tubing and spot-welded. The tubing of the frame is welded together, forming rather unreliable joints. The entire bike is heavy, unresponsive, and far too weak to withstand the rigors of touring.

Even within the category of sophisticated, lightweight bicycles, however, there are significant differences. Bicycles designed for racing are different from those designed for touring. This is especially true in the United States, where most racing during the last few years has been of the criterium type, involving many laps around a relatively short circuit and therefore requiring a very stiff bike that is quick in the corners. The touring bike is more closely related to machines used for multi-day road races. Another difference is that racing bikes usually are designed with quicker, more sensitive steering, which is less forgiving of inattentiveness on the part of the rider.

American roads generally are smooth and well maintained. (Everything is relative!) Because of this fact, it is possible to ride rather stiff bikes comfortably on these roads. For touring on rougher roads, it is better to ride a bike that absorbs more of the bumps and chattering, rather than jarring the rider and bouncing the bike into the air half the time. This is even truer when a heavy load of touring gear is carried. Thus, the old, classic touring bikes tended to be rather long, to have frames designed to absorb a fair amount of shock and vibration, and to use wheels and tires that also were intended to dissipate chattering from the road. Older racing designs also had to take road conditions into account, but they were stiffer in order to transmit as much of the rider's energy into forward motion as possible.

Several factors account for subtle changes in the standard designs of both touring and racing bikes in the past few years. Lightweight touring and camping gear has made it possible to tour with much lighter loads than were possible even a few years ago. Components have become more reliable and bicycle shops specializing in quality bikes are more common, so the amount of spare equipment and repair gear that need to be carried also has been reduced. Along with good roads, these factors have made it possible to tour comfortably on far stiffer and more responsive frames than were used a few years ago. Since a light and responsive bike is more fun to ride, there is now a major trend toward taking long tours on bikes that would have been considered racing machines a few years ago. The general tendency has been for both racing and touring bikes to become stiffer and more responsive.

This trend also is a function of taste. As you ride more, gaining experience and conditioning your body, your perceptions naturally change. A forty-mile tour may seem monumental when you first begin to ride, but once you have gained a certain amount of experience you are likely to view the same tour as either an easy day or a short training ride to be finished before breakfast. As you bicycle more often and travel longer distances, you learn the advantages of a high-performance bike. This is true for any experienced rider, not just for people who ride a couple of hundred miles in a day. A well-built, responsive bike is appreciated just as much by the cyclist who rides fifty miles per day, though he or she probably uses a gearing system different from the one used by the long-distance fanatic. For hill climbing, the rider with modest expectations and abilities probably appreciates light weight in a bike and equipment even more than the really strong rider does. Riders who aren't as strong have less energy to waste. In the past, cyclists in incredible physical condition used to accomplish amazing rides even when roads and bikes made the feats far tougher than they are now; today, modern equipment has made it possible for more people to ride long distances and enjoy it.

What to Look for in a Touring Bike

Specialized bicycles can be made to meet unusual circumstances, ranging from riding logging roads to bicycling on beaches. For most bicycle touring in the United States and Canada, however, the same general design meets the requirements of most people very well. There are a lot of fine points on a bike that can be changed, and some of these are discussed in the chapters that follow. For a beginner, however, any good-quality bike of the appropriate general design is suitable if it is the right size and has a gearing system that is matched to the terrain to be traveled and the capabilities of the rider.

The key word in this description is "good-quality," surely an imprecise term. The minimum standard is that a bike be strong enough to hold together through the rigorous demands of touring. A beginner does not need a frame custom-made

by a famous builder, but if you can possibly afford it, you should buy a bike that meets fairly
high standards in materials and construction
techniques. Department-store ten-speeds can be
used, but they really are not made to withstand the
hard use that a serious touring bike receives; so if
you have to ride one, you should recognize its
limitations. High-speed descents with such a bike
are unwise, and the possibility of frame breakage
should be considered on long trips. This type of bike
also is heavy and unresponsive compared to those
that are somewhat more expensive. In general, if
you want to save money on a bike, the best way to do
so is to learn enough to be able to judge the quality of
secondhand machines and then shop around until
you find a bargain.

Whether you are planning to buy a secondhand
bike or a new one, spend some time looking at and
learning about bicycles. Ride different bikes and
learn to recognize the feel of a good machine. The
basic components of a touring bike are discussed
briefly below and are covered in detail in the
chapters that follow.

The *frame* of a bike is its heart; components can
be changed to upgrade a bike, but a weak, heavy, or
unresponsive frame will remain the central feature
of a bad bike no matter how fancy the brakes and
crankset are. The standard diamond-shaped frame
has proven over many years to be the strongest
construction for its weight. Unless you feel strongly
about wanting a *mixte* ("women's") frame, avoid
buying one; it is weaker than the standard type. The
construction, fitting, and alignment of frames,
which are all critical, are discussed in Chapter 4.
Reject a bike with a frame deficient in any of these
respects, unless you are buying it only for the parts.

Adequate frames for touring bikes must be made

from steel with a high tensile strength, and the tubes must be brazed together so that the joints are strong. Both the tubing itself and the joining process are expensive, and this is the major reason that a bike of reasonable quality costs so much more than a kid's ten-speed, even though the two bikes may look superficially alike. A department-store bike has a welded frame, which is inherently quite weak, even though it weighs a lot.

Anyone planning extended bike tours needs to be as concerned with the strength of the frame as a hotshot racer. Though the average tourist doesn't pedal as hard as a racer, riding on rough roads with touring luggage subjects the frame to just as much stress. Luggage weight is harder on a frame than the weight of the rider simply because it is dead weight. When you hit a chuckhole, you raise yourself off the seat, allowing each wheel to pivot on the other one as it travels over the bump, and you absorb some of the shock with your arms and legs. The load on the luggage racks crashes directly down with the wheels, however, so the peak loads on the bike are higher.

The Basic Machine

Though there are many subtleties in the manufacture of each component of a touring bike, the basic design is quite simple, with the major components illustrated in Figure 6. The frame essentially consists of three triangles. One side of the *main triangle* is formed by the *seat tube,* which tilts back a little from the vertical and into which the *seat post* holding the seat fits. The *top tube* extends forward from the seat tube, usually horizontally, while the *down tube* runs at an angle from the front of the frame to the bottom of the seat tube. At this bottom juncture, the two main tubes

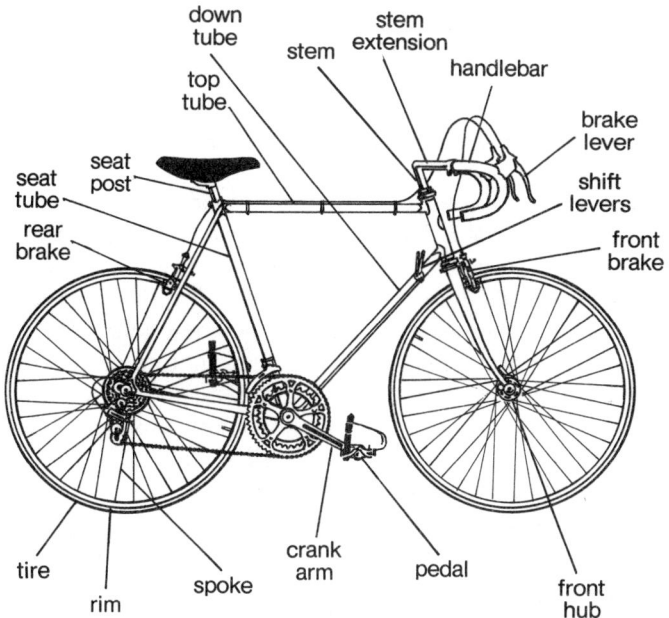

down tube
stem
stem extension
top tube
handlebar
brake lever
seat tube
seat post
seat
shift levers
rear brake
front brake
tire
spoke
rim
crank arm
pedal
front hub

6. A touring bike with most of the main parts labeled. The short tube at the front of the frame, into which the fork and stem fit, is the head tube. *The bearings that fit into it are known collectively as the* headset. *Note the toe clips and straps on the pedals; these are standard equipment on a touring bike because they improve pedaling efficiency.*

connect to the side of a short piece of larger-diameter tubing in which the axle for the pedal and crank assembly turns. This short piece of tubing is called the *bottom bracket.* At the front of the main triangle, the juncture of the top and down tubes usually is truncated slightly where it connects with another short, larger-diameter tube called the *head tube,* in which the assembly holding the handlebars and front wheel pivots. The *fork* holding the front wheel is attached to the *steering tube,* which pivots inside the head tube. The *stem* that holds the *handlebars* is inserted into the top of the steering tube and is clamped with a wedging device.

Two rear triangles made of smaller-diameter tubing extend on either side of the rear wheel. Each connects at the lower front with the bottom bracket and uses the seat tube for a third side. The lower tubes are called the *chainstays* and the upper ones are the *seatstays.* The axles of the wheels clamp into the *fork ends* at the ends of the fork and the *dropouts* at the lower back junctures of the rear triangles.

The rider propels the bike by pushing on *pedals* screwed into two arms called *cranks,* which rotate on the *crank axle* inserted in the bottom bracket. The cranks drive the front gears, called *chainwheels.* On a standard ten-speed there are two chainwheels, while the fifteen-speeds popular among tourists in hilly country have three. The *chain* itself is made up of links that fit over the teeth of the gears and pivot on the pins between. The chain drives the rear wheel with a ratchet device called the *freewheel.* (See Figure 8). Two *derailleurs* are used to push the chain from one gear to another, and the rear one also serves to take up slack in the chain. *Brakes* usually are a simple caliper type, using two pads to squeeze against each of the rims. Both the brakes and derailleurs are operated by means of cables connected to levers within reach of the rider.

Most of the moving parts of a touring bicycle operate on some sort of bearings, usually ball bearings, to minimize friction. There are bearings in the wheel hubs, freewheel, pedals, bottom bracket, and headset (in the head tube). In the chain, special rollers over the pivot pins minimize friction, and nylon or ball bearings are used for the wheels in the rear derailleur. The brake and derailleur assemblies, which move independently of the forward motion of the bike, have some parts in which friction is minimized and others in which it is desirable.

Buying a New Bike

It is worth getting the best bike you can afford. The "best" does not mean the "most expensive," however, particularly for touring purposes. There is a vast difference in price between components that are most fashionable among trendy riders and other brands of equal quality. Fashions generally are set by the top European professional racers, who use the brands they are paid to use. Furthermore, such equipment is designed to meet the needs of the racer rather than the tourist.

Though you should make every effort to get a good-quality bicycle, there is little reason for most beginning tourists to spend extra money for a custom-built machine, except in special circumstances. Of course, if money is no object, such a bicycle provides excellent service and is a pleasure to own. In general, though, there are presently enough suitably equipped bikes that can be purchased off the shelf that there is no need to have a bike specially built. You may want to specify a few changes, particularly in gearing, when you are pricing bikes and testing them, but it is not necessary to start from the ground up.

The single most important criterion for buying a bike is the fit, which is discussed in Chapter 4. All other considerations should be secondary to this one when you are shopping for a bike. No matter how low the price, a bike that doesn't fit is no bargain. Thus, some short people may find themselves to be exceptions to the statement that custom bikes are not needed. Most manufacturers make bikes with frame sizes ranging only down to 21 inches, and it is very hard to find anything lower than 19 inches or higher than 25 inches. If you are very short, you may need to query mail-order suppliers or have a frame specially made. Very tall people also may have a problem, though it is not quite so severe, since more adjustments are possible to accommodate their needs with a stock frame. People with bodies that are unusually proportioned—having long or short trunks compared with their height—also may have difficulty. The great majority of cyclists, however, can ride comfortably on a standard bike with the correct frame size, fine-tuning the fit by changing the length of the stem extension (see pages 179–80).

Even if you are going to put yourself in the hands of a salesperson, it is a good idea to learn as much as you can about bicycle design and equipment beforehand. You are likely to get a better-equipped bicycle and a better deal if you demonstrate a real interest in bicycles when you are shopping. Don't try to pretend that you know more than you really do; ask a lot of questions and find out all you can. Most people who work in bike shops do so because they love cycling. Many of them know a great deal about bicycles and love to talk about them. The different viewpoints you get from people may be somewhat confusing at first, but in the long run the things you learn this way wil serve you well.

The remainder of this section briefly describes the features and relative cost of the various grades of touring bicycles. Specific price ranges aren't given because they are changing so rapidly that they probably will be outdated by the time this book is read. Inflation affects the bicycle market more than it does most other markets since nearly all frames and components are imported; therefore, changes in the value of the dollar against Japanese and European currencies are crucial in the prices you have to pay. Even if you have a frame custom-made by an American builder, the materials used will be imported. This situation is beginning to change, but we still have a long way to go to regain the pre-eminence we had in the bicycling market at the beginning of the century.

Low-Cost, Quality Bikes

As was already mentioned, you should avoid mass-produced, department-store bikes. It is worth buying a really well-made bicycle if you can afford it. The chapters that follow provide many details concerning the features that are desirable in a touring bike, but there are a few obvious features you can look for to form a general idea of the category into which a particular machine falls.

The minimum standards necessary for adequate strength are that the bike be made from seamless, high-tensile-strength, steel-alloy tubing that is joined by brazing rather than welding, with separately made dropouts brazed in. A look at the dropouts and fork ends will reveal the cheapest bikes. Another obvious indication of low-quality bikes is the fork crown, the crosspiece linking the two fork tubes and the steering tube. In cheap bikes it usually is made of two or three plates of stamped, welded sheet steel. Better-quality bikes use cast or forged crowns or a piece that is stamped, formed, welded, and machined to form a one-piece crown.

Most bikes with brazed joints use lugs at the joints (see Chapter 4). The lugs are angled fittings into which the frame tubes slide and are brazed. Lugless brazed joints can be equally strong, though they are trickier to assemble. You can distinguish a lugless brazed joint from a welded one, but it takes a little practice. The brazing alloy fills the joint smoothly, with none of the tube metal cut away and without the sharp edges that welding produces.

Most low-quality bikes have one-piece cranks;

the cranks bend as they go into the bottom bracket and form the axle. Low-cost, quality bikes rarely use one-piece cranks. They may employ steel cranks attached to the axle with wedge-shaped pins called cotters, or they may use aluminum-alloy, cotterless cranks as shown in Figure 10.

The other components on low-cost bikes of satisfactory quality are likely to be somewhat heavier than the ones supplied with higher-priced machines. A low-cost bicycle is likely to have steel rims, though the tire size usually is 27 inches rather than 26 inches. The seat usually is made of plastic, perhaps with padding, with a steel seat post and clamp. The handlebars generally are made of steel, though the stem may be aluminum alloy.

Medium-Priced Bikes

Though the prices of everything associated with bicycling have gone up, one major improvement has been in the availability of high-quality components at relatively low prices. Up until quite recently, high quality was available only at premium prices. The Japanese have made many design innovations, but more important has been their raising of the standards of reliability, design quality, and attractiveness of moderately priced derailleurs, cranksets, stems, etc. This is a real boon to touring cyclists of modest means.

The components on most medium-priced bicycles are very good these days, differing from top-of-the-line products only in fine details, not in basic function or durability. In some cases they are better than their higher-priced competition in every respect except for snob appeal. Medium-priced bicycles should have cotterless, aluminum-alloy cranks; well-designed cranksets, headsets, and hubs; and aluminum-alloy seat posts, stems, handlebars, and rims. The brakes and derailleurs should be of good quality as well. The tubing usually is made by one of the well-known companies in the field, such as Reynolds, Vitus, Tange, and Ishiwata. The lugwork should be good, though it cannot be expected to be fancy. Fork ends and dropouts should be of the forged type rather than stamped. (For more details concerning frames, see Chapter 4.)

The next step up in quality is a bike on which the three tubes of the main triangle are made of double-butted tubing (see Chapter 4). Bikes at the upper end of the medium-priced range should have this feature and often include slightly better accessories and extras.

High-Quality Production Bikes

There is a wide range in price and quality at this level. Some differences are real, while others exist mainly as gleams in the salesperson's eyes. These bikes are made with high-quality double-butted tubing, such as Reynolds 531, Tange, and Columbus. The lugs, fork crowns, dropouts, and the like all should be of high quality, and the brazing should be impeccable. Some frames may be partly silver-brazed (see Chapter 4). The quality of all the components should be excellent. Such features as sealed bearings or brazed-on fittings for cables, brakes, water-bottle cages, and derailleur levers cost extra.

Where to Shop for a Bike

Spend some time visiting local bicycle shops and comparing the available bikes within the price range you can afford. Make notes of the differences in features. Ride the bikes you are serious about; there is no better way to judge them. Find out whether you can have any changes you might want made and what, if anything, they are going to cost. Inquire about tools and spare parts (see Chapter 10). The best time to get a good deal on equipment changes, spare parts, and tools is at the time you are buying the bike. Some changes, such as modifications in gear ratios, usually can be made at no cost when you purchase a bike. If you make them later on, however, the cost will be substantial. Once you have shopped around enough to have narrowed the choice down to a few bikes, price the total package you are interested in, not just the bike. You often can save a surprising amount of money this way. Bike-shop owners frequently have spare parts and tools, such as freewheel removers, lying around which they will throw in free or at low cost to get you to buy a bike.

Be sure to find out about the service and guarantees that you get with the bike. Most shops include adjustments after you have ridden the bike a few hundred miles, when a number of things need to be tightened or realigned. Also heed the suggestions in Chapter 10 about checking all thread standards and other specifications at this time.

There are several sources of bikes, including small bike shops, large discount bike stores, mail-order bike suppliers, sporting-goods stores, some regular discount houses, and secondhand sources. The cheapest possibility is a secondhand bike. Unless you buy a secondhand bike from a shop and get a guarantee, this is the trickiest way to buy, but you really can save a lot of money. It usually is better to avoid discount houses that sell everything from washing machines to toilet paper; their bikes rarely are much of a bargain, it is impossible to get service, and it often proves difficult to get satisfaction on a guarantee. These stores don't carry bike parts, so they can't replace or adjust a component that is defective. They have no choice but to replace the entire bike or to refuse to honor the guarantee. These same comments usually apply to sporting-goods stores, too, unless they truly specialize in bicycles.

Large discount bike stores may be quite good or rather difficult to deal with. Ask friends who recently have purchased from such a store about its reputation. Mistakes are bound to be made, and the question is whether anyone at the store has enough personal interest to care. In general, an experienced cyclist is safer in dealing with such places than a beginner is. You can get some excellent bargains, though, if you know what you are looking for.

If you buy a bike by mail order, you have to either assemble it and check it out yourself or hire someone to do so. This can negate some price advantages. You cannot examine such details as lugwork and alignment until you get the bike, and returning a bad bike costs time and money. (Even if you return the bike and receive a refund or a new bike, you probably have to pay shipping costs.) If you put the bike together, you have to be careful to check for mistakes as you go along. If you force a mismatched thread or glue a sew-up tire before finding the leak in it, the mail-order house probably won't take responsibility.

If all this sounds negative, it is. Though it is possible to make satisfactory mail-order purchases of complete bikes, there are some very strong arguments for dealing with a local bike shop: they can be very helpful; you can inspect the bike you are buying; changes you want can be made on the spot; and the shop usually makes a special effort to satisfy you because they want you to come back. By the time shipping charges are added in, mail-order houses often are not very cheap places to buy bicycles. Be sure you really are saving a lot of money before you order this way. (Components are a different story, however. You often can get excellent deals by mail order.)

Secondhand Bikes

If you want to buy a decent bike at a reasonable price, the best opportunities lie in the secondhand market, but there are qualifications. You must be able to wait until the right bike comes along. You have to learn enough about bikes to be able to analyze them carefully yourself, or have a knowledgeable friend who is willing to come along to check out the more likely possibilities with you. You need to be cool enough to avoid buying on impulse and must live in an area where there is a reasonable supply of bikes.

A good way to locate secondhand bikes for touring is to check bulletin boards in bike shops, classified ads, and college bulletin boards. Police sales of confiscated, unclaimed bikes are held in many cities. Garage sales are productive occasionally, but really are a long shot if you're going just to look for bikes. Do some checking before you bother to make a special trip to look at a bike. Ask about the frame size if the person selling the bike knows it; many people list tire size instead.

If you are thinking about buying a very high-quality secondhand bike from a local rider, it is a good idea to get a feel for the kind of person you are talking to. The ideal person to buy a bike from is someone who does more talking than riding and changes bikes frequently. A serious racer who puts in a lot of training miles every week will soften up a frame quite a bit in two or three years of hard riding, and it is best to steer clear of this type. Remember,

though, there are a lot more people around who talk
a good race than who actually ride one.

Thoroughly check over any bike you are
thinking of buying. Take your tools with you and
come back again with more tools if necessary. First
make sure the frame is the right size; it is all too
easy to rationalize when you find a sweet deal. Then
ride the bike around, paying attention to the
operation of all the bearings. Spin each moving part
independently, checking for binding, sticking,
hesitancy, and grinding noises. See if the headset
(the front steering assembly bearings) produces a
series of little hesitations when it is turned under a
load; such catching indicates brinelling (pitting) of
the bearing races. Pick up the front of the bike and
drop it to see if there is any rattling of the headset
when the bike bounces. If there is, it is out of
adjustment, and you should pull the headset apart to
check for brinelling. Any bearings that show any
stickiness should be pulled apart and checked. Make
a list of everything that needs to be replaced and the
estimated cost.

Be sure to check the frame alignment carefully.
This can be done in the manner described in Chapter
4, though riding the bike to see whether it tracks
well when you take your hands off the handlebars
gives a fairly good indication. A bike that cannot be
ridden hands-off is either badly aligned or designed
poorly. Look at the frame for dimples, paint blisters,
or other evidence that the bike has crashed.

One last note on buying secondhand bikes: ask
for the bike's original sales slip and get a signed
receipt. Many people won't have sales slips, of
course, but try your best not to buy a stolen bike.
Bicycle theft is a major problem for all of us who
ride, and you owe it to your fellow cyclists and
yourself not to reward the thieves. If you come across

a really suspicious situation, report it to the police; then follow up later to see whether they investigated. Most police departments don't take bike thefts very seriously, and they won't begin to unless they feel pressure from irate citizens.

If you are buying at a police or city auction, arrive early and carefully check out the bikes in which you might be interested. Make notes and decide what your maximum bid will be in each case. Don't go any higher in the heat of the auction. At some police auctions you can get incredible deals. Others have been "discovered" and attract people who pay far too much. You can find out if and when auctions are held by calling local police departments. Be sure to check in advance on acceptable means of payment. Usually you are required to pay on the spot with either cash or a certified check.

Changing Components and Outfitting a Custom Bike

If you decide to upgrade some components on your bike, replace worn parts, or begin to outfit a custom bike, you are likely to become unpleasantly aware of the lack of standardization of threads and dimensions on bicycles. The situation can be horribly confusing, inconvenient, and expensive. In a few instances, the differences reflect legitimate disagreements concerning proper design. In most cases, however, they simply are due to the fact that no one is willing to adopt anyone else's arbitrary standards.

For example, there are four common bottom-bracket threadings when considering quality bikes only. Since there also are different widths of bottom brackets, and since different cranksets require different lengths of axle to protrude from the bottom bracket, bike-shop owners have to carry a wide variety of parts for each crankset model they choose to stock. You have to pay the cost of all that slow-moving inventory when you buy parts, *if* you can find them. You also may have difficulty matching the threads on your bike if the combination is unusual.

There isn't nearly enough room in this section to begin to go into detail about fitting problems. The following list is intended to alert you to possible problems. Before you order any components from a mail-order house, check the catalogue carefully for information concerning different sizes and threadings. Be careful to try out anything you order by mail very gingerly. If you start to thread in a part without checking, it is easy to badly damage both the bike and the component. You won't be allowed to return the cross-threaded part. If you buy from a shop, take your bike along and make sure the parts fit before buying them.

Some Common Size and Fitting Variations

Rims and Tires

The common diameters are for 27-inch or 700C tires. Rims may be designed for sew-up (all 700C) or clincher tires. Clincher rims and tires vary in width; the extra-narrow rims (approximately 13-mm inside width) should not be used with larger tires. Bikes designed for a low clearance with 700C wheels may not accept 27-inch wheels, and, when possible at all, switches between the two may require changing brakes (see Chapter 6). Presta or Schrader valves cannot be inflated with a pump that has the opposite fitting without an adapter. The number of holes in the rim should match the number in the hub.

Spokes

Diameters are determined by the wheel builder, depending on the rider, use, and wheel construction. Length depends on the lacing pattern, size of the flange, and construction of the rim. (See Chapter 6.)

Hubs

Flange diameters vary and are discussed in Chapter 6. The width of the rear hub must match the distance between the dropouts and is larger if a standard six-cog freewheel is to be used. The threading on the rear hub must be compatible with the freewheel threading: French, Italian, or British. British threading is most common on bikes imported to the United States. British and Italian are compatible, with a less than perfect fit, but French is not compatible with either. Tandem rear hubs normally are threaded on both sides to permit fitting the freewheel and a hub brake. Spoke holes in hubs may not be large enough to fit thicker-gauge spokes, though they can be drilled to a larger size. The number of spoke holes drilled into the hub should match the number in the rim.

Brakes

The reach of brakes has a limited range of adjustment, which must be compatible with the size of the rims used and the design of the bike (see Chapter 7). For cantilever brakes, pivots must be brazed on the fork and seatstays.

Freewheel

The sizes of cogs have to be chosen. Cogs from one freewheel do not fit another. The width of the freewheel usually is different for five- and six-cog models; this width must match the distance between the rear dropouts. See the comments on threading under "Hubs" above. Freewheel removers normally are unique to a particular model, and methods of dismantling vary. The new Ultra-6 freewheels require a chain with a narrower outside dimension. The Ultra-6 chain works with other freewheels, but not vice versa.

Bottom Bracket

There are different widths and four common threadings: English, French, Italian, and Swiss. The English and some Swiss types employ a right-handed thread on the left side and a left-handed thread on the right; others use right-handed threads on both sides. Axles must be the correct length for the shell and crankset. Both the width between the bearing races and the length past them must be correct. Various tools fit the cups and lockrings.

Crankset

The crankset must match the bottom bracket. Though there is some interchangeability, parts and tools for different cranksets usually cannot be mixed. The length of the crank arms should be chosen with the characteristics of the frame in mind, with 170-mm arms being standard. The threading in the crank arms must be compatible with the pedals installed (see below).

Pedals

The pedals on most bikes imported into this country have English threading (9/16-inch with 30 threads per inch). Some, however, have French threading (14-mm by 1.25-mm). A crank with French threading can be tapped by a bike mechanic to change it to the more common English. Italian threads also are slightly different but are compatible with English. All right pedals are left-hand threaded and left pedals right-hand threaded so that they cannot accidentally unscrew.

Handlebars

Besides differences in shape, the centers of different handlebars vary in diameter. Unless you have checked the measurement, use the same brand handlebars as the stem.

Seat and Seat Post

The clamp on the post has to be compatible with the rails on the seat. Most modern racing and touring seats use rails the same distance apart, but some older seats and unusual leather models aren't compatible with standard integral posts and clamps. The diameter of the seat post must closely match the inside of the seat tube. These diameters vary in 0.2-mm increments from 26 to 27.2 millimeters.

Chapter 4

The Frame

THERE ARE A number of basic approaches to buying a bicycle. One is to put yourself in the hands of a competent shop, explain what kind of riding you want to do, the experience you have had, and how much you can afford to pay, and ask the shop people to put together the best possible bike for you with the money you can afford to spend. This is a pretty good way to get a decent bike, if you find a reliable shop. There are a lot of good bike shops around because many are run by bicycle enthusiasts who will do a good job for you.

If you take this approach, you may prefer to ignore the technical aspects of frame construction altogether. It is important to learn how such components as derailleurs and brakes work because you may have to fix them on the road. The frame, however, despite its importance, is not something you have to understand in order to enjoy yourself on bicycle tours. Once built, it may need an occasional dab of paint on chipped spots and a coat of wax once in a while if you want to preserve the finish. Otherwise, you should be able to ride the bike for a long time without giving the frame much thought, unless you have an extra-close encounter with a car.

Since the frame is by far the most important part of a bike, however, you may want to learn more about it. Frame building and design make up a sophisticated and subtle art, and very small differences in construction produce bikes that ride quite differently. This chapter provides an elementary introduction to frames. Those who are interested in getting on with the tour may prefer to skip it, while those who want to be able to judge the quality of a bicycle for themselves should learn as much as possible about frames. If you are buying an expensive machine or a secondhand bike, you must look at the frame particularly carefully. No matter how good the other components are, a bike with a poor frame is a lousy bike. A good frame, on the other hand, can be worth buying even if every accessory has to be replaced.

Shape

The basic configuration of the one-person bicycle frame has remained about the same for a long time. Many variations have been tried, but none has performed nearly as well as the standard configuration. The differences between most frames are subtle. Among quality touring bicycles, the only common variations are the mixte (or "women's") frame and the various tandem frames. The mixte frame eliminates the top tube and employs a weaker triangle with two small-diameter tubes running from the headset back to the rear lugs. Satisfactory touring bikes are available for those who really want this style, but the design is inherently weaker and less rigid for a given weight. It has advantages as a utility bike if you want to be able to ride with a skirt, but it makes little sense as a touring machine. Tandems involve a completely different set of design problems and are not covered here.

Basic frame configuration is discussed in Chapter 3. Most of this chapter concentrates on steel frames, with a brief description of some exotic materials later in the chapter. Steel is the standard against which other types of frames are judged, and it is still the least expensive material for building quality bikes.

Tubing

Steel with a very high tensile strength is used to make the tubing in good-quality bicycles. The alloys used in suitable tubing have tensile strengths in the neighborhood of 100,000 pounds per square inch (psi). The maker of the tubing must choose an alloy which is not only strong, but which can be used by the frame builder without losing its strength. Thus, some of the alloys used on bicycles made for the world's top racers are not generally available. Manufacturers sell them only to selected builders because they are difficult to work with. The same is true of some of the thinner tubing sets, which may not be durable enough for general use and may require special skills to braze.

The steels generally used for bicycle tubing and chrome-molybdenum (chromolly) and molybdenum-manganese alloys. More malleable steels are used for lugs and similar parts. The strength of a tube is dependent upon the steel, tube diameter, and thickness of the tube walls. Since the greatest stress on a bicycle occurs at the ends of the tubes near the joints, a lighter and livelier bike can be fashioned if the tubes are thicker at the ends only, where the extra strength is required. Thicker ends lend extra rigidity to the frame where distorting stress is greatest and allow a larger margin for error if the builder overheats the metal slightly and weakens it. The extra thickness also makes overheating less likely.

Tubing with thicker walls at each end is called *double-butted* tubing. The extra thickness is inside the tube and cannot be seen from the outside. Such tubes are difficult and expensive to make, so they naturally cost more. The butting is achieved by compressing the tube with great force around an interior bar called a mandrill and then running the tube between rollers that spring one end open momentarily while the mandrill is drawn out.

There are a number of makers of quality double-butted tubing. They supply decals to the frame makers who purchase their products so that they can indicate the type of tubing used in a particular bike. Since double-butted tubing is quite expensive and is one of the marks of a quality bicycle, if a bike is made with double-butted tubing, it nearly always has a decal that says so. Any unmarked bicycle is probably not made with double-butted tubing, regardless of the claims of the seller.

The most common type of tubing used in high-quality bicycles is Reynolds alloy 531, made in Great Britain. A Reynolds decal indicates whether the bike is made from 531 or another alloy. If it says nothing else, the tubes are not butted. The decal also indicates whether the three main tubes are butted or whether the tubes, forks, and stays are butted. (Seat masts, stays, and fork blades actually are tapered rather than double-butted.) Other companies use similar systems to distinguish between their various types of tubing. Tange,

Ishiwata, Falk, and Vitus are other good
manufacturers of tubing. The most prestigious
tubing manufacturer is Columbus of Italy. Decals
usually don't indicate tube thickness, but touring
bikes should be made from medium- to heavy-duty
butted tubes. Superlight tubing sets are for special
racing uses, such as time trials.

After selecting the dimensions and angles
desired, a frame builder cuts the tubing to length,
miters the joints (cuts the ends of the tubes so that
they fit together perfectly), and brazes each joint
together. (Brazing is similar to welding, but
the bonding material requires much lower
temperatures.) The brazing compound usually is
brass, an alloy of copper and zinc, and the work is
done at a temperature of between 800° and 900° C.
The mitering is critical for a strong joint, and so is
the way that the pieces are held together while each
joint is brazed. This can be done with a precision jig,
forming a "lugless" joint that relies only on the close
fit of the tubes and the strength of the brazing
material to hold it together, or a combination of a jig
and a steel lug can be used. The lug is a soft steel
joint into which both tubes fit. Depending on the way
it is made, it may be fixed at the desired angle or the
frame maker may have to modify it. Excellent
frames can be made either with or without lugs. It is
easier to make a good joint with lugs—or at least it
requires less elaborate equipment—but it is easier
to conceal sloppy work too. Internal reinforcement or
inside lugs also may be used, particularly in making
ultralight frames.

Whether the joints are lugged or not, their
strength depends on the closeness of the fit of the
tubes, the preparation of the surfaces, and the
brazing technique of the builder. At a well-brazed
juncture, brass fills the joint and creates a smooth

curve that melds into each tube, so that the distribution of stress is gradual and even. Gaps, irregularities, or poor adherence of the brass due to incorrect preparation of the steel or bad brazing technique result in a joint that is not as rigid as it should be and that may even fail under stress. Unfortunately, lugs and paint can hide some of these imperfections. Excessive heating or bending of the tubes after completion of the frame to correct mistakes made in alignment usually cannot be detected by the buyer of the finished bike, but they also seriously weaken the frame.

Good finish work on a bike does not give you any guarantee that mistakes have not been hidden underneath the paint, but at least it can give some indication. Fine hand-finishing of a frame takes an incredible amount of time. Lugs are thinned out and brazing cleaned by hours of hand-filing and sanding. Sloppy brazing requires more time to conceal. Even when these processes are imitated with the assistance of power tools, the process is neither quick nor cheap. Learning to look carefully at the detail work on a bicycle is therefore a good way to judge the quality of the bike. The brazing at the joints or the lug edges should be smooth and uniform, with no gaps or blobs. On the best frames, the lugs are thinned gradually to merge with the frame, making stress distribution more even. Cutouts in lugs and bottom bracket shells are largely cosmetic. Some cutout patterns weaken bottom brackets considerably, so it is best to avoid them since this is the part of the bike that most needs to be rigid.

Careful examination of the frame should reveal each part to be a mirror image of the opposite side, except for the indentations on the right chainstay that make space for the chainwheel. Thus, the right

and left fork blades should look exactly the same, as
should the seat stays, etc. Alignment and fit are
absolutely essential and are discussed later in the
chapter. Finally, of course, the name of the builder
may be of some worth. Builders with high standards
rarely let a bad bike go out of their shops, although
some large, well-known European manufacturers
have sent some real junk to the United States in past
years, presumably on the theory that Americans
don't know a good bike from a bad one.

Important Design Considerations

The bicycle's basic design really is amazingly
efficient; the machine easily carries a load ten times
its weight with strength to spare. Its structure
is a compromise, however, and many of the
arguments about bike design result primarily from
disagreements concerning which features should
predominate. Clearly, the frame must be strong
enough to support the rider and any luggage with no
danger of failure on bumpy mountain roads or after
tens of thousands of miles of road shocks. Except for
specialized bikes designed mainly for record
attempts or racing under controlled conditions, it is
never wise to compromise this basic strength. The
characteristics most desired in bike design are that:
(1) the bike support the rider in the optimum
position for delivering power; (2) as much power as
possible be translated into forward motion, rather
than being dissipated in rear-end whip and other
deflections; (3) road shocks be cushioned; and
(4) the bike be both maneuverable and stable.

Compromises among these features occur in any
specific design, as well as prejudices that aren't truly
relevant to the function of the machine. One
example is the common misconception surrounding

the idea of "stiffness." A stiff frame, in the positive sense, refers to one that has a lot of side-to-side rigidity in the rear end, so that there is little whip as the rider pushes down hard on the pedals, particularly when power is needed for hill climbing or for sprinting during a race. Unfortunately, the same qualities that contribute to rigidity and thus to a more efficient transfer of power also often make the bike transmit the bumps of the road directly to the cyclist's body. Consequently, some riders influenced by current racing fashions often irrationally seek a harsh, uncomfortable ride, because a "stiff" frame is identified with high performance. The desirable feature is not the harsh ride but rather the efficient power transfer. In fact, some frames that have a very harsh ride are not particularly efficient, so the rider gets the worst of both worlds—an uncomfortable ride *and* poor power transfer.

To return to genuinely desirable characteristics, some of them do entail clear-cut choices to be made by the rider from the beginning. For example, it is always desirable for a bike to track straight if you ride with your hands off the handlebars. It also is essential to be able to maneuver a bike well. The criterium racer, who must ride around tight corners at high speed while maneuvering within a pack of riders, needs a bike that can turn on a dime. Such a rider doesn't care much whether the bike can be easily kept on course with relaxed and casual steering. If you are a tourist, on the other hand, you prefer the opposite steering characteristics. You don't want a bike that needs constant attention to the steering. You want to be able to ride down the road with your hands in the middle of the bars and look at the scenery without the bike tending to turn toward a ditch. There is a definite difference, therefore, between the ultra-quick steering found on a criterium bike and the more stable feel of a good touring bike; in terms of steering design and many other factors, a road racing bike is likely to fall between the two.

You may need to compromise one desirable design feature for another to meet your needs. Everyone would like to eliminate whip and also

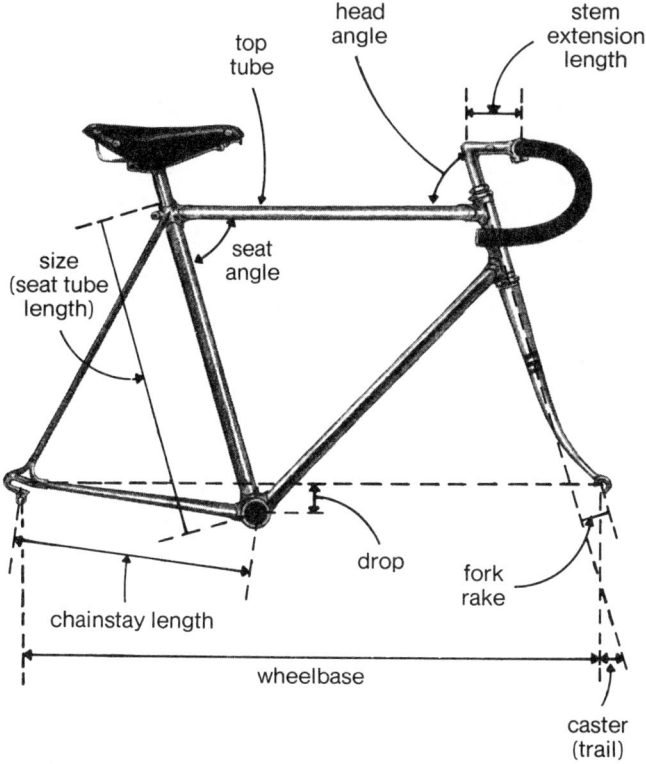

7. *The proportions of the bicycle frame, as well as the materials and quality of construction, determine the ultimate performance and handling characteristics of the bike.*

have plenty of cushioning, but in balancing the two, a racer concentrating on hill climbing is likely to be more concerned with rigidity while the long-distance tourist may be more interested in cushioning.

The bicycle designer has a limited number of variables to work with, and tolerances are close. For example, the differences in frame angles among various cycle designs are minimal. The angle of the seat tube to the horizontal might be 74 degrees in a rather uncompromising criterium racing bike and 71 degrees on a soft, easy-riding touring machine. The average person wouldn't even be able to tell the difference between the two without taking exact measurements.

A number of important frame dimensions are dictated in great part by your size and by other constraints. The length of the seat tube cannot be increased more than a small amount, since you have to be able to reach the pedals from the seat and to stand on the ground while straddling the top tube. Similarly, the length of the top tube is determined primarily by the length of your upper body, with only small adjustments possible in the length of the stem extension and movement of the seat. Wheel size usually is fixed. The builder has to work within all these limitations in designing the frame.

The main variables with which the builder can work are the angles of the seat tube and the head tube, the fork rake, the length of the chainstays, the length of the top tube, the length and angle of the down tube, and the height of the bottom bracket shell above the ground (see Figure 7). Each of these variables influences the others.

To obtain a soft ride, for example, several things can be done. The wheelbase can be lengthened a bit by extending the chainstays and the top tube a little, lowering the angle of the headset, and increasing the fork rake. The fork rake is the distance produced by the forward bend of the fork. It is measured from the center of the axle to the steering axis, which is a line drawn straight down from the center of the head and steering tubes. The more rake and the more the fork is inclined from the vertical by a decreased head tube angle, the more it deflects in response to the shock from a bump. Similarly, longer chainstays deflect upward more, and they also bring the rear wheel farther back and less directly under the rider.

Frame Size

While several dimensions of the frame affect the suitability of a bike for a particular rider, the most important is the length of the seat tube. The *frame size* of a bike is the distance between the center of the bottom bracket shell and the top of the seat tube.

Desirable frame size can be determined in a number of ways. A common formula is to subtract ten inches from the inside length of your leg, crotch to floor, measured in stocking feet. There are more elaborate methods, but this one works fairly well. Taller riders commonly get a frame an inch larger, preferring the more upright riding position and improved clearance for luggage. You must be able to comfortably straddle the top tube. Also, the frame size cannot be larger than your inside leg length minus the height of the seat and the crank length to the top of the pedal, a distance that usually works out to about 8½ inches less than your leg length.

Of course, a much smaller frame can be ridden by raising the seat, but this is undesirable for several reasons: the other proportions of the frame are going to be wrong, the seat positioning and stem extension length probably have to be extreme, and since long stems are hard to obtain, the rider probably has to bend over too far to reach the handlebars. A shorter-than-normal seat tube may be required if the bike has unusually high clearance or if a stock bike is chosen and the rider has a short torso and arms. In this latter case, the top tube length—which usually is matched to the cyclist's long legs—may be excessive, and the best solution may be to pick a somewhat smaller frame and then raise the seat.

The length of the top tube normally is increased with the length of the seat tube, but not quite so rapidly. The ideal is for the rider to be able to comfortably reach the handlebars from his or her position on the seat while leaning forward at about a 45-degree angle. The arms should angle forward but not have to strain. This position depends on both torso and arm length, and some adjustment is possible to accommodate individual body pro-portions and riding style by choosing different handlebars and stem extension lengths. The stem also can be adjusted up and down, as long as a minimum of 2½ inches remains in the steering tube. These adjustments are discussed further in Chapter 8 and should enable most touring cyclists to find an adequate fit within the proportions of stock frames. Tourists of average height usually don't have to bother with custom-made frames unless they are very unusually proportioned. Riders who are shorter than about 5'2" or taller than about 6'5" may have some difficulty because stock frames are not designed for their heights.

Clearances

There are several important clearances on every frame design, and it is important that the ones on the frame you select are commensurate with your needs. The clearance between the tires and the fork crown in front and the brake bridge in back can vary quite a bit, even on standard-sized bikes. Wheel sizes vary somewhat, a subject discussed in detail in Chapter 6. The most common size among American tourists (27 inches) is slightly larger than the one generally used by racers and European tourists (700C—the 700 is a *nominal* diameter in milli- meters; for more on tire sizes see pp. 144–45). Since a frame designed for racing normally is made with a very low clearance to permit the use of side- pull brakes with a high mechanical advantage, it may be impossible to put 27-inch clincher wheels on a bike made for 700C sew-ups. Brakes are designed for particular clearances, so the choice of brakes has to be compatible with the frame design. Finally, if you expect to do some touring in wet climates where you may want to mount fenders, you have to make sure the bike is made with enough clearance at the fork crown and the rear bridge to permit them.

The height of the bottom bracket shell above the ground is not of great concern to most tourists unless they are planning to do a lot of riding on very rough dirt roads, for which high clearance may be desirable. Racers in events that require pedaling through very sharp turns need bikes with a bottom bracket high enough so that the pedals won't hit, since hitting the pavement with a pedal while accelerating through a curve causes a certain spill. Tourists can be a bit more moderate. If you are going around a corner that is fast enough and tight enough to require a severe lean, you can stop pedaling. The average height of the center of the bottom bracket above the ground usually is about 10½ inches. Lower placement tends to make the bike a little more stable, while higher bottom brackets provide a bit more clearance. Anything much lower than 10¼ inches or higher than 10¾ inches should be avoided unless there is a special reason for the dimension. (Exact clearance depends on tire and wheel size, and frame builders prefer to specify the drop of the bottom bracket below the axles. The height of the bottom bracket is approximately 13 inches minus the drop.)

Finally, the clearance between the toe clip and the front wheel during sharp turns is of some importance. A frame with a steep head tube angle and minimal rake may bring the front wheel close enough that the toe clip can hit it if the pedal swings forward when the bike is turned hard. The problem is more likely to occur if longer than normal cranks are used or if you have big feet. Check the clearance with the length of the cranks and toe clips you plan to use. Such interference usually is not a problem, but it can cause a nasty tumble as you come around a hairpin turn while pedaling slowly uphill.

Steering

The steering characteristics of a bike are complex, and everything from the weight of the rider to the height of the bottom bracket has some effect on the steering. The main determinants, however, are the head tube angle, the fork length, and the rake; these must be carefully balanced to achieve the desired handling. Replacing one fork with another of the same length can radically change the steering if the second has a 1¼-inch rake instead of a 2½-inch one.

All bicycles are built so that the front wheel has some *caster* or *trail,* meaning that the actual point where the wheel makes contact with the ground is behind the turning axis. If you extend a line down from the axis of the head tube, around which the

fork, stem, and handlebars turn, the line reaches the
ground in front of a line dropped vertically from
the center of the axle (see Figure 7). If a bike were
not built with some caster, it would be almost
impossible to steer. As soon as you started into a
turn, the bike would tend to turn more and more
sharply. Caster produces the self-steering tendency
you use when you ride without hands.

A bike built with a vertical head tube and a
straight fork would have zero caster. As the angle of
the head tube becomes less than 90 degrees, caster
increases, but it is reduced by the introduction of
fork rake. Increased fork rake and steeper angles
both reduce caster and quicken the steering. Thus, if
a builder wants to increase rake in order to soften
the ride, he or she must decrease the angle of the
head tube at the same time; otherwise the steering
would become erratic. Increasing the fork length
also increases the caster.

A correct balance between the head tube angle,
fork length, and rake is essential if a bike is to have
proper handling characteristics. If you look at the
dimensions of touring and racing models designed
by the same builder of high-quality frames, you will
note that the racing models with steeper head tube
angles and shorter forks also have less rake.

Extra Features

There are a host of fancy extras that can be put on a
bike frame, some very useful for the touring cyclist.
Many special features are a matter of fashion more
than anything else, however, and you must decide
for yourself whether they are worth the money.

A good finish on a bike may give some indication
of quality in other areas, though the relationship
does not always hold. The tougher the finish and the
better it is applied, the easier it is to keep the bike

clean and untarnished. There are a number of ways of applying a quality finish, ranging from new technologically sophisticated methods to old-fashioned spraying, sanding, and baking of many coats. If the dropouts aren't chromed, you can take a sharp object and test the adherence of the paint where the wheel clamps on, an area that is going to lose its paint anyway. A chrome finish requires the least care if it is well applied, but it also is heavy and does not appeal to many cyclists. Chrome is attractive and makes excellent sense when applied to areas that normally receive a lot of dirt and wear, such as fork ends and dropouts.

Fancy cutout work on the lugs often is the mark of a fine bike, though the weight saved is negligible. Cutouts in the underside of the bottom bracket shell can seriously weaken the frame at a place that requires maximum strength. Such "relieving" of the bottom bracket is used on some of the finest frames, such as Colnago's famous clover cutout, and the patterns can be assumed to be safe, if not particularly functional. It usually is wiser not to have relieving done, however, even by a good custom frame maker, since he or she may not have tested various cutout patterns carefully, and some of them can significantly reduce the strength of the bottom bracket.

There are a number of special types of fork crowns, dropouts, and methods of finishing the chainstays and the top of the seat tube. Most of these are more a matter of taste than of structural importance. Investment casting of such parts as the dropouts and fork crowns can produce a lighter and stronger product than other methods can, but the same amount of weight can be saved in other ways far more cheaply.

More important to the tourist are the various

fittings on the bike. The fork ends and dropouts should have eyelets, preferably threaded ones, for attaching racks. It is a nuisance to mount luggage carriers without them, though Blackburn makes some fairly effective fittings for bikes that follow racing fashion and omit mounting eyelets. It is convenient to have double eyelets if you want to mount fenders, but only custom-made bikes are likely to be equipped with this feature.

There should be a threaded mounting hole for the derailleur on the right dropout; otherwise a special claw has to be used on the axle with added weight and reduced convenience. Dropouts with slots that extend straight down make removal and mounting of the wheel simpler, but most frame makers avoid them because they require a much more precise building technique. Conventional dropouts with slots extending forward permit minor adjustments of the wheel to compensate for slight differences in chainstay length.

Additional fittings are convenient to avoid the need for many clamp-on fittings, saving weight and preserving the paint on the frame. They have to be properly mounted and chosen to be compatible with the hardware to be used on the bike. Furthermore, fittings that are attached near the center of butted tubes have to be put on very carefully, since it is easy to overheat the thinner center sections of the tubing. Commonly used fittings include a cable stop for the derailleur on the right chainstay, derailleur cable guides just above the bottom bracket, a stop at the appropriate place for the front derailleur (varies with the model of derailleur), guides for brake-cable housings on the top tube, water-bottle fittings on the seat tube, down tube, or both, bosses for the shift levers on the down tube, fittings for direct attachment of pannier racks, a cable stop between the seatstays for center-pull or cantilever brakes, and perhaps posts for these same types of brakes (see Chapter 7).

Because of the danger of overheating, it usually is best if these fittings are attached with a brazing compound that has a high silver content, which requires a lower temperature for bonding. This is particularly important for water-bottle or lever fittings on the thinner center sections of the down tube. The overheating danger is one reason that racers avoided such fittings for a long time. They probably are best avoided on mass-produced bikes because of the niceties of brazing technique that are required; builders in production lines may accidentally overheat the thinner central sections of tubing while brazing on such fittings.

Some builders use a brazing compound with a high silver content on some of the frame joints as well, because of the lower temperature required. However, in addition to being more costly, a brazing compound with a high percentage of silver does not bridge nearly so wide a gap and requires much more care in surface preparation. Therefore, except for special purposes, such as attaching bottle fittings, brazing compounds with a high silver content are best left to master frame builders who know how to use them and where they are needed. Ultralight tubing sets often are assembled with a silver solder because of the greater danger of overheating the thinner tubing, but such tubing usually is not the best choice for a touring frame.

Recommended Frame Dimensions

For the type of bicycle touring emphasized in this book, 72-degree frame angles usually give the best compromise between responsiveness and riding comfort over the miles, perhaps with a somewhat steeper seat tube angle on very small frames. (Head and seat tube angles do not have to be the same, though this is the most common configuration. Of the two, the head tube angle probably influences the ride more.) Combined with chainstays of about 17 inches or a little more and a fork rake of about 2 inches, this should produce a bike that climbs well and responds in the curves without transmitting an unreasonable amount of road shock, particularly if the bottom bracket is fairly low, around 10¼ inches. The wheelbase of such a bike should be about 40 inches for shorter frames and a little longer for those frames over 22 inches.

Angles of 73 degrees are a little steep for a touring bike, though they can be used if they aren't accompanied by very short chainstays and short fork rakes. Seventy-three-degree angles combined with chainstay lengths of 16½ inches or less, a short rake, and a high bottom bracket are better suited for criterium racing than for long tours.

For those who prefer a more comfortable bike that is a bit less responsive, 71- to 72-degree angles with a rake of 2½ inches, chainstays of 18 to 19 inches, and a wheelbase in the neighborhood of 42 to 43 inches give a very comfortable ride without sacrificing performance too much. If you plan to ride on a lot of rough roads and to carry heavy loads, this might be about right. For most touring in the United States, I don't recommend bikes with a wheelbase much longer than this.

Angles of 74 to 75 degrees combined with very short chainstays are going to jar your teeth and bruise your crotch by the end of a long tour or several days of road racing. On rough surfaces they also dissipate a lot of energy because of bouncing. Leave these machines to track racers and self-styled hard-guy club racers.

All the dimensions given above must be revised a bit for extremely small or large frames. Except where specified, they apply to frame sizes of about 22 inches. A 25-inch frame naturally has a bit longer top tube and therefore a bit longer wheelbase, though chainstay lengths should increase only ½ inch or so between a 19-inch frame and a 25-inch one to maintain similar handling. Frames shorter than 19 inches are very hard to find and must be specially designed to be used with standard wheels and tires. Wheel clearance must be cut to a minimum, perhaps with the use of cantilever brakes (see Chapter 7), and bottom bracket height probably needs to be reduced to about 10 inches. Chainstays need to be a little shorter than 17 inches to give a ride equivalent to that of the designs recommended above. Unfortunately, a short person may have to have such a frame custom-built.

Alignment

Any bike frame should be perfectly aligned, although there is no way to tell whether some corrections have been made by bending after construction. The simplest overall alignment test is to ride the bike with no hands. A properly aligned bike tracks easily, rather than pulling to one side or feeling as though it is about to swerve out of control.

There are other tests that you can make quite simply. If the wheels are properly trued, the rims should be equidistant from the fork blades and the chainstays. If one side is closer than the other, reverse the wheel to see whether the fault is in the wheel or in the frame. If the short side remains next to the same frame member, the error is in the frame. The wheels should be easy to mount and remove without pressing in on the fork ends and chainstays or spreading them apart. While someone holds the bike, pointing the front wheel straight ahead, sight along the two wheels from the front and back. They should line up perfectly in exactly the same plane. The head tube and seat tube also should line up precisely in the same plane.

Stretch a string around the front of the head tube and back on either side of the bike to the rear dropouts. The string should be the same distance from the seat tube on each side. The cranks should pass the seat tube and down tube at exactly the same distance, otherwise the bottom bracket shell is not oriented exactly at a right angle to the plane of the main triangle.

Remove the front wheel and the stem and rest the fork ends on a bench about a foot high. If possible, check to see that the bench is perfectly level. Sight from above the fork to make sure that a line drawn across the tips of the forkends would be parallel to the front of the fork crown. Hang a weighted string through the steering tube; it should fall exactly down the center of the fork.

Exotic Frame Materials

Builders have experimented with a number of special materials as complete or partial re-placements for steel in bike frames, with varying degrees of success. The most promising seem to be aluminum alloys, titanium, and composites using carbon or boron fibers bonded with epoxy resin. All these materials pose special design and production problems that generally add up to a very high price for any weight saved. Furthermore, the most successful of the exotic frames have been built chiefly with the racer in mind, so the ride is less than ideal for the touring cyclist.

A full discussion of the unique design problems and manufacturing techniques for exotic frames is outside the scope of this book, but I will indicate a few of them. One of the major challenges in using these materials is that traditional specifications for steel frames need radical reconsideration to effectively accommodate other materials. These changes in turn are complicated by the fact that other bicycle components are designed to fit standard frames. Prototypes and tooling are expensive, and therefore the cost of reaching the production stage is often prohibitive.

So far, the most successful titanium frame has been the Teledyne Titan (not currently in production), which uses larger than normal tube diameters to overcome the reduced stiffness, compared with steel, of the metal. Of the aluminum frames, the most competitive in terms of price at the time of this writing is the Alan. It uses screwed and epoxied joints in aluminum alloy lugs, which facilitate the joining of thick-walled aluminum tubes and compensate for the metal's lack of stiffness. The Alan frame weighs less than its steel counterparts, and its price is comparable to equivalent steel frames. This construction method is not well suited to modification of frame geometry, however, and great care is necessary to avoid scratching, which can lead to tube failure.

In many ways the most interesting of the exotic materials are carbon and boron fibers, which are very light for their strength and stiffer than steel. Perhaps even more important, they have better damping characteristics, which should make it possible to build bikes that not only weigh less but also combine great responsiveness with a comfortable ride. Some bikes have been made with tubing composed solely of epoxy-bonded graphite fibers (graphite is a form of carbon), but so far the only successful production models have used metal tubing stiffened with graphite fibers. (These include the Klein and Graftek models.) The frames that employ carbon and boron have been designed solely for racing up to now, and most cyclists would find them too harsh and skittish, as well as too expensive, for touring.

Chapter 5

The Drive Train

THE BASIC PROPULSION system on a touring bike is quite simple and straightforward, though there are thousands of variations and nuances. Because the derailleur and chain system has proved to be so effective, none of the more exotic systems are considered here. At the moment, the derailleur and chain provide the most practical and efficient drive available with variable gearing.

Planetary gearing systems,* such as the well-known three-speed hub, are used for some

---

* A planetary gear-drive system consists of a central gear (the "sun" gear), several smaller gears (the "planet" gears) that mesh around the sun's circumference and roll around it, and, outside these, a "ring" gear with interior teeth that mesh with the planet gears. The planet gears can be considered as a unit, and their axes are usually connected with some sort of frame.
All three components of the system are interconnected but move at different speeds; if two move with respect to each other, the third is driven. A three-speed hub uses this type of system with a clutch that connects different combinations to change gears. The gears themselves are always connected and move in the same relation to one another; only the linkage to the bike's sprocket changes.

100

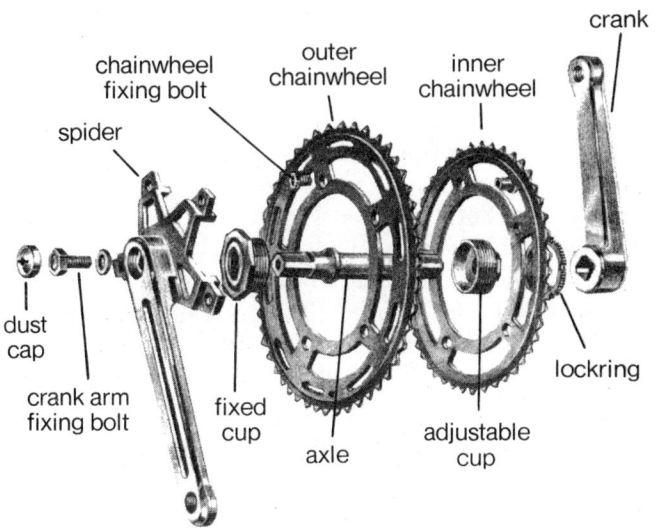

10. A typical cotterless crankset. The hardened steel axle in the center is held in the bottom bracket by threaded cups. Ball bearings run between the machined races on the axle and the races on the insides of the cups. The lockring fits over the adjustable cup to hold it in position after the tightness of the bearings is adjusted. The crank arms mate with the square ends of the axle and are held in place by the fixing bolts. The chainwheels attach to the spider. A dust cap protects the threads on each of the crank arms.

cause the square holes in the aluminum to become rounded so that the cranks have to be replaced. In the better cotterless cranks, the *spider,* to which the chainwheels bolt, is forged in one piece with the right crank arm. Cheaper cranksets may have either the spider or the entire large chainwheel pressed onto a projection from the arm.

Crank length can be varied somewhat by experienced riders to fit individual riding style and taste, but standard lengths really work quite well.

Longer cranks provide more leverage, but they also require the feet to travel in larger circles. The standard crank length for people of average height is 170 millimeters. Frames for very short people may be made for, and equipped with, slightly shorter cranks. Measurement of a crank is from the center of the bottom bracket's axle hole to the center of the hole for the pedal spindle.) Larger frames made for taller people generally are built to permit somewhat longer cranks to be used. Exact measurements are a matter of opinion and taste, but a person 5'9'' or 5'10'' tall might want to use 172.5-mm cranks, while a six-footer might want 175-mm cranks. Really tall people may want still longer cranks, but these can be hard to find. Many standard crank-sets come only with 170-mm cranks. 177.5-mm and 180-mm lengths can be found if you look hard enough. The T. A. Cyclotouriste crankset, one of the best for tourists, has cranks available from 165 to 180 millimeters in 2.5-mm increments.

Between the two cranks are the axle and bearings which fit into the bottom bracket. The large tube forming the bottom bracket on the frame itself is threaded to accept the bearing cups. There are four common threadings, which are not interchangeable: French, English (and Japanese), Italian, and Swiss. The normal arrangement is to have the ball bearings run between the screw-in cups and the flanges machined onto the axle. Sealed bearings use a different configuration. The major advantage of sealed bearings is that they are far less vulnerable to water and grit and need servicing less often. However, the ease of servicing the bracket in case of a breakdown should be considered, particularly if specialized tools are required to remove a sealed bottom bracket.

Most bike frames have at least one opening through which water and dirt can get into the

bottom bracket. If the bearings are of the conventional unprotected type, this water and grit
can rapidly ruin them. Because moisture and dirt
can remain trapped for some time, it is a good idea to
use as many protective measures as possible. If you
do not have sealed bearings, inexpensive plastic
sleeves can be purchased to help keep conventional
bearings clean and dry. If your seat post is open at
the top, plug it, since water and dirt can enter
through the hole and slide down the seat tube into
the bottom bracket. Chainstays and the cross-tubes
between them often have holes through which
foreign matter can enter. These can be plugged with
silicon adhesive or caulk.

The front chainwheels are attached to the
right-hand crank arm. This is done in different ways
by the various crankset manufacturers. Generally,
five arms, called the *spider*, extend outward from the
inside of the crank. All the chainwheels may bolt to
the spider, or one chainwheel may do so while the
others are attached to the first with a separate set of
bolts. Ten- and twelve-speed bikes have two front
chainwheels, while fifteen- and eighteen-speed
models have three.

In choosing a crankset, it is important to pick
one with a reputation for strength and reliability.
Some models are recommended below. You also must
find a model that offers chainwheels with the
number of teeth you want. Many sets designed
primarily for racers do not take chainwheels with
less than 42 teeth. You may want much smaller
forward cogs than this, especially if you plan to ride
through mountainous terrain and are not very
strong. If you think you may want to change
chainwheel sizes later, be sure the sizes you may
want are available for the crankset you contemplate
buying.

For tourists who want fairly low gears, the

most common method is to use the same large chainwheels as racers do, but to substitute larger rear cogs. Since this solution adds weight without any real advantages, it makes better sense to buy a crankset designed to permit smaller chainwheels, so that smaller rear cogs can be used as well. (Gear ratios and recommended systems are discussed later in the chapter).

One final point worth considering in choosing cranksets is the availability of replacements, even though chainwheels are not likely to cause trouble during a tour. Each of the major crankset manufacturers offers several models. The parts usually are not interchangeable among the different designs, and a model number often is not even placed on the set. The long-time standard for touring is the T. A. Cyclotouriste, which offers chainwheels ranging from 26 to 55 teeth in either double or triple models. Stronglight also has made good cranksets for touring, most recently the 105 Bis, with chainwheels down to 38 teeth. Several Japanese manufacturers are now making excellent touring sets at much more reasonable prices than European models. These include the Sugino Mighty Tour and the SR Super Apex Tourist; the former goes down to 34 teeth and the latter to 28. The SR model is an excellent bargain.

When buying a used bike, check the entire crankset carefully, since replacement can be expensive. The cranks on any bike should turn freely under pressure, with virtually no play.

Chains

Power is transferred from the front cog to the rear one by means of the chain, which consists of rollers held together by pivoted links so that the distance between rollers is exactly the same as the distance between the teeth on any of the cogs. The chain thus serves to drive the back wheel of the bike at a rate equal to the pedaling cadence times the ratio between the number of teeth on the front cog and the number of teeth on the rear cog. Or, expressed as a formula:

$$\text{Speed of back wheel (in rpm)} = \text{pedaling cadence} \left(\frac{\text{number of teeth on chainwheel}}{\text{number of teeth on freewheel cog}} \right)$$

The more friction-free the chain, the more efficient the power transfer. For a discussion of chain maintenance and lubrication, see pages 221–23.

Standard chains for touring bikes are 8 millimeters wide, which is narrower than the chain widths used on many children's and utility bicycles, and no spring-clip key link normally is used. The chain is opened or closed by using a special tool to push one of the rivets in or out. Chains usually come with 116 links, and if all these are not required, some simply are removed from one end by driving out the appropriate rivet. Until recently, chains did not differ significantly except in workmanship and strength, though some were drilled to remove a few ounces. The Japanese have made several major innovations, however.

Shimano's Uniglide chain has outer plates that are raised in the center so that they drop more quickly onto the teeth of a larger gear when they are being shifted. This makes shifting faster and smoother and reduces the tendency of the chain to ride past the larger cog when being shifted to a higher gear on the front chainwheels. This can be useful to the tourist who wants more precise shifting. The derailleurs employed by tourists because of their larger capacities often are sloppier and slower to shift than are racing derailleurs.

Another innovation is found in Maeda's Sun Tour Ultra-6 system. By flattening the ends of the rivets, the outside width of the chain is reduced without changing the inside dimensions. The outside width is thereby cut from 8 millimeters to 6.9 millimeters. The chain fits cogs with standard tooth widths, but because of the smaller external dimension you can use a special freewheel with six cogs instead of five. Though the Ultra-6 chain can be used with any freewheel, it has few advantages unless the matching freewheel also is used.

Freewheels

The rear cluster of gears is mounted on the freewheel, a ratchet device which transfers power to the rear hub when you pedal forward and which allows the wheel to turn alone when you are coasting. The body of the freewheel screws into the hub, and the gears are mounted on the freewheel by some combination of screw threads and splines. (Splines are projecting ridges on the freewheel body which mate with corresponding notches in the cogs.) Choosing the method for mounting the cogs is particularly important for racers and other riders who might want to change cogs frequently, but most tourists tend to stay with one or two gear combinations. You do need to be able to find the combination of gears you want for a particular freewheel. Cogs are not usually interchangeable between freewheels, and some standard touring configurations are not available on all freewheels.

Freewheels are threaded so that the force of pedaling screws them more tightly into the hub; otherwise they would come loose the first time you pushed hard on the pedals. This causes the freewheel to lodge very tightly, so that removal can be a major problem. The freewheel body is keyed in

some way with notches or splines, so that a
freewheel remover can be inserted into the body and
used to unscrew it. A freewheel remover should be
purchased at the same time as the freewheel since
there are a number of non-interchangeable removers. The most common types have either a
set of splines on the outside of the remover that
correspond to a set of slots on the freewheel body
or a pair of teeth on the remover with matching
indentations on the freewheel. The splined type is
less likely to strip, though the ones with larger
teeth, such as the Sun Tour Pro Compe, are adequate
if you use them carefully.

The methods required for removal of either the
entire freewheel body or the cogs are important,
because you have to get one or the other off to
replace the spokes on the freewheel side of the rear
wheel. A tourist usually carries a freewheel remover
and uses a makeshift method to reach a service
station, where a large wrench or vise can be
borrowed to hold the freewheel remover and allow
the body to be taken off. Carrying a large enough
wrench is impractical unless you have a sag-wagon
or a large group of riders. A second method is to
dismantle the cogs, leaving the freewheel body
attached to the hub. With most hubs this leaves
enough room to insert spokes with no difficulty. The
technique is discussed more fully on pages 217–21
and is applicable only to freewheels whose outer cogs
are screwed on and whose inner ones are attached
with splines. Most modern freewheels are made this
way, but a few, such as the Regina, Cyclo 72, and
Atom, employ a different system.

Virtually all of the freewheels sold these days
are dependable, and the likelihood of having the
freewheel either freeze up or lock open so that you
cannot pedal forward is very slim. A few years ago,

there were quite a few bad freewheels on the market, but Japanese competitors' inexpensive, reliable models have greatly improved overall quality standards. The main considerations in choosing a freewheel are the ease with which it can be removed or dismantled, its weight, and the availability of cogs, in case you want to change gear ratios.

Some important innovations have been made recently by the two major Japanese competitors in the field, Shimano and Maeda. Other manufacturers can be expected to come up with better designs also. Shimano's Uniglide freewheel has teeth that are slightly splayed in alternate directions. When combined with the Uniglide chain, which has side plates that curve outward, this freewheel permits much easier shifting. (Shimano also makes a hub–freewheel unit that offers several advantages; see Chapter 6.)

The Sun Tour Ultra-6 freewheel also requires a special chain, one that has a narrower outside width created by shaving the ends off the rivets. Since the inside width remains the same as on standard chains, the chain can be used with normal front gears and other freewheels besides the Ultra-6. This narrower chain, however, permits you to use the Ultra-6 freewheel, which has six cogs instead of five but is no wider than a standard five-cog freewheel. Other six-speed freewheels have been used in the past, but they all required the wheel to be built differently and needed a wider than normal space between the rear dropouts of the bike. The Ultra-6 and the copies that certainly will follow permit the cyclist to switch from a ten-speed to a twelve-speed simply by changing the freewheel and chain. In fact, since the same cogs and freewheel bodies are used as in Sun Tour's standard systems, you might need only a narrow set of spacers and a few additional cogs. Seven-speed freewheels that require the same space as current six-speeds are now appearing as well.

Gearing Systems

Before discussing the final parts of the drive train—the gear shifting mechanisms—we must consider gear ratios and how they are obtained. Your choice of derailleurs depends upon the gears with which your bike is equipped. Though gear ratios can be changed fairly easily, alterations can be expensive, especially if the bicycle was not equipped originally with some thought given to changes that could be made later. Racers frequently change the gears on their bikes to deal with different kinds of courses. However, the tourist, particularly the beginner, probably is better off learning to use one system effectively. Later on, if you make many long rides on a regular basis, you may find that you can profitably use different gearing systems for various kinds of rides.

Gearing systems occasion more arguments than any other topic of debate among cyclists. There are literally thousands of possible combinations of gears, and all of them reflect compromises of one sort or another. The most important thing to realize from the beginning is that there is no ideal system. You must pick a setup that seems to meet your needs fairly well. Once you've done that, learn to ride well with the gears you have and forget the subject for a while. After you have become a good cyclist and are thoroughly familiar with one gearing system, you'll be much better able to judge the advantages and disadvantages of other possibilities.

Remember that the standard ten-speed gearing system consists of two large gears driven by the

pedals and a cluster of five smaller gears on the
freewheel driving the rear wheel. Before you try to
sort out various gearing setups, make sure you know
how the basic system works. Hang your bike from
the seat or turn it upside-down and run it through
the gears a few times. All normal-range gears drive
the rear wheel of the bike faster than the pedals. If
this weren't so, bikes with conventional wheels
would travel very slowly. In the days of direct-drive
bikes, when the pedals were connected directly to
the axle of the wheel as on a child's tricycle, reasonable speeds were achieved only by making the
driving wheel very large. The resulting bikes were
called *high-wheelers* and had small rear wheels
and huge front ones. Just getting up on a high-
wheeler and starting to ride is quite a trick since
the wheel often is nearly as tall as the rider.

The gearing terminology currently in use in the
United States is derived partly from the days of the
high-wheelers. In referring to a particular gear, we
call it a 100-inch gear, 80-inch gear, 60-inch gear,
etc. This means that the distance traveled with one
turn of the pedals using that gear is the same as on a
direct-drive bicycle, such as a high-wheeler, which
has a wheel of the specified diameter. Thus, if you
are riding a bike with a 60-inch gear, you travel the
same distance with each turn of the pedals as you
would if you were riding a high-wheeler with a
60-inch tall front wheel. The actual distance
traveled with each revolution of the pedals is this
distance times pi (3.1416). This probably is not the
most useful way of talking about gears, but it is well
established in this country, so we are stuck with it
for the time being.

The gear, expressed in inches as just described,
depends on the ratio of the number of teeth in the
front sprocket to those in the rear and on the

diameter of the bicycle wheel. The way the tire is made has some effect also; however, because construction differences are minor, the nominal size of the tire is all that is considered. Since most touring bikes in the United States employ 27-inch tires, the following discussion is based on a 27-inch tire size to keep things a little simpler. (Other tire sizes are considered in Chapter 6. The most common is 700C, which is slightly smaller than 27 inches and does not greatly affect gearing. Some touring bikes use 26-inch tires, which are enough smaller to make a particular gear ratio into a significantly lower gear; these tires are used on many inexpensive ten-speeds.)

Suppose you are riding with a chain driven by a front chainwheel having 52 teeth. If the chain drives a cog in the rear with 26 teeth, then the rear wheel of the bike turns around twice for each revolution of the cranks. The number of revolutions is always in the same ratio as the teeth in the front gear to the teeth in the rear cog because the spaces in the chain are fixed and can't slip or stretch unless the chain breaks or comes off a gear. Thus, for bikes with 27-inch wheels:

$$\text{gear in inches} = \frac{\text{number of teeth on front chainwheel}}{\text{number of teeth on rear cog}} \times 27 \text{ inches}$$

A bicycle with only one front chainwheel and one rear cog has only one gear ratio and is called a *fixed-gear* bike. Examples are standard children's bikes and track-racing cycles. (Bikes with three-speed hubs have concealed shifting mechanisms, and the formula above applies only to the middle of the three gears.) Ten-speeds have ten possible gear ratios, one for each of the combinations of front chainwheels and rear cogs. If the number of chainwheels is increased to three, you have a fifteen-speed bike. If there are six cogs in the rear, the bike can have twelve or eighteen theoretical speeds. The advantages and disadvantages of these combinations are discussed later in this chapter.

If you carefully examine the formula above or think a little about the mechanism, it is obvious that the same gear can be obtained from a number of combinations. Your 27-inch bike wheel will go the same distance at a given pedaling speed whether you have a 52–26, 50–25, 48–24, or 36–18 combination. It is the *ratio* that is important in determining the gear, together with the wheel size. The art of designing gearing systems lies in choosing the combination that gives the most useful set of ratios.

Ideally, it is desirable to have the gears on your bike closely and evenly spaced over the entire range you need, so that you can maintain a high cadence with approximately equal effort whether you are climbing a hill, going down the other side, or traveling on the flats. It also is desirable that the shifts from one gear to the next be easy, involving only one of the two gear derailleur levers at a time. It is never possible to meet all these requirements, so the cyclist has to make some sacrifices to secure other advantages.

Table 1 gives the resulting gears in inches for various combinations of front chainwheel and rear sprocket teeth, based on a bike with 27-inch wheels. For 700C wheels, these numbers must be multiplied by .987, and for 26-inch wheels, by .963. From this table you can construct smaller tables showing the gears provided by particular combinations.

Many good-quality bicycles designed for beginning and intermediate cyclists are equipped with what usually are called *alpine gears*. In a typical alpine combination, the front chainwheels are 52- and 40-tooth ones, and the teeth on the rear gear cluster number 14–17–20–24–28. The resulting gear table looks like this:

	14	17	20	24	28
52	100.3	82.6	70.2	58.5	**50.1**
40	**77.1**	63.5	54.0	45.0	38.6

The lowest gear in this setup is a 38.6-inch one, quite low for a strong cyclist but not very low for a beginner, especially when pedaling a bike loaded with touring gear. In the 38.6-inch low, the rear wheel is turning around almost one-and-a-half times for each revolution of the cranks. The high gear is a 100.3-inch one. Hundred-inch gears are traditional high ratios, but they really are larger than either the beginner or the tourist needs. A beginner is likely to use the gear while pedaling with much too low a cadence, while an experienced tourist rarely uses it at all, except while descending steep hills. By the time this high a gear is required, the bicycle can just as well be allowed to coast. As we shall see below, the cyclist has to sacrifice other options to get a 100-inch gear. It makes more sense to have a 90-inch high, even for a very strong cyclist; it is a far more useful gear and is high enough for any touring needs. The alpine setup has no 90-inch gear; it jumps from 82.6 to 100.3.

Overleaf: Gear chart for 27-inch wheels. This chart shows the gears obtained by using normal combinations of chainwheels and freewheel cogs. The gears are shown in "inches" which is the standard mode of reference in the United States and which refers to the diameter of the equivalent wheel in a fixed-gear bike. The larger the number, the higher the gear.

GEAR CHART FOR 27-INCH WHEELS

Number of Teeth on Rear Cog

	13	14	15	16	17	18	19	20	21	22	23
26	54.0	50.1	46.8	43.9	41.3	39.0	36.9	35.1	33.4	31.9	30.5
27	56.1	52.1	48.6	45.6	42.9	40.5	38.4	36.5	34.7	33.1	31.7
28	58.1	54.0	50.4	47.3	44.5	42.0	39.8	37.8	36.0	34.4	32.9
29	60.2	55.9	52.2	48.9	46.1	43.5	41.2	39.2	37.3	35.6	34.0
30	62.3	57.9	54.0	50.6	47.6	45.0	42.6	40.5	38.6	36.8	35.2
31	64.6	59.8	55.8	52.3	49.2	46.5	44.1	41.9	39.9	38.0	36.4
32	66.5	61.7	57.6	54.0	50.8	48.0	45.5	43.2	41.1	39.3	37.6
33	68.5	63.6	59.4	55.7	52.4	49.5	46.9	44.6	42.4	40.5	38.7
34	70.6	65.6	61.2	57.4	54.0	51.0	48.3	45.9	43.7	41.7	39.9
35	72.7	67.5	63.0	59.1	55.6	52.5	49.7	47.3	45.0	43.0	41.1
36	74.8	69.4	64.8	60.8	57.2	54.0	51.2	48.6	46.3	44.2	42.3
37	76.8	71.4	66.6	62.4	58.8	55.5	52.6	50.0	47.6	45.4	43.4
38	78.9	73.3	68.4	64.1	60.1	47.0	54.0	51.3	48.9	46.6	44.6
39	81.0	75.2	70.2	65.8	61.9	58.5	55.4	52.7	50.1	47.9	45.8
40	83.1	77.1	72.0	67.5	63.5	60.0	56.8	54.0	51.4	49.1	47.0
41	85.2	79.1	73.8	69.2	65.1	61.5	58.3	55.4	52.7	50.3	48.1
42	87.2	81.0	75.6	70.9	66.7	63.0	59.7	56.7	54.0	51.5	49.3
43	89.3	82.9	77.4	72.6	68.3	64.5	61.1	58.1	55.3	52.8	50.5
44	91.4	84.9	79.2	74.3	69.9	66.0	62.5	69.4	56.6	54.0	51.7
45	93.5	86.8	81.0	75.9	71.5	67.5	63.9	60.8	57.9	55.2	52.8
46	95.5	88.7	82.8	77.6	73.1	69.0	65.4	62.1	59.1	56.5	54.0
47	97.6	90.6	84.6	79.3	74.6	70.6	66.8	63.5	60.4	57.7	55.2
48	99.7	92.6	86.4	81.0	76.2	72.0	68.2	64.8	61.7	58.9	56.3
49	101.8	94.5	88.2	82.7	77.8	73.5	69.6	66.2	63.0	60.1	57.5
50	103.8	96.4	90.0	84.4	79.4	75.0	71.1	67.5	64.3	61.4	58.7
51	105.9	98.4	91.8	86.1	81.0	76.5	72.5	68.9	65.6	62.6	69.9
52	108.0	100.3	93.6	87.8	82.6	78.0	73.9	70.2	66.9	63.8	61.0
53	110.1	102.2	95.4	89.4	84.2	79.5	75.3	71.6	68.1	65.0	62.2
54	112.2	104.1	97.2	91.1	85.8	81.0	76.7	72.9	69.6	66.3	63.4
	13	14	15	16	17	18	19	20	21	22	23

Number of Teeth on Rear Cog

Number of Teeth on Chainwheel

GEAR CHART FOR 27-INCH WHEELS

Number of Teeth on Rear Cog

24	25	26	27	28	29	30	31	32	33	34	
29.3	38.1	27.0	26.0	25.1	.24.2	23.4	22.6	21.9	21.3	20.6	**26**
30.4	29.2	28.0	27.0	26.0	25.1	24.3	23.5	22.8	22.1	21.4	**27**
31.5	30.2	29.1	28.0	27.0	26.1	25.2	24.4	23.6	22.9	22.2	**28**
32.6	31.3	30.1	29.0	28.0	27.0	26.1	25.3	24.5	23.7	23.0	**29**
33.8	32.4	31.2	30.0	28.9	27.9	27.0	26.1	25.4	24.5	23.8	**30**
34.9	33.5	32.2	31.0	29.9	28.9	27.9	27.0	26.2	25.4	24.6	**31**
36.0	34.6	33.2	32.0	30.9	29.8	28.8	27.9	27.0	26.2	25.4	**32**
37.1	35.6	34.3	33.0	31.8	30.7	29.7	28.7	27.8	27.0	26.2	**33**
38.3	36.7	35.3	34.0	32.8	31.7	30.6	39.6	28.7	27.8	27.0	**34**
39.4	37.8	36.3	35.0	33.7	32.6	31.5	30.5	29.5	28.6	27.8	**35**
40.5	38.9	37.4	36.0	34.7	33.5	32.4	31.4	30.4	29.5	28.6	**36**
41.6	40.0	38.4	37.0	35.7	34.4	33.3	32.2	31.2	30.3	29.4	**37**
42.8	41.0	39.5	38.0	36.6	35.4	34.2	33.1	32.1	31.1	30.2	**38**
43.9	42.1	40.5	39.0	37.6	36.3	35.1	34.0	32.9	31.9	31.0	**39**
45.0	43.2	41.5	40.0	38.6	37.2	36.0	34.8	33.8	32.7	31.8	**40**
46.1	44.3	42.6	41.0	39.5	38.2	36.9	35.7	34.6	33.5	32.6	**41**
47.3	45.4	43.6	42.0	40.5	39.1	37.8	36.6	35.4	34.4	33.4	**42**
48.4	46.4	44.7	43.0	41.5	40.0	38.7	37.5	36.3	35.1	34.1	**43**
49.5	47.5	45.7	44.0	42.4	41.0	39.6	38.3	37.2	36.0	34.9	**44**
50.6	48.6	46.7	45.0	43.4	41.9	40l5	39.2	38.0	36.8	35.7	**45**
51.8	49.7	47.8	46.0	44.4	42.8	41.4	40.1	38.8	37.6	36.5	**46**
52.9	50.8	48.8	47.0	45.3	43.8	42.3	40.9	39.7	38.5	37.3	**47**
54.0	51.8	49.8	48.0	46.3	44.7	43.2	41.8	40.5	39.3	38.1	**48**
55.1	52.9	50.9	49.0	47.2	45.6	44.1	42.7	41.3	40.1	38.9	**49**
56.3	54.0	51.9	50.0	48.2	46.6	45.0	43.6	42.2	40.9	39.7	**50**
57.4	55.1	53.0	51.0	49.2	47.5	45.9	44.4	43.0	41.7	40.5	**51**
58.5	56.2	54.0	52.0	50.1	48.4	46.8	45.3	43.8	42.5	41.3	**52**
59.6	57.2	55.0	53.0	51.1	49.3	47.7	46.2	44.7	43.4	42.1	**53**
60.8	58.3	56.1	54.0	52.1	50.3	48.6	47.0	45.6	44.2	42.9	**54**
24	**25**	**26**	**27**	**28**	**29**	**30**	**31**	**32**	**33**	**34**	

Number of Teeth on Chainwheel

Number of Teeth on Rear Cog

The two combinations printed in bold type in the alpine gear table represent the gears in which the chain runs from the smaller chainwheel to the smallest rear cog and from the larger chainwheel to the largest rear cog. These two combinations usually are avoided because they force the chain to work at a rather extreme angle, resulting in increased friction and more rapid wear of all the parts, especially the aluminum-alloy teeth of the front chainwheels. The combination of the large front gear and the large rear one is the most damaging and should not be used. The other combination may not be too bad on some bicycles, depending on the gears involved and the length of the chainstays. You can tell if the combination is acceptable by the way the gears sound while you are riding. If it is quiet, the combination is usable; if it is noisy, it will cause too much wear. The following discussion assumes that neither of the extreme combinations are going to be used. On most touring bikes, then, there are actually only eight workable gears.

Gear Spacing

Using the alpine gear example above, note the spacing between the gears. In the first shift, from the lowest gear to the next lowest, the jump is 6.4 inches, from a 38.6 gear to a 45.0 one. The next jump is 9 inches, then 4.5, 5, 6.7, 12.4, and 17.7 to cover the seven shifts between the eight usable gears. The shifts are far from even, though this is not a particularly bad combination. There are differing opinions as to the ideal relationship. My own feeling is that, for touring, it is best to have movements of about five inches in each shift in the middle of the gearing range, where most of the pedaling is done. This allows you to make a fairly small adjustment as the grade or the wind changes a little, maintaining the same cadence and energy output. If you have a gearing arrangement with large changes, especially in the middle of the range, you often find that you have to strain at a gear that is too high or spin wastefully in one that is too low.

It is nice to have close gears at the top and bottom of the range, too, though not so important. You are likely to use your lowest gears only when climbing steep hills. As you move onto a hill, you tend to slow down rather quickly, and you usually shift down rather rapidly. Thus, a narrower range in the low gears is missed only when the grade is such that you could pedal in a little bit higher gear and don't have it available. Similarly, a moderately large jump at the high end is less of an inconvenience than it is in the middle of the range.

Naturally, the larger the range you are trying to span, the more large jumps you have to tolerate. One mistake is to demand a wider range than you really need. The alpine gearing system we have been examining is a good example of this type of error, though it is not nearly so bad as many other combinations. The 100.3-inch high gear definitely is larger than anything required by people who are likely to need a low gear of less than 40 inches. Racers do require high gears in the hundreds, but even in the mountains they never use gears lower than 40 inches. Tourists can do very nicely with a high gear of 90 inches or less, and this includes tourists who do much of their riding as racers. If you want to travel fast, learn to increase your cadence rather than carrying around gears you need only on downhill stretches.

Shifting Sequences

Another feature of any gearing system is the sequence of shifts. Ideally, you should have to move only one gear lever at a time, avoiding the necessity to *double shift*. Racers in particular try to stay away from sequences that require the chain to be moved on both sets of sprockets in order to change to the next gear. A racer has to make a lot of fine shifts to maintain the highest possible power output, and a double shift requires a break in pedaling that can cost precious time and interfere with rhythm.

Even though tourists also like to avoid double shifts, the problem is not nearly so critical as for racers. A tourist generally has adequate time to plan shifts in advance and does not have to be nearly so quick in making the changes. However, I do like to avoid doubleshifts at the low end whenever possible, since it can be important to make a fast shift on a steep hill, when a hesitation can cause the bike to nearly stop.

It is a good idea to examine the shifting sequence in any gearing system you are considering. Looking at the alpine gearing system again, you can see that three double shifts are required to take advantage of all the gears.

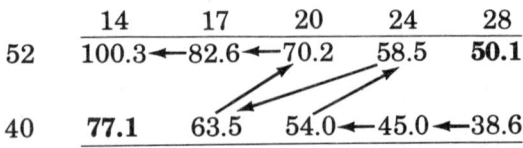

The first shift, from 38.6 to 45.0, requires that you move the chain in the rear from the 28-tooth cog to the 24-tooth one, requiring only one of the two derailleur levers, the right one. The same is true of the next shift, from 45.0 to 54.0, in which you move the chain in the rear again from the 24-tooth gear to the 20-tooth one. In the next change, however, from 54 to 58.5, the chain has to be pushed back to the 24-tooth cog in the rear and up to the 52-tooth chainwheel in the front, requiring you to shift with both levers. The next change is worse yet, since the chain has to go back to the smaller chainwheel in front and down two cogs in the rear. On the other hand, these problem shifts occur in the center of the shifting sequence, where you generally have more time to make them work.

To get some idea of the way a racer's gearing system differs from the one we have been discussing, consider one of the standard racing setups:

	13	14	15	16	17
52	108.0 ← 100.3 ← 93.6 ← 87.8				**82.6**
42	**87.2**	81.0 ← 75.6 ← 70.9 ← 66.7			

Note that the spacing is much closer. The jumps are 4.2, 4.7, 5.4, 6.8, 5.8, 6.7, and 7.7 inches and are even closer if the two high-friction combinations are permitted. More important, there is only one double shift, when the rider goes between the large and the small chainwheels. The racer can even take the double shift at a different time if necessary by using one of the high-friction combinations. The sequence also is easy to remember; shifts always are made with the rear derailleur except for one range change. A reasonable touring sequence with a fairly wide range can be constructed on the same principle, as follows:

	14	16	18	21	24
48	92.6 ← 81.0 ← 72.0 ← 61.7				**54.0**
34	**65.6**	57.4 ← 51.0 ← 43.7 ← 38.3			

As with the racing model, the shifts are easy, with only one double shift. The range is quite wide, but there are some large jumps in the middle of the gearing: 5.4, 7.3, 6.4, 4.3, 10.3, 9.0, and 11.6. Still, this is a much better touring combination than the alpine system.

How Low a Gear
Do You Need?

In choosing a gearing system, the low that you require determines a lot of the other compromises you have to make. Racers manage to achieve both a simple shifting sequence and close gears by eliminating the lower gear ratios. The touring cyclist should not try to do this. Trying to push too high a gear is an excellent way to develop knee trouble, so it is important to be sure that you have low enough gears to pedal at a good cadence rather than straining at the gears. A loaded bike clearly has to be geared lower than an unloaded racing machine, even if you keep your equipment light. Finally, your tours are not akin to short, hard training rides. You'll be riding most of the day, sometimes for many days at a time, and after a number of hours on the road, your enthusiasm for pumping a high gear over a pass is likely to wane.

The size of your lowest gear should be determined by your condition, your technique, and the steepness and duration of the hills you are likely to be riding. A 40-inch gear is low enough for a strong rider in almost any terrain, and it should be low enough for average cyclists as long as the hills are not too steep nor too long. There is no point in letting your ego interfere with choosing appropriate gears, however, and the beginner should not be swayed too much by this writer or by someone's claims that he or she never uses less than such-and-such a gear.

Many experienced tourists demand a "granny gear" of 30 inches or less to handle long mountain passes and very steep grades. Such a solution makes particular sense if you start touring at an older age. It takes you longer to develop strong conditioning, and it is extremely important not to tax your knees too much by hard pedaling. Learning to pedal a lower gear at high cadences will make you a far better and happier cyclist than straining to use someone else's gears.

If you already have a bike with a reasonable gearing system, such as the alpine gears mentioned earlier, I recommend that you ride it for a while on day tours to get some idea of your needs before spending a lot of money on a different system. Then, if you find that you have a hard time managing the hills in your area without luggage, you know that you need a significantly lower gear before heading out with full touring gear. If you are starting with a bike equipped with racing gears, you usually can switch to alpine gearing fairly cheaply by changing the freewheel cluster. You'll probably have to change the rear derailleur at the same time to handle the extra chain slack produced by the larger range.

Recommended Gearing Systems
In this section, several good gearing systems are recommended. The fairly close ratios they exhibit are important for the tourist, and if you find you need lower gears than the high 30's, I recommend that you change to a twelve- or fifteen-speed system rather than sacrificing the moderate jumps in the middle of the range. A weaker cyclist needs close ratios even more than a strong one does. Some recommended twelve- and fifteen-speed arrangements are included later in the chapter.

The earlier example of 48–34 chainwheels and a 14–16–18–21–24 cluster is a reasonable gearing system with an easy shifting sequence, though the jumps at the top end are rather high. The other disadvantage to this system is that the large jump between the chainwheels requires hard shifting on the front derailleur and may cause fairly rapid wear on the front chainwheels and derailleur cage. The standard alpine setup also is quite workable, though not as good as the one just described because of the somewhat larger range and the awkward shifting pattern.

My favorite ten-speed gearing system is as follows:

	14	17	20	24	28
46	88.7	73.1	62.1	51.8	**44.4**
42	**81.0**	66.7	56.7	47.3	40.5

When shifting from the low gear up, the jumps are 6.8, 4.5, 4.9, 5.4, 4.6, 6.4, and 15.6 inches. If the small-chainwheel-to-smallest-cog combination is usable, the last jump is split into steps of 7.9 and 7.7 inches. The other jumps are almost perfectly spaced, and the high gear is just about the right one for touring. Strong riders should find the 40-inch low to be adequate even for long days in the mountains. In regions where the hills are shorter, any rider in reasonable condition should be able to use this system. The first two changes do not require double shifts, so there are no awkward pauses on hills. Thereafter, every second shift is a double, so the pattern is easy to remember and there are no large, awkward jumps. I find this sequence easy to use.

A somewhat weaker rider can gear this same setup a bit lower. The easiest way to do this—and save weight at the same time—is to use slightly smaller chainwheels:

	14	17	20	24	28
44	84.8	69.9	54.4	49.5	**42.4**
40	**77.1**	63.5	54.0	45.0	38.6

This yields very similar jumps, but with everything geared a little lower.

A still lower gear and a wider range can be achieved without too much sacrifice of close ratios by leaving the chainwheels at 46–42 and using a freewheel with larger jumps. For someone who likes the 46–42 chainwheels and 14–28 freewheel but wants a larger range for mountain riding, this can be achieved simply by buying three larger cogs for the freewheel:

	14	17	21	26	32
46	88.7	73.1	59.1	47.8	**38.8**
42	**81.0**	66.7	54.0	43.6	35.4

The jumps are now 8.2, 4.2, 6.2, 5.1, 7.6, 6.4, and 15.6 inches. I also recommend this arrangement for an inexperienced rider, with the idea that after some training he or she might want to change the three larger cogs on the freewheel to the closer spacing. This is an inexpensive conversion.

Finally, a strong rider on flatter terrain might want to gear up the arrangement as follows:

	13	15	18	21	24
46	95.5	82.8	69.0	59.1	**51.8**
42	**87.2**	75.6	63.0	54.0	47.3

This gives a high gear in the middle 90's and jumps of 6.7, 5.1, 3.9, 6.0, 6.6, 7.2, and 12.7 inches. For hilly country with touring gear, however, you need the low gear of 40 inches.

Twelve-Speed Systems

Until recently, the problem with twelve-speed systems has been the extra space required by the additional cog. To accommodate an extra gear in the

conventional freewheel cluster, the space between
the rear dropouts of the bike has to be wider than
normal, and there also are complications in wheel
building, discussed in detail in Chapter 6. Chain
angles are increased, too, causing extra friction and
cog wear.

The new Ultra-6 system eliminates these
difficulties, however, because a six-speed freewheel
can be installed in the same space normally occupied
by a five-speed. Shifting actually is easier, and the
extra gear can be used either to increase the range of
a gearing system or to make the shifts closer. The
only real disadvantage is the weight of one extra
rear cog. An excellent twelve-speed touring setup is:

	14	16	19	23	27	32
46	88.7	77.6	65.4	54.0	46.0	**38.8**
42	**81.0**	70.9	59.7	49.3	42.0	35.4

The jumps in this system are 6.6, 4.0, 3.3, 4.7, 5.7,
5.7, 5.5, 6.7, and 11.1 inches, without the two
extreme combinations. An even lower gear of 33.4
inches can be achieved by changing the largest rear
gear from 32 to 34 teeth. To gear the system higher,
you can either substitute a 13−15−17−20−24−28
freewheel or change the chainwheels to 48−44 or
50−46.

Fifteen-Speed Bikes

By adding an extra chainwheel in the front, a
bicycle can be made into a fifteen-speed. This
sounds instantly attractive, but there are some
disadvantages you should be aware of before
choosing this option. The crank axle has to be made
longer to accommodate the extra cog and the chain
line is moved out somewhat from the bike, so that

unless the frame is beefed up, there is more whip. The tension on the right side of the bike between the crank axle and the rear wheel axle is given increased leverage by the longer dimension. The angle of the chain also is greater from either the largest or smallest front chainwheel, and the extreme combinations are considerably worse than they are with a ten-speed or an Ultra-6 twelve-speed. The largest chainwheel is likely to wear quickly, and friction is significant in some gears. In the past, triple chainwheels have been rather expensive and hard to come by, but this situation is improving.

Finally, since the main reason for going to a fifteen-speed usually is to gain really low gears for hill climbing without losing a close range on flat terrain, it is important to consider the effect of such a large range. The discussion of derailleurs below points out that the rear changer has to be designed to take up all the slack chain that results from the difference between the lowest and highest gears. Derailleurs with large capacities generally are heavier and less precise than those which take up less chain. It follows that you should not add the extra gears unless you really need them.

In general, if you do decide to add an extra chainwheel, it is best to add a really low gear and to plan to do most of your riding using the two larger chainwheels. It may be possible to almost center these in the normal double chainwheel position, with the third wheel placed as far inside as possible and used only with the two largest rear cogs. Usually, however, the center chainwheel is lined up with the center of the rear cluster. The geometry of the bicycle often does not permit the crankset to be moved any farther left.

Following is a good fifteen-speed configuration:

	13	15	18	22	26
46	95.5	82.8	69.0	56.5	**47.8**
42	87.2	75.6	63.0	51.5	43.6
26	**54.0**	**46.8**	39.0	31.9	27.0

The bottom gear is a true wall climber; with it you should easily be able to take a full touring load up a 25-percent grade. Such steep hills are quite rare, however, and the main advantage of this system is that cyclists who are not fanatics about training can still ride up long mountain roads and enjoy them. If you do need very low gears, a triple chainwheel is a better way to get them than using an overly wide spread that distorts the rest of the gearing system. The intervals in this system are 4.9, 7.1, 4.6, 7.9, 5.0, 6.5, 6.0, 6.6, 7.2, 4.4, and 8.3 inches. If you don't feel the need for the 95-inch high gear, you can make the ratios a bit closer with a 14−16−19−22−26 freewheel.

Derailleurs

Derailleurs are being discussed after gearing systems because they should be chosen to match the gears rather than the other way around. The finest racing derailleur in the world cannot be used with a wide spread of touring ratios because it cannot handle the large range.

There are two derailleurs on any ten-, twelve-, or fifteen-speed bicycle—one to move the chain between the front chainwheels and the other to move the chain among the rear cogs. The rear derailleur has the additional function of taking up the slack that develops in the chain when it is moved to smaller gears. The rear derailleur is thus somewhat more complex than the front one.

Normally, each derailleur is moved in one direction by a cable attached to the control lever and returned the other way by a spring. A few derailleurs have double cable systems instead, so that the motion in each direction is positively directed by the lever.

Most serious cyclists prefer to have the cable levers located on the down tube of the bicycle. This is an inconvenient position for beginners, who have a hard time getting used to it until they have practiced awhile. The location is a good one, however, since the cables can be run to the derailleurs with a minimum of bending and only one short length of housing, so there is less cable stretch and friction to interfere with efficient shifting. Positioning the cable levers on the handlebar stem, as is done on many inexpensive bikes, is a poor arrangement; it is convenient only to novices.

A third possibility, however, does have some special advantages and is preferred by some experienced bicycle tourists. Special levers can be installed in the handlebar ends so that shifting can be done while riding on the drops without removing your hands from the bars. Advocates argue that this position is far safer in difficult situations if you're riding a heavily loaded bike. Handlebar shifters have either spring or ratchet devices to hold them in position. Cables are run under the handlebar tape or are led out through holes drilled in the handlebars with sleeves to reduce friction. The disadvantages of handlebar shifters are the extra weight, cable stretch, friction, and complexity they introduce. Personally, I never load my bike so heavily that I feel the need for handlebar shifters, and I prefer the standard type.

Down tube shifters are quite simple and have the advantages of light weight and smoothness of operation. Normally, an easily adjustable friction screw is attached to the pivot of the lever, but some levers use heavier ratchet mechanisms instead. On the best touring bikes, the cable stops for derailleurs are brazed on and may limit the types of derailleurs that can be used, especially in front. Various models use different means for transferring the force of the cable, so be sure any front derailleur you are considering will fit your bike.

Most of the front derailleurs made by reputable manufacturers work adequately. Since the front derailleur simply pushes the chain back and forth, it is rather simple. Look for light weight and smooth operation. Be sure that the cage is built to accommodate your lowest front gear, especially if you have large differences in front chainwheel size. With triple systems, check to see that the back-and-forth range is enough to shift over the wider distance, regardless of the position of the chain on the rear cogs. Most front derailleurs are built so that the derailleur goes into high gear when the lever is pushed forward and the cable tension is reduced. A few work the other way. It isn't too important how yours works, but people used to one system may not want to switch.

The rear derailleur is more complex and is composed of two main parts. At the bottom is an arm or cage with two pulleys around which the chain is threaded. This arm pivots on the body of the derailleur and is spring-loaded so that it can take up the slack in the chain. The lower pulley, called the *idler pulley,* thus moves forward and back as you shift between larger and smaller gears. The upper pulley, or *jockey pulley,* and the cage around it serve to actually push the chain from one cog to another. Since the arm between the pulleys must take up all or most of the slack in the chain, the length of this arm is the main determinant of the total capacity of the derailleur. This capacity is expressed in *teeth:* the total number of links of slack chain the derailleur can take up. The capacity must be at least as great as the sum of the differences between the largest and smallest cogs in the front and rear. Thus, for the fifteen-speed recommended earlier, the capacity must be $(46-26) + (26-13) = 33$ teeth. In contrast, the ten-speed system most highly recommended here requires a capacity of $(46-42) + (28-14) = 18$ teeth, just a little more than half as many. Compare both of these with the racing pattern mentioned earlier: $(52-42) + (17-13) = 14$ teeth. Clearly, a derailleur with an arm just long enough to handle this racing pattern would not even come close to taking up the slack in the fifteen-speed gearing system. A derailleur with an arm long enough to work on either touring system would work with the racing gears, but not nearly so precisely, so the racer would avoid it.

The upper part of most rear derailleurs, the part that is attached to the frame dropout, consists primarily of a metal parallelogram. The parallelogram is spring-loaded so that it swings the pulley arm out toward the smallest sprocket when it is permitted to. The cable from the control lever extends diagonally across the parallelogram and compresses it in the opposite direction when the cable is tightened, shifting the chain inward toward the larger cogs.

There are several important design features on the rear derailleur besides those already mentioned. The derailleur can be directly attached to the dropout by means of a threaded hole that is machined in the better dropouts or it can be secured with a mounting claw that hangs over the axle. The derailleur may have an additional pivot point at this attachment that swings it back and allows it to take up more chain, but which also then causes the chain to engage fewer teeth on the cog, increasing wear on both the cog and the chain.

When the bike is in low gear, the jockey pulley should be positioned in front of the largest cog and rather close to it. The best position permits about three links of straight chain (1½ inches) to show between the pin where the chain starts to bend around the cog and the point at which it starts to wrap around the pulley. When a close fit such as this is achieved, a derailleur that is built to fit a 17-tooth large cog perfectly will smash right into a 32-tooth cog. Thus, there is an additional derailleur capacity, also expressed in teeth, which describes how large a cog can be used on the freewheel. Often only one of the two derailleur capacities is listed in catalogues, and if the fit is likely to be close, you should check carefully to be sure that a particular derailleur works with your gearing system.

It is desirable for the forward swing of the rear derailleur to be adjustable, but most are not, except by doing a lot of unreasonable fiddling. A few Sun Tour models are the only exceptions at the time this is being written.

Once you have determined that a particular derailleur has the capacity you need for your gearing system, the important features to look for are durable construction, light weight, and smooth, positive shifting. Derailleurs chosen to work very close to their capacity usually do not function as well as those with a few teeth more capacity than what is required. Most manufacturers now produce a large line of derailleurs to handle most needs, but it is a good idea to check the reputation of a particular model with someone who has a gearing range similar to the one you want to use. A good design for racing is not necessarily good if the arm is length-ened to handle a touring range.

A fair amount of friction is caused by the jockey wheels supplied with derailleurs and can be reduced significantly by replacing the wheels with Bullseye sealed ball-bearing pulleys. These are made of an aluminum alloy and seem to last indefinitely.

Chapter 6

Wheels and Their Components

THE WHEELS OF a bicycle are truly amazing structures; they are built from light, fragile components but exhibit amazing strength and resilience when correctly assembled. The proper choice of wheels is especially important to the cyclist for a number of reasons. Since they are moving parts, the wheels must turn with as little friction as possible so that energy is not wasted in overcoming unnecessary drag. Besides the friction of the bearings, the wheels also cause more wind resistance than one might guess, and, most important, the tires have a rolling resistance as they move along the road. This rolling resistance is an inevitable consequence of the grip and cushioning that the tires provide; in choosing tires and other wheel components, the cycle tourist has to balance these desirable features against the rolling resistance that accompanies them.

A bicycle wheel transmits forces between the bicycle and the pavement through a clever system designed to be as light as possible. Light weight is more important in the wheels than anywhere else on the bike, because in order to make the bicycle roll, the wheels must be given angular momentum as well as forward momentum, and that requires energy. The heavier the wheels, the more energy required. Weight in the tires and rims is particularly critical because more energy is required to spin mass that is farther from the center of rotation.

Structurally, your weight and that of the bicycle are borne by the axles, which rest on the bearings in the hubs. The hubs themselves turn around these bearings and are suspended from the spokes above. The spokes, in turn, hang from the arch formed by the rim. The weight is then transmitted through the rim, which is prevented from distorting by the tension of the spokes. The design of all these elements and of the tires is discussed in the rest of this chapter.

The fundamental design consideration for any cycle tourist is the weight of the wheels. You want the lightest wheels that can do the job, with special attention given to the tires and rims, because each time you stop, all the energy stored in the revolving wheels must be dissipated in the friction of the braking system. You then must replace that energy from the muscles in your legs when you start up again. The lighter the wheels, the less energy required whenever you accelerate the bike.

Hubs

The weight of the hubs is important, as all weight on a bicycle is. However, because a hub rotates at the center of the wheel, additional weight there is not as critical as it is at the rim and tire. The most important considerations in choosing a hub are its mechanical efficiency and ease of maintenance. The design and type of bearings and quality of finish are the main determinants of these qualities. The diameter of the flanges on a hub is also of some importance to the rigidity and strength of the wheel.

Traditional hubs are hollow and rotate around a central axle cup that takes a set of free ball bearings (see Figure 11). A cone screws onto each end of the axle to form the inside rolling surface for the ball bearings, and a system of washers and nuts locks the races into proper adjustment. (The races are the grooves in which the balls run.) When they are

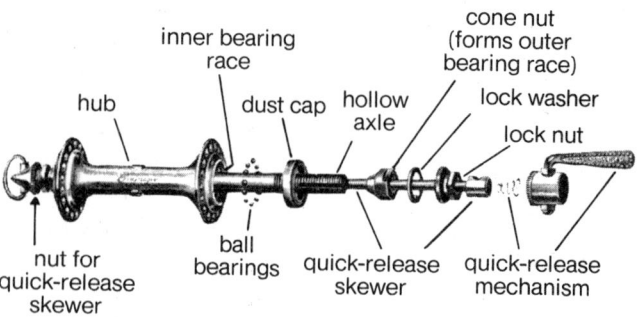

inner bearing race   cone nut (forms outer bearing race)   hub   dust cap   hollow axle   lock washer   lock nut   nut for quick-release skewer   ball bearings   quick-release skewer   quick-release mechanism

11. A conventional low-flange hub with loose ball bearings. The balls ride between a race pressed into the aluminum-alloy hub and the cone, which is screwed onto the hollow axle and used to adjust the tightness of the bearing. A dust cap covers the bearing, and a set of lock washers and a locknut fix the position of the cone. The quick-release mechanism permits the wheel to be removed or mounted with a flick of the lever.

properly machined, lubricated, cleaned, and adjusted, such bearings have very low friction and work well. They are relatively easy to maintain and to obtain parts for. However, such bearings are quite vulnerable to penetration by dirt and moisture, and they may need fairly frequent disassembling and cleaning to keep them running smoothly and to prevent excessive wear due to grit. Some of the newer hubs employing sealed bearings have the distinct advantage of being essentially maintenance-free.

Some tourists don't like hubs with sealed bearings and prefer the traditional variety for three reasons. The first reason is that such hubs generally are more expensive. Second, the best conventional hubs usually have had slightly less rolling resistance than sealed types because the seals on the bearings cause a slight drag. This concern affects racers more than it does recreational riders, but the newer sealed-bearing hubs, such as those designed by Avocet and Durham, have solved this problem. Finally, and most important, some tourists are nervous about using a hub that is hard to repair in the field should anything go wrong, even if the equipment tends to be more trouble-free. Earlier sealed-bearing hubs had to be sent to the factory if the bearings needed servicing, while the newer designs mentioned above use bearing sets that are widely available throughout the United States and that can be replaced in the field. My own experience with the original Phil Wood sealed bearings has been excellent, however; I have ridden on them for five or six years, including a good deal of foul-weather cycling, and have had no problems.

In general, I recommend sealed-bearing hubs if you can afford them, particularly if you ride a good deal in bad weather or on dirt roads, or if you don't like to do regular maintenance on bearings. If you want to get maximum performance at minimum cost and don't mind keeping your hubs clean and well lubricated, choose conventional hubs. There are some good ones that are relatively inexpensive. It is a good idea to get several replacement balls when you buy conventional hubs and to keep them in a plastic bag with your tools. In foul weather make sure there is plenty of grease in the bearings, preferably the water-resistant type marketed by Phil Wood. It also is helpful to wrap a little grease-impregnated thread around the outside edges of the cone nuts to partially protect the grooves through which water can enter the bearings.

Most quality hubs employ a hollow axle that is clamped into the dropouts with a special quick-release mechanism. Quick releases are handy to use for some purposes, though they are essentially a carry-over from racing, in which they are neces-sary to permit lightning-fast wheel changes. The tourist can do perfectly well with either conven-tional nuts or Allen-head screws for mounting. Wing nuts are adequate on the front wheel, but they cannot be tightened sufficiently for use on the rear.

The best hubs are made primarily from aluminum alloys to save weight, but use bearings, races, and axles composed of steel. Titanium can be substituted for steel at a premium price in order to shave off a few more ounces.

There is a wide range of flange diameters available. The various sizes generally are categorized as either *high flange* or *low flange,* the former projecting considerably farther from the axle than the latter (see Figure 12). Flange size is related to the spoke pattern of the wheel and is discussed

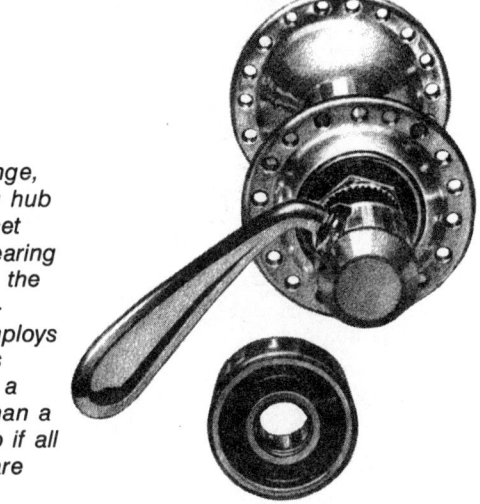

12. A high-flange,
sealed-bearing hub
made by Avocet
along with a bearing
that is used in the
hub. The high-
flange hub employs
shorter spokes
and produces a
stiffer wheel than a
low-flange hub if all
other factors are
equal.

later in this chapter with spokes, lacing, and wheel
building.

Tires

The standard racing bicycle tire is known as a
sew-up or *tubular tire* (see Figure 13) because it
consists of a tubular casing, sewn together with an
inside seam, which completely encloses the lightweight tube that holds the air. The sew-up is
mounted on a lightweight rim that is troughed on
the outside to accept the tire. The tire is held firmly
with glue, shellac, or a special tape with adhesive on
both sides.

The other common type of bicycle tire usually is
called a *clincher* (see Figure 13), though technically
the name refers to an earlier type of rim that has
not been used for many years. A modern clincher
tire is made much like an automobile tire; it has a
U-shaped cross section with a wire molded into each

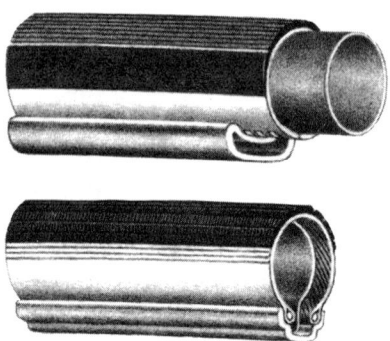

13. *A cross section of a sew-up, or tubular, tire* (top) *and a wired-on, or clincher, tire* (bottom). *Most modern clincher rims incorporate a channel construction patterned after the sew-up rim.*

side that locks into a channel in the rim. A separate tube fits into the tire for inflation.

Sew-ups always have been preferred by racers for several reasons. The tires themselves are very light, can carry extremely high pressures, and employ rims that are light for their strength because they are constructed with a hollow cross-section. An additional advantage, especially for racers not being followed by a car carrying spare wheels, is that a flat tire can be switched for a fresh one in a very short time. Finally, sew-ups have a wonderful lively feel that only the newest clinchers come close to reproducing.

Until quite recently, clinchers were much heavier than sew-ups, required considerably heavier rims to achieve the same strength, and could not be inflated to nearly so high a pressure. It was harder to carry a spare tire because the wires prevented clinchers from being neatly folded, as sew-ups could be. Clinchers take longer to *change* because the wired edge must be carefully pried off

the rim. However, they are much easier and faster
to *repair* because the tube is readily accessible once
the tire has been removed. With sew-ups, the
stitching on the tire has to be cut and later resewn;
moreover, the location of the puncture may be hard
to find since air can migrate and escape through
stitching some distance from the puncture itself.

Clinchers always have been the tire of choice
for tourists needing a heavier tire relatively resistant to road hazards or one that cushioned the ride
when traveling on rough surfaces. The new, narrow,
high-pressure clinchers, however, have eliminated
most of the advantages of sew-ups for touring
cyclists because the weight of some light tires and
rims has been reduced to a range only slightly
heavier than sew-ups designed for road use. In most
touring situations, particularly on long trips,
clinchers are more convenient to repair than sew-
ups because the total time required is far less.
The few more minutes required at the time of the
puncture to remove the tire usually are not significant in touring situations. Finally, clinchers
are far cheaper than sew-ups, which cost two or
three times as much as clinchers do. The initial
investment required for sew-ups is even greater
than these figures indicate since more spares have to
be carried to make up for the time required to
patch a tire.

With the advent of modern, lightweight
clinchers, there appears to be little reason to tour
on sew-ups. The new, narrow clincher rims
incorporate sophisticated designs that achieve the
necessary strength with less weight. These rims
can be matched with light, high-pressure tires so
that the tourist can choose wheels that are almost
as light as touring sew-ups with neither their
expense nor inconvenience.

Wheel and tire sizes are not standardized between the United States and Great Britain on the one hand, and continental Europe and other countries that have completely converted to metric measurements on the other. In the United States, relatively light, high-pressure clinchers usually are the 27-by-1¼-inch size. The tires used on most ten-speeds intended for young people, which have a wider profile and use softer pressures, are the 26-by-1⅜-inch size. These latter tires are of a considerably smaller diameter. Their wider profile makes them more suitable for riding on dirt roads and soft surfaces, so that those planning to do a lot of such touring may want to consider equipping their bikes with steel rims and 26-inch tires. The tires are enough smaller, however, that you will have problems fitting brakes to a bike designed for 27-inch tires but using 26-inch ones. Lower pedal clearance from the ground also may cause difficulties.

The corresponding Continental sizes for tires are 700C for 27-inch tires and 650B for 26-inch ones, but these sizes are not interchangeable with their American counterparts. Sew-up tires and rims always come in the 700C size (considering the diameter of the rim only), and the rims for these tires are just a little smaller in diameter than the rims for 27-inch tires. While the same frame size can be used easily, brakes have to be realigned if you switch from one wheel size to the other. For this reason, many racers who use sew-ups for racing and switch to clinchers for touring and training prefer to use clinchers in the 700C size. The disadvantage when touring in the United States is that 700C tires are less widely available. You can find them in good bike shops, but even there the selection is more limited than that of 27-inch tires. The latter can be found even in standard discount stores in emergencies, though the quality of the tires naturally is poor.

Most of the new, narrow-profile clinchers fit on standard 27-by-1¼-inch rims, but narrower, lighter rims are made especially for them. The narrow tires typically are designated 27 inches by 1⅛ inches or, for still narrower models, 27 inches by 1 inch. Any good catalogue indicates which rims and tires are compatible, however, and the sales-people at a good bike shop can tell you. Remember that the 27-inch size and the 700C size are not interchangeable, though the same inner tubes can be used with either tire.*

There is no perfect choice of tire for touring. The larger, semi-balloon sizes, together with stronger and heavier steel rims, are well suited for people who plan to tour a lot on rough roads, especially when soft dirt or gravel surfaces also

---

*The confusion in the designation of tire sizes is incredible. The 27-by-1¼-inch designation, for example, is supposed to indicate that the outside diameter of the tire is 27 inches and that the height and width are each 1¼ inches. This becomes particularly confusing since a 27-by-1-inch tire can fit on the same rim and is allegedly an inch in width and height yet still presumably 27 inches in diameter. Since the continental European system is completely different, the confusion becomes even greater.

The European Tire and Rim Technical Organization (ETRTO) has developed a new system of nomenclature that may help clarify things a little if it comes into general use. The size is designated with two numbers—32–630, for example. The first number indicates the nominal height and width of the tire in millimeters. The second designates the diameter of the rim in millimeters *where the inside of the tire contacts it.* Thus, the 32–630 (27-by-1¼-inch) tire fits a rim on which the channels for the tire edges are 630 millimeters in diameter and the tire is nominally 32 millimeters wide and high. Thus, 27-by-1-inch tires are 25–630's in the ETRTO system, while 700C tires are 25–622's. Actual widths of the tires vary somewhat, but 25-mm tires generally should be mounted on the new narrow rims, while 32-mm ones should be mounted on 1¼-inch rims.

are anticipated. Since most touring in the United States takes place on quite good roads, however, such tires rarely are used by cycle tourists. The most versatile choice for most purposes is a set of good-quality alloy rims and high-pressure, 27-by-1¼-inch tires with a substantial tread, but not a knobby, heavy tread. The best tires of this type hold up well, can be used on fairly rough ground, can tolerate quite a few road hazards without excessive numbers of punctures, and can be ridden at pressures of 100 pounds per square inch (psi) or so with no problem. Ridden at slightly lower pressures, they can get you by on some dirt roads without too much difficulty.

For fast day tours and longer trips on reasonably good roads, you may want to tour on lightweight, high-pressure clinchers with light, narrow rims. These tires work well for cyclists experienced enough to avoid most road hazards and touring with light loads. They make a bike very responsive and are a joy to ride, especially if you like to cover distances of more than 100 miles a day regularly. They must be ridden at fairly high pressures (90 psi or a little higher) to prevent rim damage from chuckholes, and because of this and their thin walls, they are punctured easily by glass, gravel bits, and thorns. Thus, if you have to ride much at night, when you can't see broken glass and other road hazards, or if you are riding in areas where there is a lot of debris coupled with heavy traffic that keeps you stuck on the shoulders, you may want to stay with 27-by-1¼-inch tires. Narrow-profile tires also are hard to control on soft and irregular surfaces, such as dirt roads, because they sink in more and are easily deflected by bumps. On the generally good roads in the United States, however, most touring is done on fairly smooth surfaces with only occasional chuckholes, and the narrow-profile clinchers are quite suitable.

The narrow clinchers also make excellent spares, whatever type of clincher tire you use. They are light and can be coiled into a small package, unlike the heavier types. Since these tires (in the appropriate size) can fit on the standard 27-by 1¼-inch or 700C rims, they are ideal for this purpose.

Rims

Most of the variations in rims have been discussed in conjunction with the corresponding tires. The rim and tire must be of matching size, though labeling often proves rather confusing. Rims are made either of steel or of an aluminum alloy, the latter sometimes reinforced by inserted material, such as wood strips. Although steel rims are cheaper, this fact should not influence the tourist. Remember that light weight is especially important in the wheels, and if you are trying to get by on a budget, spend the extra money for alloy rims rather than for a lighter seat, stem, or sleeping bag. The only reason to use steel rims is for durability on extremely rough terrain. Thus, if you are planning cross-country trips with heavy loads, extensive touring on jeep roads, and other forms of hard traveling, get steel rims; otherwise, stick with alloy ones.

Rim sizes have been discussed already. Tourists who insist on using sew-up tires for touring will want to build a set of wheels with relatively heavy, durable rims (compared with other sew-up rims), probably close to 400-gram ones, such as the Mavic Montherly or the Fiamme red label. The lightweight, narrow clincher rims, such as the Mavic Modular, Rigida, and Super Champion, employ special hollow reinforcing channels or a hollow cross-section to lend rigidity. Weinman uses a concave surface facing the hub to gain still more rigidity for the weight. Clincher rims have to be stronger than sew-up rims to withstand the spreading force of the pressurized tube, a force absorbed by the thread and tape in sew-ups.

Spoke holes for touring should be reinforced with steel ferrules or eyelets for extra durability; otherwise the spoke nipples will gradually distort the holes, causing the wheel to lose its trueness, and will eventually break through.

The braking surfaces of the rims should not be covered with small indentations, a feature usually found on steel rather than alloy rims. Such indentations are designed to provide better braking, but they do the opposite in wet weather, trapping water on the braking surface. Since wet weather creates the most critical braking condition, the braking surfaces should be smooth.

Spokes and Lacing Patterns

The art of wheel building is well worth learning, both to give you a general understanding of the bicycle's functioning and to enable you to make repairs in the event of serious wheel damage on tour. Once you have properly built a set of wheels, you will find the job of *truing* a wheel after replacing a few broken spokes to be much easier. Instructions and illustrations for building and truing a wheel are given in Appendix II; the present discussion covers spokes and the various spoke lacing patterns that can be used.

Spokes are those wonderful gadgets that mysteriously hold the wheel together. The spokes radiate out from the hub to the rim. They are tightened by screwing the nipple at the rim end of each spoke onto the threaded end of the spoke itself, so that each spoke is in tension. As long as the wheel is properly put together, with enough tension in all the spokes and equal force being exerted by each one, it will stay round and remain very strong. Since the spokes pull the rim to either side as well as toward the center of the hub, the rim also is held centered between the flanges. Spokes are strong only in tension, so when you are sitting on your bike, it is not the lower spokes in the wheel that are bearing most of your weight directly, but the upper ones, on which you are hanging. The lower ones do serve at the same time to hold the rim's round shape so that the rim remains in an arch from which the upper spokes are suspended.

The choice of ideal lacing patterns is one of the standard subjects of debate among bicycle freaks, along with the related issue of flange size. When all other conversation fails, lacing patterns and flange size are always good for a few hours of heated exchange. Try it sometime and see. Just walk into a local bike shop and casually remark, "I really think high-flange, cross-four wheels are the only good touring pattern!" Then lean back and watch the sparks fly.

The lacing patterns in wheels are referred to by indicating the number of spokes that cross any one spoke. Wheels can be laced radially (no crosses), cross-one, cross-two, cross-three, or cross-four. In the rear wheel, the spokes on the two sides may use different patterns, as will be discussed later. Take a look at the front wheel of your bike or any bike and check the cross pattern. Start where the mushroom-shaped end of a spoke (the *head* of the spoke) is anchored in the hole in the flange. The spoke you are examining probably crosses the paths of one or two others very close to the hub. The other spokes are inserted in the same flange of the hub but on the opposite side, and they lean in the opposite direction. A little farther out, the spoke you are following most likely crosses one or two more spokes going the other way. The total number of intersections gives the cross pattern. On touring bikes, the two common patterns are cross-three and cross-four. The illustrated description of wheel-building in Appendix II depicts a cross-three wheel.

Spoke Dynamics

As a bicycle rolls along freely, the spokes are loaded dynamically, with shifting tension in each one. In an older wheel in which the surfaces have corroded a bit, you can hear the spokes shifting against one another at the intersections. The load is dependent on speed, frame design, your weight, your riding position, luggage weight and distribution, and the angle of the slope. Bumps in the road which suddenly force the wheel to rise introduce complicated shock loading in a few spokes. This shock loading is affected by the tires and rim design, the pressure in the tires, the rigidity of the frame, and the way you are riding. If, for example, you are sitting solidly on the bike with your arms stiff, the spokes have to lift much of your weight to get over the bump; if you rise onto the pedals and hold the bar lightly, the bike rotates under you, placing far less stress on the spokes.

The shifting forces in the spokes are complicated further when you are pedaling or braking rather than just coasting. In this case, rotational forces also are being transmitted through the spokes. When you are pedaling forward, the spokes in the rear wheel are being used to transmit rotational acceleration from the hub (driven by the freewheel) to the rim and tire. When you brake, the spokes in both wheels are used to transmit the braking force from the rims, on which the brakes press, to the hubs.

Wheel Design

There are a number of factors involved in choosing spokes and lacing patterns for a wheel; that is why there are no universally accepted formulas for construction. Wheels have to be stiff enough to transmit pedaling and braking forces as efficiently as possible. Too much distortion of the wheel under these forces wastes energy and causes metal fatigue in the shifting components of the wheel, with the likelihood of later failure. Excessive flexibility also may contribute to instability of the bicycle, especially during high-speed descents. On the other hand, a wheel that is too stiff does not absorb road shocks, making for an uncomfortable ride, possible damage to the bicycle, dangerous bouncing in descents, and loss of pedaling energy due to bouncing and vibration. The wheels are not the only components involved in determining this stiffness–shock absorption balance. The stiffness of the frame, size and pressure of the tires, riding style, load, and many other factors are all inter-related. Nor is there an ideal balance. The hard-riding, performance-oriented tourist is likely to want a stiffer bike that transmits pedaling force with little energy waste and responds quickly to steering. Other riders may prefer less high-strung and more forgiving mounts. Just as there is no one perfect frame for everyone, there is no one ideal wheel structure.

For the tourist, stability and durability are particularly important. A well-designed and

well-executed wheel should stay true for a long
time without constant readjustment of spoke
tension. The spokes should not break very often.
Breakage usually occurs in the rear wheel on the
freewheel side, where spokes can be hard to replace
on tour because of the difficulty of removing the
freewheel. (The reason these spokes break most
frequently is discussed further on.) Thus, it is
worth using slightly heavier spokes if necessary to
avoid having to fuss frequently with broken
spokes.

Cross Patterns

Radial spoking is not common; it most often is seen
on the front wheels of track bikes. It produces a
very stiff wheel, not desirable on touring or
road-racing bikes. More important, no pedaling or
braking force can be transmitted through a spoke
that travels radially between the rim and hub. If
such force is applied, the wheel distorts somewhat
and large forces of tension appear in the spokes. In
general, as the angle the spokes make with the rim
becomes sharper, pedaling and braking forces are
transmitted with smaller increases in the tension of
the spokes. These sharper angles accompany a
greater number of crosses and require longer spokes.
Such patterns produce wheels that absorb shocks
a little better and enable peak loads to be shared
more equally among the spokes. Sharper angles
tend to stress the spoke ends, however, where there
is some sharp bending, especially with cross-four
patterns on high-flange hubs.

Flange Size

The size of the flanges used is another factor
influencing wheel design. With a larger flange the
spoke comes into the rim at a greater angle from
the plane of the wheel, giving the wheel more

side-to-side stability with the same spoke tension. Because a large flange spans part of the distance to the rim, the spokes are shorter and develop higher tension in response to road shocks than if a low flange is used. (More force is required to stretch a shorter spoke of the same diameter a certain amount.) Thus, with other things being equal, a high-flange, cross-three wheel is the stiffest of the normal patterns and the least shock absorbent, followed (in my experience) by low-flange, cross-three; high-flange, cross-four; and low-flange, cross-four.

The exact measurements between opposite spoke holes in low- and high-flange hubs vary somewhat with the brand, but typical ones are 40 to 44.5 millimeters for low flange and 67 millimeters for high flange. Some manufacturers also use intermediate sizes, such as Phil Wood's 48-mm sealed-bearing hubs. High-flange hubs naturally are heavier. There is no general agreement on which type is better for touring, and the fashion seems to change from year to year. Personally, I prefer to use low-flange hubs with a cross-three lacing pattern, perhaps using a cross-four on the freewheel side of the rear wheel (about which more later).

Spoke Number and Size

The number of spokes used in each wheel also can be varied. More spokes mean that loads are distributed better and that spoke breakage is less frequent. Wheels with more spokes are less likely to be damaged if they hit rocks or chuckholes. They also are naturally heavier. Thirty-six-hole flanges and rims (often confusingly abbreviated as 36°) generally seem best for touring, with 40-spoke rear wheels sometimes used by heavy riders carrying a good deal of luggage and commonly used on tandems.

Spokes of various lengths, materials, and thicknesses are available. Proper length is determined by flange size, rim design, wheel diameter, and cross pattern. All spokes should be galvanized, plated, or made from stainless steel to prevent rusting and weakening. Stainless-steel spokes are attractive, but they are weaker and more expensive than galvanized spokes. Chrome-plated types are weaker than either stainless-steel or galvanized types. Spoke thickness normally is specified by gauge; the smaller the gauge number, the thicker the spoke. Spokes are either *straight gauge,* which are much cheaper to make and should be much cheaper to buy, or *butted,* with thinner centers to reduce weight. Butted spokes usually are described by giving the end-center-end gauge, as with 15–16–15 or 14–15–14 spokes. The weight advantage of butted spokes is quite small, but they are so common that you may not be able to purchase straight-gauge spokes at a significantly cheaper price. Nipples that fit on the screw ends of spokes should come with them. Aluminum-alloy nipples are not a great deal more expensive, but they do save a significant amount of weight: 40 to 50 grams per wheel near the rim, where weight is most critical.

As with other factors in wheel design, there are no hard and fast rules in choosing spoke thickness because of the many variables involved, but most riders who keep their luggage weight down find straight 15-gauge spokes or butted 15 -16 -15 ones to be strong enough. If you are heavy, have a heavy riding style, or expect to place unusual stress on the spokes because of heavy luggage or bad surfaces, you may want to use 14-gauge or

14–15–14 spokes. A tandem generally has spokes at least this thick on the rear wheel.

The Rear Wheel

The structure of the rear wheel is complicated by the space required for the drive chain on the right-hand side. The wheel itself is centered between the two sides of the frame, not between the hub flanges, from which the spokes radiate. Since the entire freewheel cluster has to fit on the right side, the right-hand flange of the rear wheel is much closer to the rim center than the left-hand flange is. When the wheel is built, the actual centering is done by adjusting the tension of the spokes so that equal sideways pull is exerted from either side, all the way around the wheel.

The sideways pull each spoke exerts is dependent upon the tension of the spoke and the angle at which it meets the rim. A spoke that meets the rim at a greater angle to its plane pulls the rim harder to the side for each pound of tension in the spoke. What all this means is that the spokes on the freewheel side, which have to come in at a much flatter angle, have to be screwed in a lot tighter.

Building the rear wheel so that it can be correctly centered with the spokes flatter on the right side is called *dishing*. The right-hand spokes also are a bit shorter, so they have less length to stretch with the bumps. This results in even higher loading compared with the spokes on the other side whenever you accelerate or hit bumps in the road. As a result, the freewheel-side spokes are always the most prone to breakage. They are the hardest spokes to replace, because unless the hubs are specially drilled with a keyhole arrangement to allow the heads to be keyed in without threading an entire spoke through the hole, the freewheel has

to be removed or disassembled to replace a spoke.
This is difficult to do in the field without access to a
vise or a large wrench to hold the freewheel
remover (see pages 217–21 for repair techniques).

    There is no perfect solution to the problem of
building the right side of the rear wheel, but
several techniques often are used to make this side
stronger. A rear hub may be used that has a low
flange on the left side and a high flange on the
right. This reduces the difference in the angle at
which the spokes from the two sides enter the rim,
though it also reduces spoke length and increases
the bending angles at the ends of the spokes. Some
wheel builders use a cross-four lacing on the right
side of the rear wheel combined with a cross-three
on the left. Heavier spokes also may be chosen for
the right side.

Recommendations

For a cyclist who wants a responsive bike and
is willing to keep his or her luggage light, I
recommend a pair of the new, narrow clincher rims,
preferably with a hollow cross-section. One of the
new, lightweight, high-pressure clinchers on this
rim makes for a lively bike on decent roads.
Low-flange hubs laced cross-three with galvanized
15-gauge or 15–16–15 spokes using aluminum-alloy
nipples should provide a good balance of weight,
strength, and shock absorption for most riders.
Vary the tire pressure with the road surface and
load. On smooth roads, you can probably run the
front tire at about 100 psi and the rear at 110, but
when it gets a little bumpier, you may want to
reduce the pressure 10 to 15 pounds for each one. For
an extremely strong wheel, use one of the slightly
heavier rims with a concave inside surface. They are
as strong as conventional steel rims.

It is a good idea to carry both a spare tube and tire on long tours. In a group that has interchangeable equipment and that stays close enough together, carrying one spare tube and tire usually is enough for several riders, unless someone is trying to get the last few miles out of an old set of tires. Most punctures can be patched easily, so more spares usually are required only for very remote areas and those with a lot of debris on the road.

Most punctures can be prevented by watching the road and taking elementary precautions. If you spot one piece of glass, there is sure to be a lot more around, so try to avoid the patch. If you do hit bits of glass or are riding in sharp gravel, wiping the tires with your glove or something else often removes pieces that are stuck in the rubber before they have a chance to work through. Many cyclists use small wire gadgets called *tire savers;* these attach to the brake bolts and ride lightly on the tires to knock off gravel, glass, and nails. I usually carry one of my tire irons in my pocket and use it to clean my tires.

Chapter 7

Brakes

THE IMPORTANCE OF brakes to cyclists is obvious, particularly when you realize that bicycle racers travel at speeds of more than fifty miles an hour on steep, winding, mountain descents. Bicycle tourists keep their speeds at a somewhat more reasonable level (by using their brakes), but they often carry loads on their bikes that create even greater demands on the braking system than racers do.

All braking systems on bicycles operate by slowing one or both wheels, and this fact imposes some fundamental limits on the slowing force that can be applied. Since the brakes do not have any direct contact with the ground, they ultimately depend on the friction of the tires against the road surface as the first link in the chain of forces that operate to slow the bicycle and rider. No matter how efficient other elements of the braking system may be, the slowing force that can be applied never can be greater than the maximum adherence of the

158

tires to the road. If you are riding down a gravel road in the mountains, the limiting factor in your ability to stop is not a function of the design of your brakes, but rather of the loose surface of the road itself.

The limit of adherence of the bicycle tire to the road is even more important with bicycles than with automobiles. When a car starts to skid because of either too much pressure or uneven pressure on the brakes, it is more difficult to control and braking is less effective, but the driver usually can control the skid. Because the bicycle is a two-wheeled vehicle, any skid that is not stopped immediately will cause a crash.

The standard brakes for touring bicycles are *caliper brakes,* which squeeze pads of rubber or some other material against both sides of each wheel rim, using one of several methods of leverage. Cables are used to transmit the force from the brake control levers to the brakes themselves. Within the category of caliper brakes, there are a number of mechanisms that can be used to operate the brakes, and the merits of the different types often are the subject of a good deal of controversy. The resulting arguments generally shed more heat than light on the subject. The various types of caliper brakes include side-pull brakes, center-pull brakes, and cantilever brakes, which are discussed in detail farther on.

Various types of disc brakes also have been developed, in which brake pads squeeze against a disc attached to the hub of each wheel. These brakes are capable of exerting greater braking force, particularly during wet weather, when caliper brakes become far less effective. Most of the disc brakes made are quite heavy, however, so they have replaced caliper brakes only on bicycles that require the extra stopping power, primarily tandems. A tandem carries twice the load of a standard bike and can reach very high speeds on downhill grades because the wind resistance and friction are not much greater than for a single-person bike, yet the force exerted by gravity on the bike is doubled. Thus effective brakes are essential, since the problems associated with caliper brakes become hazardous to tandem tourists in the mountains. Some touring cyclists who carry extremely heavy loads choose disc brakes for the same reasons. Lightweight disc brakes are available but are very costly. As for the hand-operated drum brakes which have been developed for tandem bicycles, they are effective but quite heavy.

The hub brakes commonly used on children's bicycles have the advantages of being weathertight and relatively maintenance-free, and they do not require any strength in the hands to operate. They can burn out easily on steep hills, however, and are not suitable for touring bikes.

With brakes of any kind, it is desirable to be able to exert pressure on the brake pads smoothly and with steadily increasing force so that the braking is controlled exactly, without grabbing or chattering, either of which could initiate a skid, make the steering erratic, and stress the frame unnecessarily. The brakes should not fade during long descents and ideally should be as effective in wet weather as in dry. If the brakes can exert enough force on the wheels to equal the grip of the tires on the road, then they have sufficient power, since maximum stopping force is achieved when the wheels are restrained enough so that they come just short of skidding.

Besides providing adequate stopping ability, the brakes must be properly matched with the rest of the bicycle design. Some types of brakes exert strong forces on the parts of the bike to which they are mounted, so they can be used only with a bike designed to withstand those stresses. Disc brakes, for example, put a lot of lateral stress on the bottom of the seatstay when the mechanism is mounted there. Cantilever brakes mounted with fittings to the fork and seat tubes require both that the correct fittings be brazed on and that these tubes be strong enough to ensure reliability. If a bike is built with sufficient clearance to allow fenders to be mounted, the brakes must be of a type that also provides enough clearance.

Characteristics of Caliper Brakes

All caliper brakes are operated by the rider squeezing a lever or a pair of levers on the handlebars. This force is transmitted to two pairs of brake pads that squeeze against the rims of the bicycle wheels. Caliper brakes usually have adequate stopping capacity in all cases on dry pavement, providing they operate smoothly enough. They lose a great deal of friction in wet conditions, however, because the rim area is large and is constantly rewetted as it passes near the road surface before returning to the brake. Much greater force has to be exerted in order to brake in wet weather, even if the cyclist has the foresight to pump the brakes lightly in anticipation of the need to stop, in order to wipe the rims. Because great forces are exerted on the mechanism when the brakes are squeezed hard for a wet-weather stop, any part of the linkage that can deform may do so under the pressure of hard braking—stretching of cables and bending of brake arms, for example —and reduce braking force. Riders without a great deal of grip strength may have particular difficulty exerting enough force to brake effectively in wet weather or on long downhill runs, during which caliper brakes exhibit some fading due to overheating of the rims and pads.

It appears, therefore, that there would be a major advantage in having as much leverage as possible in a caliper braking system so that considerable force could be exerted when needed. The greater the mechanical advantage in the system, the higher the actual force on the brakes is when maximum pressure is exerted by the hands.

The desirability of a large mechanical advantage has to be balanced against another factor, however. Mechanical advantage is gained by having the brake levers travel farther for a certain distance traveled by the brake pads. Therefore, the mechanical advantage that can be used is limited by the reach of the hands while gripping the handlebars, the distance the brake blocks have to travel to get to the rim, and the sum of all the deflections in the brake mechanism. A large mechanical advantage does no good if the brake levers bottom out against the handlebars before full force is applied to the rims. Since the reach of the hands is quite limited, not much mechanical advantage can be built into the brakes, even when mechanical deformation is kept to a minimum.

Brake Levers and Linkage

The standard brake levers for touring bikes are hooded levers that are mounted at the downward curve on each side of the handlebars. These levers

can be operated fairly effectively from above,
particularly by a rider with strong hands, and they
give excellent performance when operated from
the drops (the lowest position on the handlebars).
The levers could be given greater mechanical
advantage by making them longer, but then the ends
would be out of reach. There are alternative types
of levers, but these rarely are chosen by tourists.
Some riders do like to attach supplementary levers
that extend under the upper portion of the
handlebars and allow the brakes to be operated
from the top of the bar. Such "safety levers" are
inadvisable for several reasons: they often are
weak or too flexible; they are hard to adjust so that
they don't bottom out in hard braking; and they
cause the rider to develop the bad habit of braking
from the top of the handlebars. The lower position
is more effective because it allows a good grip on the
brakes and because the body's center of gravity is
lowered.

The linkage is responsible for much of the
deformation limiting the mechanical advantage that
can be built into brakes. Some excellent bikes
made with durability in mind rather than light
weight use a linkage of rods that offers very little
loss due to deformation. This system is too heavy for
a light touring bike, however. Racing and touring
bikes normally use cables to transmit force from
the brake levers to the brakes themselves. Cables
do stretch somewhat, especially during the first few
weeks of use, so fairly heavy cable should be used
to reduce this stretch. Since the pull on the cable
cannot be transmitted directly to the brakes along
a straight, fixed line, the cable has to be enclosed in
a housing to transmit the squeezing force. The
housing is fixed at both ends and the cable is pulled
through it. Cable housing compresses somewhat

when you squeeze the brake levers, and there also is friction between the cable and its housing. Therefore fittings often are brazed or clamped onto the frame along the long cable route to the rear brake in order to reduce both compression and friction. Brazed fittings are excellent, if the brazing is well executed, but the frame tubing can be weakened if it is heated too much. The linkage also can be achieved much more efficiently by using a hydraulic system, but no hydraulic linkage designed for touring bikes is available in the United States at the time of this writing.

The deformation of fittings used to stop the motion of the housing under hard braking also obviously reduces the efficiency of the brakes and the mechanical advantage that can be built into them. This is particularly true of the housing stops used with center-pull brakes. If the stops are too flimsy, they will deform badly during fast stops in wet weather.

Side-Pull Brakes

Side-pull brakes (see Figure 14) are the most common type on inexpensive ten-speed bicycles and also on the most expensive ones. The curved arms or yokes to which the brake pads are attached cross one another at a pivot bolt in the center which also serves to attach the brake to the frame. The brake cable is attached to the end of one of the two arms and the housing is stopped by the other arm, so that when the lever is operated, these two ends are squeezed together, causing the brake pads at the other ends of the arms to pivot toward one another. This mechanism has the great advantage of simplicity and minimum weight. A spring returns the brake to its original position when the pressure is released.

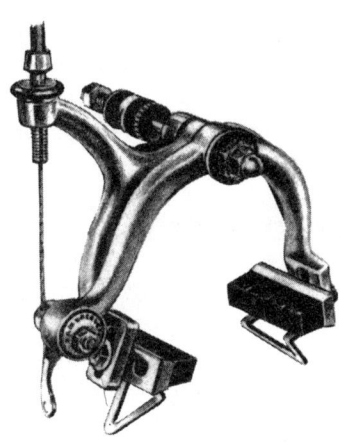

14. A high-quality side-pull brake. This model includes a screw to adjust cable tension and a quick-release lever at the bottom. The guides below the brake pads are designed to permit very rapid wheel changes for racers.

Simple side-pull brakes are inexpensive to manufacture, which is why they are used on cheap bicycles, but they have several disadvantages. Because the center bolt is both the pivot and the attachment device, the brakes often become misaligned, so that one brake pad accidentally rubs against the rim. Good-quality, modern side-pull brakes are carefully designed to pull smoothly from both sides and return the same way, avoiding this problem.

A more serious problem with side-pull brakes is that the leverage available is determined by the ratio of the length of each arm on the cable end of the pivot to that on the brake pad end. Since the amount of travel of the upper ends of the arms is limited by the size of the rider's effective grip, the leverage possible with a side-pull design is dependent on the length of the lower parts of the arms. If they are short, the brakes can be made with good leverage, but if they are made longer to allow space for fenders and larger tires, the available leverage is reduced. This problem does not occur with center-pull brakes because the pivot points are separate from the attachment, so the brakes can be designed to give both the desired clearance and the exact amount of mechanical advantage desired.

Inexpensive side-pulls made with enough clearance to accommodate large tires and fenders thus have rather poor leverage, and their stopping power is not adequate for difficult braking conditions involving a loaded bicycle in wet conditions or on long, steep descents. The high-quality, modern side-pulls, such as Campagnolo and Dura Ace, have minimal wheel clearance. They can be mounted on a bicycle that is made with greater clearance by using a specially designed spacer, but not if you wish to use fenders or large tires.

Good-quality side-pulls provide excellent stopping power, but they are very sensitive to a wheel that is slightly out of line and afford less control at intermediate levels of braking than center-pulls do. For a racer riding in a pack, the time from reaction to actual hard braking may be a split second faster with side-pull brakes, but for a bicycle tourist the grabbier action of the side-pulls can be a distinct disadvantage. An even gradation of braking power is desirable. Thus, despite the fact that Campagnolo side-pulls are far more fashionable (and expensive), you may want to consider center-pull brakes instead.

Center-Pull Brakes

Center-pull brakes (see Figure 15) offer several important advantages. The most important already has been mentioned: the pivots can be set by the designer so that they permit exactly the desired amount of leverage, even if some clearance is

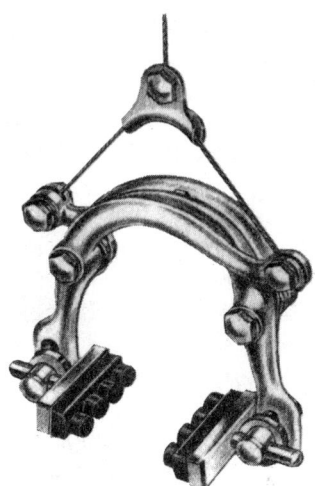

15. *A typical center-pull brake. Each arm pivots around the bolt on the opposite side, and the brake is attached to the bike with a separate bolt.*

needed for mudguards or fenders. Center-pulls also are considerably more tolerant of slight wobbles in the rims of the wheels than side-pulls are, and the progression from moderate to strong braking is smoother than with side-pulls, an advantage for the tourist riding a loaded bike. The stopping power with center-pulls is just as good as with high-quality side-pulls. The price for center-pull brakes usually is a good deal lower than for side-pulls of comparable quality, one reason for their low status appeal.

Because of their greater complexity and more elaborate lever system, center-pulls are likely to be a little heavier than side-pulls, though not decisively so. The close clearance of the two brake arms and the bridge allows the brake to be more easily fouled by mud and makes the brake harder to clean. Center-pull brakes tend to have a bit more play than good side-pulls, so that reaction time is an instant longer.

With a custom-built frame, center-pull brakes can be mounted directly to brazed-on fittings, eliminating the need for a bridge piece in each brake; however, if brazed-on fittings are used, the bike probably will be fitted with cantilever brakes.

Cantilever Brakes

Custom-made touring bikes frequently are made with brazed-on posts to permit the mounting of cantilever brakes. These brakes employ a cable system exactly like the one used with standard center-pull brakes, but most of the rest of the mechanism is eliminated. Each brake pad is mounted on its own spring-loaded lever arm, which is attached in turn to the brazed-on post. Cantilever brakes function in much the same way as center-pull types, but they are less affected by mud or snow than are other caliper brakes.

The only significant drawbacks to cantilever brakes are that they tend to protrude a little more than other types, that brakes and parts are harder to find in the United States, and that brazing the fittings onto the seatstays and fork blades to make them secure without weakening the frame requires a skilled builder.

A few inexpensive bicycles are equipped with cantilever brakes. This is undesirable because the fittings are not likely to be reliable on a mass-produced frame. Catastrophic failure might easily result.

Maintenance and Braking Techniques

Always be sure to keep your brakes perfectly adjusted. The blocks should be as close to the rims as possible without rubbing so that there is no chance of the levers bottoming out during hard braking. Remember that you are going to have to squeeze much harder to stop when the rims are wet. It is easy to let the cables stretch and the blocks wear without bothering to readjust the brakes if they are providing enough stopping power for average conditions. Make it a point, therefore, to check the brakes every time you ride and keep them adjusted properly, so that when a difficult braking situation occurs you will have plenty of reserve. Replace cables that are beginning to fray and housings that are developing too much play. Keep all the brake parts clean and well lubricated.

During steep descents, both the brake blocks and the rims tend to overheat. This causes the blocks to melt or glaze slightly so that the brakes begin to fade. Some glues used with sew-up tires may be softened by the heat, which may cause a tire to twist off its rim during cornering, with unpleasant consequences. Overheating may cause blowouts with either sew-ups or clinchers. To help alleviate these problems, keep your speed at a reasonable level during descents, particularly if you are carrying a heavy load. Brake intermittently, allowing some cooling period between applications. If your brakes start to fade or you have some doubts as to their effectiveness, slow down and then stop for a little while to allow them to cool. A bicycle rider sailing down a hill headfirst at fifty miles an hour is in a very vulnerable position if he or she hits a patch of gravel on a turn or meets a car coming up the wrong side of the road. Make some allowances for the surprises that may await you around the next bend.

Those who feel the need for more efficient brakes can switch to the special pads made by Mathauser or Kool-Stop. They use special high-friction materials and designs that permit much better heat dissipation than conventional brake blocks.

Chapter 8

Where You Meet the Bike

YOUR CHOICE AND fitting of the seat and handlebars on your bike contribute a great deal to either your comfort or misery on long tours. Proper fitting and adjustment make a lot of difference to your efficiency, since you can pedal well only in a position that permits your legs to work as effectively as possible. It is surprising how much difference small changes in the position of the saddle can make in your pedaling. The handlebars should be positioned so that the bicycle fits your body. Incorrectly placed handlebars can adversely affect your handling of the bike and also cause fatigue and cramping in the muscles of your arms, shoulders, and back. You spend many hours sitting on your saddle and leaning on the handlebars, so it is worth taking the time both to choose designs to suit you and to make sure they are properly adjusted.

170

Saddles

Efficient pedaling of a touring bicycle requires
that the cyclist lean forward, even during fairly
relaxed riding. The legs need to extend almost
completely at the bottom of the pedaling stroke;
when they do, the thighs drop down beside the
saddle. The front part of the saddle has to be quite
narrow to allow the thighs to slide past without
interference or chafing, and without forcing the
rider to shift from side to side on the seat. Sliding
back and forth causes a lot of abrasion and subsequent discomfort. The weight of the body is
supported by the crotch and the two crests of the
pelvic bones, not by the buttocks farther back. Wide
saddles may look more comfortable, but they
aren't.

Within the range of narrow saddles, however, there are many variations to accommodate
differently shaped bodies and different needs. Racers typically use saddles that are narrower than
tourists' because racers spend most of their time
riding on the drops (or hooks), shifting body weight
farther forward on the crotch. The tourist, who
assumes a slightly more upright position much of
the time, rests a little further back on the two
pelvic protrusions and needs a saddle wide enough
at the back to support them.

Beyond these general specifications, the process
of choosing a saddle begins to fall into the category
of a black art. You can measure the distance
between the protruding bumps at the lower rear of
your pelvis, if you like, and compare this with the
supporting surface toward the rear of a saddle, but
this dimension alone does not describe the complex
curves, relative softness and support, nor the
ability of the saddle to move perspiration away
from your skin and shorts.

Traditionally, the favorite saddles of bicycle tourists have been made from a high-grade, heavy leather (see Figure 16). The Brooks Professional and Idéale 90 are among the favorites. Because of their wider pelvises, women often are happier with a saddle that is slightly shorter and that widens more rapidly toward the rear. The advantage of a leather saddle is that it is comfortable for as many miles as you can pedal, day after day. As a porous and absorbent material, leather also breathes and permits moisture to migrate away from your skin and shorts. The disadvantages of leather saddles are that they are considerably heavier than synthetic ones, require some effort to break in, and require protection from the weather and periodic care to preserve the leather.

Leather saddles should be regularly cleaned and treated top and bottom with a leather preservative. Except when you are trying to soften a particular part of the saddle, use silicon or wax-based preservatives. Animal oils and similar compounds weaken the leather over the long run

16. The tourist's long-time favorite saddle is made from heavy leather riveted to a metal frame. It is heavier than a plastic-based saddle but eventually conforms to the rider's shape, making it very comfortable.

because of the action of the enzymes they contain. A leather saddle should be covered with a plastic cover whenever you ride or leave the bike out in the rain. Never expose a leather saddle to heat in order to dry it; the leather is sensitive to heat and can be easily ruined. The nut or bolt at the nose of a leather seat is used to adjust the tension as the leather stretches.

Several other types of saddles now available are made from synthetics or a combination of synthetic and natural materials. Saddles made from molded nylon were the first serious alternative to leather saddles. These nylon models are very light and require no maintenance. Many riders find them to be uncomfortable, however, and the fact that the material is impervious to moisture sometimes causes chafing and softening of the skin of the rider's seat, resulting in sores and discomfort. Other cyclists are able to ride comfortably on nylon saddles, sometimes after drilling a few extra holes at strategic points to increase ventilation and to make the saddle slightly more flexible in the area where most of the weight rests.

The most recent development in saddle design is to mold the saddle to better conform to the anatomy of the cyclist's rear end, using some combination of padding, variations in flexibility, and a curvature that avoids pressure on the most sensitive areas. Typically, separate touring and racing models are offered, and differently shaped seats are made for women. Many of these specially shaped saddles are covered with a lightweight split leather to help wick away moisture (see Figure 17) as are some conventionally molded ones. The newer saddles are a blessing for many people, combining the comfort of the classic leather seat with the light weight of a nylon saddle

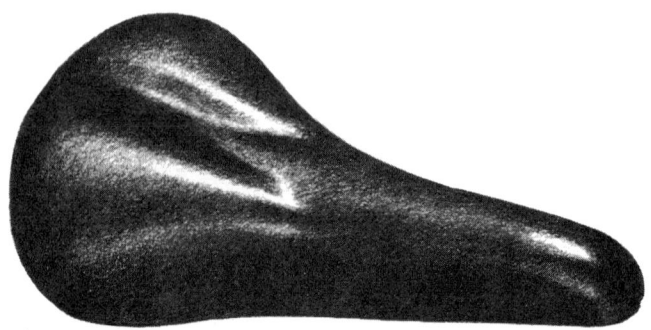

17. *Contoured saddles, such as those made by Avocet and Selle Milano, are becoming increasingly popular. A nylon base is padded with foam and covered with split leather.*

and no need for an extended break-in period. People are different, however, and not everyone finds that a particular brand of saddle fits well. It is best to try one out thoroughly before you buy it. Like the fine leather models, most of these newer saddles are expensive. Good saddles of this type include those made by Avocet and Selle Milano.

The breaking in of leather saddles, progressive conditioning of the cyclist's own posterior, and correct positioning of the saddle are critical for comfort on long tours. Most of the best leather saddles require many hours of riding to mold themselves to the shape of the rider. Some riders advocate the application of softening oils or the judicious use of a mallet or baseball bat to speed the break-in period. Oils which soften leather, however, also cause the structure of the fibers to deteriorate, as well as sometimes staining clothing. Use softening oils sparingly so that the overall stiffness of the saddle is not lost.

Toughening of the cyclist's rear end often is the

most neglected precaution against soreness, one for which there is no substitute. A well-chosen seat enables you to ride farther with somewhat less preparation than one that is not as suitable for your anatomy, but if you don't work up slowly to riding long distances, you are bound to suffer saddle sores. Be sure to start your preparatory riding well before any extended tour to give yourself time to toughen your seat. Saddle sores of various kinds are discussed more extensively on pages 385–86. A good saddle can help to prevent sores experienced by regular riders, but it won't substitute for slowly working up to longer distances. Cyclists who stay in shape during off seasons with other activities, such as running, should be particularly wary of doing too much too soon, since their good physical condition is likely to enable them to ride farther than their untoughened skin can stand.

Seat Posts and Positioning

Positioning a saddle is a very fine adjustment, and only minor changes in either its height or angle can make a great difference both in cycling efficiency and comfort. If the saddle is placed either too high or too low, the rider will shift back and forth on the seat slightly with each stroke of the pedals, or twice for each revolution. If you are spinning along at 80 rpm, that makes 9600 tiny shifts per hour, which produces a lot of shearing action on a small amount of rather tender tissue.

Most people tend to adjust seats too low. A rough approximation of the correct height can be achieved by setting the seat so that when you sit straight on it, you can just press the heel of your fully extended foot against the pedal at the bottom of a stroke. This positioning permits a slight bend of the knee when the ball of the foot is on the pedal in normal riding.

The angle of the seat is equally critical, but it is easier to feel differences as you adjust the saddle angle. In general, it is best to have a level saddle, although some people are more comfortable with a very slight forward tilt. The saddle should not tilt backward. The main difficulty in adjusting the saddle angle usually is not in feeling the proper orientation but in making the adjustment itself.

The standard seat attachment consists of a tightening bolt with two interfacing clamps that tighten on the post. Another clamp at the top of the frame's seat tube tightens on the post to adjust the height. The interfacing clamps normally have serrations that permit the seat to be clamped at many discrete angles. Unfortunately, there is an obvious cyclist's corollary to Murphy's Law ("If anything can go wrong, it will") which states that the proper seat position is always between two of the fixed angles of the clamps. Modern seat-post designs, such as the one shown in Figure 18, have the advantage of being easily adjustable to any angle. Those models with the adjusting screws placed so that they are accessible from below can be set even while riding; this sometimes is useful on long rides to relieve particular pressure points. The modern posts also are lighter, more secure, and more expensive than traditional designs.

It is important to note that not all seats can be used with the newer seat-post designs. The rails of the seat have to have the proper dimensions and configuration to fit. If you plan to install an alloy seat post with a built-in micro-adjustable clamp, be sure that the seat you buy is compatible.

In choosing a seat post, also remember that the post must be long enough so that *at least* 2½

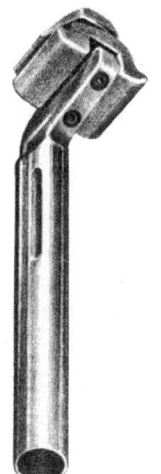

18. A modern seat post, designed by Avocet, with an integral clamp that grips the seat directly. The greatest advantage of this type of post is that it permits the seat to be adjusted to any angle. Other quality posts of this kind are made by Campagnolo, SR, and Weyless.

inches (6.4 millimeters) are held in the seat tube of the frame. If a shorter length remains in the seat tube after the saddle height has been adjusted, a longer post is required for safety.

Saddles also can be slid forward and back to accommodate for frame design, individual physiological differences, and pedaling style. A good starting position is with the saddle nose 1¾ to 2 inches (4.5 to 5.1 centimeters) back from a vertical line extending down to the center of the bottom bracket. Women using shorter than average saddles may want to use a position an inch farther back. In general, as your technique improves and you spin faster, you will want your saddle slightly farther forward.

Positioning of Handlebars

When you buy a bike, try to be sure that the handlebars are positioned correctly for the dimensions of your body. Ready-made bikes usually come

with standard handlebar stems and extensions
that may not suit you. A good bike dealer can get
different stems, though he may not stock them.
You can buy different ones later, of course, but
you'll save money if you make sure the bike is
properly equipped from the start.

The stem and extension usually are made
from a single piece, consisting of two tubes attached
at an angle of about 72 degrees. The stem and the
extension can be made from steel, but on a good-
quality touring bike they normally are cast from
an aluminum alloy to save weight. Any well-
made alloy stem with the right dimensions is
adequate, but the best ones are rounded into a
smooth curve toward the rear with an inset Allen-
head bolt, so that there are no sharp projections
that could injure the rider in an accident.

The end of the stem which has the expander
plug and which goes into the headset can be
adjusted up or down, but the stem must be long
enough so that *at least* 2½ inches (6.4 millimeters)
stick into the steering tube. Otherwise, enough
leverage can be developed to break the tube when
you are riding, a thrilling experience you probably
want to avoid. Thus, when buying a bike, be sure
that the stem is long enough so that you can raise
it to a comfortable height and still have 2½ inches
remaining in the head tube.

The tube which sticks forward from the stem and
clamps the handlebars is called the *stem extension.*
Production bicycles (those that are not custom
made) come with standard-length extensions, but a
good bike shop should stock stems with different
extension lengths. Different stem lengths are
harder to find, particularly in aluminum-alloy
models.

Stem and extension lengths are critical dimensions in fitting the bike, and the best length depends on the proportions of your body as well as your riding style and use of the bike. People with longer torsos and arms in proportion to leg length need longer extensions in order to ride in the same position as people with shorter upper-body dimensions. The length of the extension determines the angle of the arms when the cyclist leans forward onto the handlebars. A longer extension requires the rider to reach farther forward to grab a particular position on the bar. Thus, to have the same arm angle as a rider with a short torso, a person with a longer torso needs a longer extension.

Stem length needs also vary. The stem length may need to be longer for a touring cyclist riding a particular size frame than for a racer riding the same frame, given the same seat height for both riders. The tourist probably wants to be in a slightly more upright position than the racer, so the handlebars must be higher. They are made higher either by riding a larger frame or by raising the stem farther out of the head tube.

To measure the stem and extension for size and to adjust them, first be sure the seat is correctly positioned. Have someone hold the bike upright while you mount it and sit in a relaxed position with your hands on the upper part of the handlebars. Move the stem up or down in the head tube until you feel comfortable. Typically, this point is reached when the handlebars are a couple of inches below the level of the seat. Your back normally should incline forward at about 45 degrees with your hands on top of the bar. Relax your muscles, release one hand from the bar, and swing your arms, shoulders, and torso around to that side; then swing your arm back to the bar, still relaxing and maintaining as natural a position as possible. The object of the exercise is to find the position that your hand will return to naturally, without stretching or cramping. If the extension is the right length, your hand should naturally come right back to the bar. If your hand swings back in front of the bar, the extension is too short; if it returns to a spot behind the bar, the extension is too long. Repeat the maneuver several times on each side to be sure of the correct extension length. If you are an experienced rider, try the bike out after making the adjustments to see how it feels. Another way to determine extension length is to put your elbow against the nose of the seat. Your fingertips should just reach the handlebars.

It is worth spending a good deal of time making sure that the seat height, stem extension length, and stem length and adjustment are correct on a new bike. Besides having a lot of impact on your pedaling efficiency, these dimensions greatly affect your comfort after several hours of riding. Back fatigue and aching shoulders are common beginners' complaints, and they are likely to be much more of a problem if the bike doesn't fit properly.

Types of Handlebars

Within the category of racing-style dropped handlebars, there are many variations in shape and dimensions. The track racer stays down on the drops all the time, so neither the height nor shape of the top of the bars concerns the rider of a track bike. The handlebars for such a machine normally make a smooth curve from the stem extension down to the drops (see Figure 19, bottom).

Track bikes don't even have brake levers mounted on the handlebars.

Handlebars for a touring bike, however, should offer the cyclist as many different hand positions as possible, to minimize muscle fatigue and numbness caused by pressure on the nerves of the palm and the discomfort caused by hitting bumps and chuckholes. The best designs rise slightly or extend horizontally from the stem extension, providing plenty of room for the hands to rest in a high position. The bars should then bend sharply forward, so that the hands also can be rested on the forward-pointing sections. A fairly deep drop gives the tourist a choice between a comfortable high position on the top of the bar and a streamlined position when leaning on the drops. Handlebar width should be in the neighborhood of 15 to 16 inches (38 to 41 centimeters). A typical touring-style handlebar design, often known as the Maes bend, is shown in Figure 19, center. Even better for many tourists is the Randonneur bend (Figure 19, top) which has a horizontal section near the stem as does the Maes, but which bends up before curving forward and down, so that the tourist has a very slightly higher back position and an additional variation for the hands.

Positioning the Brake Levers

The brake levers should be clamped high enough on the handlebars so that you can lean comfortably on them by hooking your thumbs over the tops. This gives an extra position for the hands and a back position halfway between those used for riding on the top of the bars and on the drops. It also is the riding position normally used for honking and frequently used for mild braking when full grip strength is not required.

The levers also should be low enough so that they can be reached easily from the drops, the normal position for full braking. If the levers are placed too high, they may be hard to reach quickly for a stop; if too low, you won't be able to use them to lean on from above. Remember that braking from the drops not only gives you maximum squeezing force, but also positions the body's center of gravity as low as possible so that there is less tendency for you to pitch forward or for the rear wheel to lose traction.

Rubber hoods are available for most brake levers. They serve to cushion the hands and to help keep water from rusting the upper parts of the brake cables in wet weather. Fit these hoods onto your levers carefully, without distorting them too much, since they can rip easily during installation.

Handlebar Tape and Padding

Handlebars nearly always are taped to give a surer grip and to provide a more comfortable surface than the bare metal of the bar itself. Plastic, leather, and cloth tape are used by riders. Plastic is most commonly supplied on production bikes, but cloth is preferred by most experienced cyclists. Cloth provides a better grip, improves insulation in cold weather, and wicks perspiration away from the hands; dark colors stay presentable longer.

If standard cloth handlebar tape is used, two rolls are required to tape a bar. Make sure the

19.   Bottom: *Handlebars designed for track racing. The bar is fairly narrow, has a deep drop, and offers no good positions for the hands high on the bar or at the bends. This type of bar is ill-suited for touring, yet many inexpensive bikes are equipped with such a design.* Center: *Typical touring handlebars of the Maes type. This design permits a variety of excellent hand positions. The stem shown here*

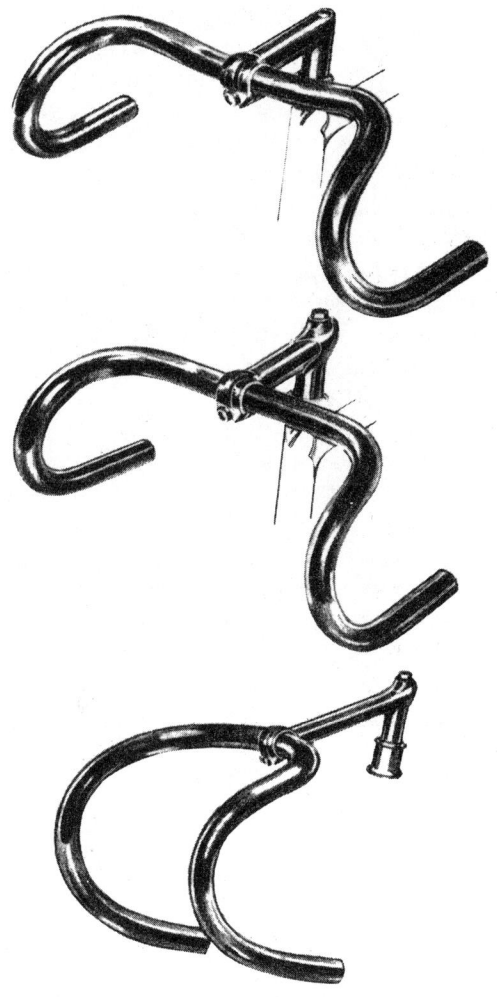

employs a standard bolt for the expansion plug; the bolt and stem are adequate, but their sharp edges can be nasty in an accident. Top: Handlebars with a Randonneur bend, probably the best for touring because of the many comfortable hand positions possible. The stem is designed with a rounded back and a concealed Allen-head bolt for the expansion plug.

brake levers are positioned correctly before taping.
Start near the stem on one side, wrap the tape
around the bar twice to anchor the end, and then
wrap it in a spiral along the bar. When you reach
the brake lever, loosen the lever slightly so you can
pass the tape between the top part of the hood and
the bar, around the back, and then between the
hood and the bar on the bottom. Tighten the lever
again, spiral the tape down to the end of the bar,
and snip off the end, leaving about an inch to spare.
Push this extra tape into the end of the bar and
insert the plastic end plug to secure the tape end.
Repeat on the other side.

It is much more comfortable on long tours, and
particularly on poor road surfaces, to pad the
handlebars so that your hands are better protected
from road shocks. Several nerves in the hands are
quite vulnerable to constant pressure and can cause
numbness after long periods of riding. Handlebar
padding greatly reduces the likelihood of this
problem. Padding also increases the circumference
gripped by the hands, and many riders with long
fingers find this larger grip to be far more
comfortable.

Several types of padding can be used. A special
handlebar tape that provides some padding is made
by Bailey and is distributed fairly widely by
cycling shops and mail-order houses. Specially
molded handlebar covers that simply slip onto the
bars to substitute for tape also have become
available recently. The old standby method is to
pad the handlebars with some cushioning material
and then tape over it. Some riders use neoprene
wet-suit material, which is heavy but which grips
the metal surface well. Others use strips cut from
automobile inner tubes or material used to insulate

heating pipes. I prefer to use quarter-inch-thick
Ensolite closed-cell foam, cut in strips which either
fit all the way around the bars or cover only the
top two-thirds. I pad the bars starting at about two
inches from the stem on either side and going as
far as the brake lever assemblies; I also pad the
lower part of the drops, leaving the portion near
the brakes clear for a hard grip during braking and
sprinting. A little contact cement prevents the
padding from shifting. If standard cloth tape is used,
three rolls are necessary to cover the larger
diameter created by the padding. Wrap the tape
tightly, with close overlaps, so that the padding
stays in position for a long time.

Toe Clips

Toe clips (see Figure 8) keep your feet in the
optimum position for efficient pedaling and also
allow you to exert force on the pedals throughout the
pedaling cycle, rather than just on the downstroke.
A strap goes through the pedal under the shoe and
then through an opening at the top of the clip, so
that it can be tightened over the instep to hold the
foot firmly in place. The straps should be of
high-quality heavy leather for durability; the best
ones use two pieces of leather laminated together
with nylon to minimize stretching.

The clips can be made from aluminum alloy to
reduce weight, but spring steel is more durable and
therefore a better choice for most tourists. The clip
should be long enough that the ball of your foot is
positioned just over the spindle of the pedal. The
length you need varies according to the type and fit
of your shoe, but usually cyclists who wear a shoe
size smaller than men's 6 or women's 7 need a small
size toe clip; those who wear sizes up to men's 9½ or

women's 10½ take a medium clip; and others need a large clip.

The clips are screwed to matching holes on the pedals, and each strap is threaded with the buckle on the upper outside of your foot. The buckles are designed so that the straps can be pulled tight or loosened with a flick of the thumb. Putting a twist in the strap where it is threaded through the body of the pedal keeps it from shifting around and pulling the buckle out of position.

Chapter 9

Accessories for the Bike

THERE ARE DOZENS of accessories for touring bikes. Some, such as pumps, are essential pieces of equipment, as necessary on a tour as the tires or pedals. Others are required for particular conditions or are handy to have. The real function of most gadgetry sold in bike shops, however, is to prime the pump of a sagging economy and to keep shops afloat that might otherwise close. Keep the little extras to a minimum and lighten your bike rather than your wallet.

The really essential bike accessories are a pump, tool kit, water bottles, lighting and other devices to make you more visible on the road, and, at times, a locking device. Tools are discussed in Chapter 10, along with some of the repair techniques that can be used on the road, while lighting, reflectors, and other devices that make you more visible to motorists are considered in Chapter 11.

Pumps

Even if you rarely use it, you should always carry a
pump on tour so that you can inflate your tire tube
after repairing a flat. Cheap pumps are barely able
to reach a pressure that allows you to make it to
the next service station; they cannot get the tire
up to full pressure. Most good-quality, modern
clincher tires should be inflated to a pressure of at
least 90 psi, and sew-ups have to be inflated at
least that high. The best narrow clinchers and all
sew-ups usually are run at 100 psi or more. Many
pumps cannot fill a tire to anywhere near that
pressure. Since riding a loaded bike with under-
inflated tires is a good way to damage the tires
and dent the rims, it makes sense to carry a pump
that can inflate your tires to full pressure.
Service-station compressors should be reserved for
emergencies. It is easier to inflate tires accurately
with a hand pump, anyway, and altogether too
easy to blow a tire with air from a gas-station hose.

There are two types of valves used on bicycle
tubes, and you should be sure that your pump and
valves are compatible. Pay particular attention to
this problem if you are carrying one pump for
several riders. All tubular tires employ Presta
valves, and, until fairly recently, most of the pumps
with high-pressure capacity have been made to fit
only Presta valves. Tubes with Presta valves can be
obtained for most clincher tires, too, so a pump
with a Presta head can be used on both types of tire.
A pump head designed for Presta valves presses
onto the valve and can be removed easily without
leaking air in the process, a feature which is
important with narrow tires since a small air loss
can easily drop the tire pressure twenty pounds.
The Presta design employs a screw nut as part of
the valve to prevent accidental leaks, and the

spring in the valve is always very light, which makes the tires easy to pump. The main disadvantage of Presta valves is that they require adapters if you want to fill them at gas stations. Since alloy adapters are very cheap, however, this is hardly a major inconvenience. Simply buy an alloy adapter, which weighs almost nothing, and a little rubber washer called an Air Nut, which prevents leaks when using the adapter, and keep them in your tire repair kit in case you ever need them.

The conventional type of valve found on automobile tires, all department store bike tubes, and many quality tubes is a Schrader valve. Schrader valves often are hard to pump, because the springs are very strong to prevent accidental air leakage. Lighter springs are made by Schrader, but I have never seen a tube that came equipped with one. You can take the valve apart and weaken the spring or install a weaker one if you want to make the valve easier to pump.

Decent bicycle pumps made to fit Schrader valves are now available, so the greatest problem associated with using them has been removed. Be sure to get a pump that can reach a high pressure, however, rather than the usual type with a hose that screws into the pump body and onto the valve, leaks air in both places, and cannot be taken off the valve without letting out half the air you just put in. The best hand pumps for Schrader valves employ a locking mechanism that seals over the valve and depresses the core at the same time. Be sure the mechanism comes off smoothly without releasing air from the tire.

The standard pump for Presta valves is the Silca, available with either plastic or metal heads. The metal heads are more reliable but heavier. Silca pumps are made from plastic and generally are quite good. Some cyclists feel that Zefal pumps are more reliable. Zefals are made from aluminum and are a bit heavier than Silcas. They are available with heads for both Presta and Schrader valves. If you like to rely on your pump as an emergency weapon against dogs, better get a Zefal; a Silca will break with the first direct hit and is rather expensive for this purpose.

Most pumps can be obtained in lengths that can be snapped into the frame along the seat tube. If you are riding in a dry area and want to carry water bottles on both the seat and down tubes, however, it is more convenient to get a fitting that permits the pump to be mounted on the top tube.

Several double-action pumps (which pump air on both down and up strokes) have been introduced recently and are reputedly easier to use than standard pumps. In general, smaller pump barrels make for easier pumping, but they require more strokes to fill a tire.

If you are traveling in a group, you can save a little weight by taking only one pump for every few cyclists. This can cause problems if you split up, however, so it usually is better for each rider to carry a set of tools, a patch kit, and a pump. Then, if you have a flat when you are a bit behind everyone else, you won't have to wait until you are missed to get hold of the tools to fix your tire so you can get back on the road. When two people are traveling together, a second pump provides insurance in case one breaks, so I recommend that both people carry pumps.

You can learn to feel a tire to roughly determine its pressure, but a gauge is more accurate. Bike stores and mail-order houses sell gauges for both Presta and Schrader valves. A couple of new pumps with built-in gauges are available; you preset the pressure you want and then pump until you reach it. To properly maintain your pump, take it apart periodically and treat the leather cups with lubricant and preservative.

Water Bottles

Water bottles also fall into the category of essential accessories. It is easy to become dehydrated while you are riding if you don't make sure that you drink enough. You lose a lot of liquid during hard riding, even in cool weather, and in hot, humid conditions, perspiration losses can be enormous. You use quite a bit of liquid even on moderate rides in cool conditions. To prevent your body from losing efficiency and possibly becoming dangerously dehydrated, it is important both to tank up at rest stops and to drink occasionally while riding. You should have at least one water bottle attached conveniently to the bike where it is easily accessible. When others are necessary, they can be carried the same way or placed in pockets in your luggage.

The number of water bottles you need depends on where you ride and on other circumstances. If water is readily available every few miles, you need only one bottle, which you can refill whenever you like. The same is true if you make your trips with sag-wagon support. For self-contained trips involving long, dry stretches, on the other hand, you may need several bottles. I usually carry one or two bottles on my bike, and on self-contained trips I carry other containers in my luggage that can be filled or left empty depending on the situation.

Standard bicycle water bottles are handy, although they aren't the only type of water containers that can be used. The cages which hold them can be attached either to the seat tube or down tube on the frame. There is enough room for three or four such bottles on the two tubes, so you can carry several in these easily accessible spots without taking up luggage space. The standard water bottle is a plastic squeeze bottle with a nozzle for squirting water into your mouth and a spray head for direct cooling. Standard cages hold the bottles firmly but allow them to be grabbed easily while you are riding. They can be made of steel wire, which is cheaper, or aluminum alloy, which is lighter. The cages are available in designs that can be clamped onto the seat tube or down tube and in designs that are made to clamp onto the handlebars for those who don't use handlebar bags. The type that fits into the main frame triangle also can be mounted on brazed fittings if your bike is equipped with them. Several cages can be mounted in the triangle if they are needed. A water-bottle cage also is convenient for carrying a fuel bottle away from the luggage if you use a white-gas stove (see Chapter 18).

Other types of water bottles also can be used. You can work out fittings on any of your luggage racks to hold water containers. A clip-on type that holds a special quart-sized bottle is available to clamp to the seat tube, but it cannot be used easily while riding. There also are many quart-sized bottles that fit in a standard cage.

Besides the water bottles on the frame, I carry a quart bottle in one of my pannier pockets. It usually is empty, but I fill it before a long, dry stretch of road or when I am nearing a camp that may not have water. I also carry a folding gallon-sized container that can be filled on the way to camp when I want more water or prior to a long desert ride between service stations. On a few trips I may add an extra quart container in the panniers. You can either purchase quart containers or salvage them from use as food containers. The one I use originally was a vinegar bottle. Folding containers can be obtained from mail-order backpacking suppliers.

For hot- and cold-weather rides, you can purchase insulated bottles to keep beverages cold or hot for a few hours. In the heat, you also can wrap a cloth or sock soaked with water around the bottle after you fill it. The moisture in the cloth keeps the bottle cool until all the water evaporates.

Fenders and Rain Skirts

Some cyclists ride without fenders all the time, whatever the weather, and others would never be caught without them. Preferences vary according to geography, personality, and the type of touring to be done. If your experience has been confined to day tours in California, you probably view fenders as a nuisance with little redeeming value. On the other hand, if you want to tour in Ireland on your two-week vacation, waiting for the rain to stop might result in your never riding at all. In this situation most tourists would consider fenders a blessing.

The advantage of fenders is that they reduce the amount of water and dirt that get sprayed on you as you ride. They do not stop you from getting wet or save you from the water and grit splashed by passing cars. Still, they may reduce the amount of splashing enough to make the situation more tolerable.

Fenders do cause significant air drag, par-ticularly if you are pedaling at a good speed. They cause *a lot* of drag when you are riding in the rain because the spray stopped by the fenders bounces against them, and the deceleration of the water translates into deceleration of the bike.

Fender weight is significant but tolerable—a little over a pound for a pair of the new, close-fitting, plastic fenders. Riders who prefer to ride without fenders regardless of the weather advocate wearing good rain garb in colder weather or as little clothing as is comfortable when the weather is warm. Their theory is that you are going to be pelted with water and grit from all directions anyway, so you might as well keep the bike operating as efficiently as possible. Fender advocates cite the advantages of less slop hitting the body and the reduction of wet grit working into the brakes, headset, bottom bracket, and pedals.

Some fender variations also are possible. For even more protection, rain skirts can be made from a coated fabric and stretched over the fender supports in the quadrants close to the rider: between the chainstays and seatstays in back, and between the fork and the fender supports in front. These further reduce spray and increase pedaling resistance, but unlike the fenders themselves, they can be removed easily and carried in luggage when they aren't in use. For those who don't want to bother with full fenders but would like to protect the brakes somewhat from dirt fouling, short fenders about nine inches long are available. They keep mud from spraying onto the brakes and clogging them. Short fenders do not cause significant resistance nor do they give any appreciable protection to the rider.

Your own preferences and the sort of tour you plan determine whether you use fenders or not. Performance-oriented fanatics always dispense with them. Check the weather statistics for the area and time of year in which you plan any long tours. If rain is infrequent you probably won't want to bother with fenders, especially if you plan to put

up a tent or head for the nearest motel as soon as
any drops begin to fall. On the other hand, if a
significant amount of rain seems inevitable and you
plan to ride most of the time, whatever the
weather, you may want to use fenders on your tour.

Plastic fenders, if they are well made, should
be light and not too fragile. They won't stand much
direct stress, however, so you have to be careful of
them. Fortunately, they are cheap. Get the kind
that fit close to the wheel, and remember that you
may not be able to use fenders on a bike with very
close wheel and brake clearances.

Security Devices

Finding an effective means of protecting your bike
from theft can be a major problem when touring.
Depending on the circumstances and the location of
the ride, you may or may not want to haul the
weight of some kind of locking device. If you decide
to take something, you also must determine how
much weight to carry. No locking device is
completely adequate against the determined
bicycle thief, and the better devices are rather heavy.
A lock and chain can easily outweigh all your
other luggage combined, so the problem is not an
easy one to deal with.

On most tours you can dispense with locking
devices altogether, keeping an eye or hand on your
bike at all times. This usually is not too much of a
problem on a camping trip. Restaurants often are
situated so that you can park your bike outside a
window, where you can watch it as you eat. When
there is no way to watch your bike you may be able
to take it inside, or there may be a separate locked
area where you can put it. Usually, if you ask nicely,
people will find a place. If you are traveling with
companions, one person can stay with the bikes

while another shops for groceries or tends to other chores. At night you can keep the bike next to you, incorporate it into one of the guylines of your shelter, or even sleep with your pillow on top of one of the wheels. One major advantage to relying on your own attentiveness is that keeping your eyes or hands on the bike makes it more secure than any lock. The greatest problems occur on solo trips when you have to go into a rest room, grocery store, or wherever. If it's impossible for you to keep an eye on your bike, you often can find someone who will agree to watch it for a few minutes. You also may be able to take your bike into a lot of places if you explain politely and smile.

Fortunately, you are likely to stay in hotels, motels, hostels, or friends' houses during any stopovers in large towns and cities, where the hazards of thievery are greatest. Locking your bike in a hotel or motel room usually is safe, and hostels have facilities for securing bikes. Don't ever leave your bike unattended and locked with an inadequate device in cities or college towns. Thieves in these places have learned the value of quality bikes and carry cutters that can quickly shear through any but the toughest of systems. If you want to visit museums, shops, or bars, get a room first and take care of your bike before doing the town. Even if the bike is well insured, your trip probably will be ruined if it is ripped off. Also be sure your room has an adequate lock on the door. Your bike could be stolen from your room, of course, but this is not very likely. It is difficult to sneak off unobtrusively with a bicycle, and hotel robbers are less likely to be oriented toward stealing bikes.

On some trips a light locking device may be useful—not for foiling serious bicycle thieves, but to discourage casual theft or to slow the thief's progress while you are in a bathroom or are picking out snacks in a grocery store. A light cable and small lock weigh very little and can be useful in such circumstances. You still have to keep your eyes peeled, but you can be a bit more relaxed. Such devices also are useful in campgrounds to prevent casual theft while you are away from the bike for short periods. To repeat my earlier warning, however: don't ever rely on a light locking device in cities and large university towns where professional bike hustlers practice their trade. People who steal bikes for a living can cut through the light cable or chain and have the bike in the back of a truck in fifteen seconds. If you have to leave your bike in such places and don't have a room or somewhere else to lock it, find someone willing to take pity on you and keep an eye on the bike. Bike shops and police and fire stations are good possibilities. Remember, too, that many people are willing to be helpful if you smile and ask.

The lightest types of reasonably secure locking devices on the market are the U-shaped locks made by Citadel and Kryptonite. A U-shaped lock weighs about two pounds and passes through the frame, rear wheel, and detached front wheel, locking them to any stationary object that is fairly small and conveniently placed. These locks are as secure as reasonably possible against the cutting tools generally used for stealing bikes. The main disadvantages, aside from weight, are that they are less versatile than chains and cables and can be used for only one bike. You can't, for example, fasten your bike to a good-sized tree or thick lamppost with one of these locks. They also are expensive. The manufacturers do offer to cover the cost of a bike if it is stolen by someone's having broken the lock, but the guarantee is good for only a year and specifies a maximum payment of $200 as of this writing. This would be enough to cover your deductible if you have homeowners' insurance, but it certainly wouldn't be enough to replace any bike that is worth buying a lock this expensive to protect.

Chains and cables each have advocates. Cables are handy to carry, and for a given weight they offer more strength against saws or bolt cutters. On the other hand, cables can be severed with small, easily concealed cable cutters. Cables should be tempered, and chains and locks should be case-hardened. Hardening makes sawing a link or shackle difficult, but hardening all the way through makes it relatively easy to break a link with blows from a hammer. The rule with both cables and chains is: thicker is stronger. Locks should latch on both sides of the shackle.

For protection from serious thieves, a solo bicyclist cannot find a lighter system than a Citadel or Kryptonite lock. If several cyclists are traveling together, however, they can carry a heavy cable or chain long enough to lock all the bikes together. Experiment with the number of bikes you want to lock and a piece of string to find out the length you need. Shackles, links, and cable with 7/16-inch diameters seem to provide a reasonable compromise between security and weight. You can lock three or four bikes with a six-foot cable or chain and four or five with an eight-foot one. If you remove the front wheels and carry them with you, so that the chain doesn't have to pass through them, you can lock three or four bikes with a six-foot cable or chain and four or five with an eight-foot one. A 7/16-inch cable six feet long weighs about 3¼ pounds with a suitable lock.

If you are making a long tour and plan to stay in a city where you really need your bike for local transportation, you might be able to persuade a local bike shop to loan or rent you a heavy locking system. You may even want to write or call some shops in advance. Other possibilities are lock shops or members of bicycling clubs, such as the League of American Wheelmen.

Remember that no lock you can reasonably carry will protect an unattended bike left out at night in a town where the theft problem is serious. Take it with you!

Insurance

Insurance is not something you carry on a tour, nor will it do you a great deal of good if your bike is stolen at the beginning of a trip you have planned for years. It is related to the subject of security, however, and therefore is discussed briefly here.

Insurance specifically for bikes is virtually impossible to obtain. There are several reasons for this. One is the narrow-mindedness of the insurance companies, but another is the susceptibility of a bike insurer to fraud. Few police departments take bicycle theft very seriously. Partly for this reason stolen bikes can be disposed of easily, and so can allegedly stolen bikes, if the owners have a sudden need for money. In the long run, the solution probably is group insurance through clubs, perhaps with length-of-membership qualifications to eliminate people who want to join simply in order to collect on insurance.

In the interim, about the only protection available to cyclists is through homeowners' or renters' insurance policies. Such policies normally insure bikes along with other personal possessions against theft, with a deductible, usually $100, applied against any claim. Losses are not limited to those that occur at home. However, there are a number of important points that need to be checked carefully before you depend on such a policy to cover your bike, and you should look at both the legal language of the policy and the actual practices of the company involved.

For example, you should know what you have to do to establish the fact of a theft and what special conditions may apply when the bike is away from home. Property in or on a car, for example, usually is covered only when there is evidence of forcible entry. Since anyone with an IQ of fifty and a coat hanger can get into most cars in a couple of minutes, the protection provided may be questionable. Similarly, there may be special conditions which apply when the insured article disappears and there is no obvious evidence of theft. If someone runs a pick-up into your garage door to obtain access and then absconds with your bike, you will have no difficulty in demonstrating theft. However, what about the more likely situation in which a thief cuts your heavy chain with a set of bolt cutters and takes both the bike and chain from a downtown bike rack? How can you prove the bike was stolen? This is one of several situations in which the practices of the company are critical.

Perhaps most important is the problem of establishing the value of your bike. Any decent bike that has been properly maintained has doubled or tripled in value during the last few years. So what happens when your prized Colnago with Campy components, bought at a good price of $300 a few years ago, is ripped off from a friend's apartment in Chicago? Even if the fact of the theft is not questioned, many insurance companies will proceed to perpetrate a nastier trick on you than the guy who stole your bike.

The more villainous sort of insurance company will reason as follows: bikes, like most property, depreciate with use over a period of time. The company is likely to consider itself generous in permitting your claim of a $300 purchase price even though you no longer have the receipt, and in depreciating the bike over a period of five years. Since the bike is three years old, depreciation at $60 per year leaves a value of $120. After the deductible has been applied, this leaves you with a settlement of $20 for a bike that will cost at least $1000 to replace and which you could have sold easily for $600. Furthermore, even if you are willing to go to the trouble of suing and could win, losses in this range are difficult to recoup in most states. They are too small to make it profitable to hire a lawyer and too large to fall into the category of small claims, even if your state has a small-claims court.

Carefully checking out insurance companies can help you avoid the complications just described. All policies are written just about the same way, but interpretation and practices can vary a good deal. Such matters can change with an agent or district manager, of course, but current and past performance are at least some indication of the way a particular company handles claims. Ask the agent trying to sell you a policy what would happen in particular circumstances, such as if your bike were stolen from home with no visible evidence remaining, or were stolen from a car rack. Ask how value is established. You also might ask to have some of the replies put in writing, though you probably won't get them, and they may not commit the company even if you do. Every little bit helps, however. Finally, you might ask for a couple of references—customers who have had their bikes stolen and claims settled. If you can get references, call the people and find out how they feel about their settlements. You also might call your state's insurance commission and ask about complaints concerning the company. Some state regulatory bodies are effective, although most are industry promotional groups funded at the taxpayers' expense. Even with the latter, however, you may be lucky enough to get a clerk who is benevolent or bored enough to give you real information on a company's performance.

It would be tremendously helpful if cycling magazines conducted a number of reader surveys to rate insurance companies on their handling of bike claims. Insurance claims are a major problem for cyclists in some areas, and it is very difficult to find out which insurance companies treat cyclists fairly and which do not. The good companies deserve our business, while the bad ones deserve publicity.

If you do have a bike stolen, be sure to file a police report immediately and then check up on the case frequently. This puts you in a better position with the insurance company and eventually may help to persuade police to deal with bicycle theft more seriously. If you are treated badly by an insurance company, creating a fuss may help. Insurance companies spend a lot of money on advertising, and it often is helpful to convince a recalcitrant firm that a fair settlement will cost them a lot less than the grief you can cause them. Finally, if you have insurance, take some good color pictures of your bike and keep a record of its serial numbers; this will help if the bike is ever stolen. If you have your purchase papers, put them away in a safe place.

When you make plans for traveling, you might want to investigate the possibility of insuring your baggage, including your bike. You may even be able to get insurance to cover some of the losses caused by baggage misrouting and the consequent disruption of your travel plans. Such insurance might cover the cost of renting a bike on a long-planned trip, such as a European tour, as well as extra ticket costs if you have to change reservations as a result of the delay.

Chapter 10

Maintaining and Repairing Your Bike

IT IS IMPOSSIBLE to include a complete handbook on bicycle mechanics in the middle of a book on touring. The purpose of this chapter is not to serve as a substitute for a repair manual, but to discuss some techniques and problems of particular concern to cyclists planning long tours and to point out the information and skills you need to acquire to maintain and repair your bike.

Bicycles are very simple machines, and with a little effort anyone should be able to learn how to care for them. The best bicycles, though their design and machining are precise, are even simpler than some less expensive bikes. Many of the complications that plague bicycle mechanics, such as the lack of standardization of threads and dimensions, do not have to trouble the cyclist working on his or her own bike. Once you have noted all the particular idiosyncrasies of your machine (preferably when you purchase the bike) and have acquired a selection of compatible spare parts and tools, you can forget about most of these problems.

I think you should do nearly all your own bicycle maintenance and repairs for a number of reasons. The most obvious is that you will learn to fix things yourself, so that if something breaks down while you are alone on a deserted road, you'll be able to pull out your tool kit and repair it. The time to learn how to adjust a derailleur, break a chain, or replace a spoke is at home, with good lighting, warm hands, and a cup of coffee or a beer. Then when you have to do it in the rain as night is falling, you will be able to work efficiently and be back on the road in the shortest possible time.

Another good reason to do your own maintenance and repairs is that it makes you a better rider. The more you understand about your bike, the more effectively you can use it. The cycle itself usually stays in better condition because you are far more likely to notice things that need attention if you do your own work; you check bearings and adjustments habitually when you ride. Most bike maintenance is so simple that it can be done quickly. Tightening a loosened headset can be completed easily in a few minutes and can save your having to replace the bearing races. Working on your own bike is satisfying and, of course, it can save you quite a bit of money.

Learning the Basics

The first step in learning to maintain your bike is to develop an understanding of the way it functions. If you buy your bike from a shop or from a knowledgeable person, spend some time with him or her and ask a lot of questions. Don't try to pretend you know more than you do. If you ask about everything, you can learn a lot. Most people who work in shops love to talk about bicycles and are happy to pass on their knowledge to a beginner. (If it happens that the person you are dealing with is trying to snow you, it becomes more apparent if you let him or her ramble, anyway.) Make sure you understand how each part works, how it goes together, and what you need to assemble and disassemble it. The best time to buy tools and spare parts is with the bicycle. That is when you easily can match the spokes, ascertain the various thread sizes and other specifications needed to replace parts of the bike, and pick out the tools that are compatible with the various parts. This is the easiest time for two reasons: the person selling you the bike has the information readily available, and he or she also has the incentive of wanting to satisfy you. You usually can get such items at a better price when you purchase them with the bike.

Also purchase a good repair manual and read it, whether you have a chance to ask a salesperson questions or not. This is a particularly good idea before buying a secondhand bike, especially an expensive one, since it gives you a better understanding of the problems you should look for. For beginners, the best book is *Anybody's Bike Book,* by Tom Cuthbertson (see Appendix V for complete publishing data and a listing of other recommended repair manuals).

Starting at the top and front of the bike, check it over and note how things work. Go back later and list what tools you need to work on each part; such a checklist is useful as you begin to purchase or borrow tools for use at home and to assemble a repair kit to carry on tours. Check things systematically when looking the bike over so that you understand everything. One excellent way to learn the basics is to watch a shop mechanic assemble a bicycle, preferably a custom-built one that has to have everything put on, from the headset to the handlebar tape. When you buy a bike at a shop, ask to see a bike being put together.

The most important single rule for maintaining a bike in good operating condition is to keep it clean and properly lubricated and adjusted. Dirt and moisture are the primary enemies. Most good bicycle parts last for many thousands of miles of riding without significant wear if they are kept clean and lubricated, but dirty parts wear out rapidly. There are many special cleaning products available at bike shops, but soap and warm water generally do a perfectly adequate job for road grit on the frame and incidental metal parts. A good automobile wax applied occasionally helps protect the finish and keep dirt and water from sticking so much. Special cleaners and polishes can be used on shiny metal parts if they become slightly discolored or corroded.

Kerosene, diesel fuel, or a commercial solvent can be used to clean greasy parts, such as the chain. *Such solvents are flammable and should be handled with care.* Except in emergencies, it is best to avoid using gasoline for cleaning parts. It is dangerous, especially if you use it indoors. You may get away with using it hundreds of times before the right mixture of air and gas happens to drift over to an electrical motor, hot plate, or water heater and explodes.

From the beginning, it is important to be sure that you have the proper tools to work on your bike. I direct this comment mainly to novices, who are not yet familiar with the horrible things that can be done to a bike by tools which don't fit or are badly made. Wrenches that are too large can round the flats of bolt heads, pliers can mutilate them beyond recognition, and so on. Many improvisations do work, but if you aren't already handy with tools, use the ones made for the job. The tools necessary for working on a bike are relatively inexpensive and are well worth the money. Some tools that you buy must be of good quality. Adjustable wrenches have to be made with close tolerances so that the jaws won't open wider as you put pressure on the handle. This is especially true of the 6-inch crescent wrench you probably will carry on tour; the smaller the wrench, the better it needs to be made. Buy good Allen wrenches (hex keys) also; the cheap ones bend and deform when you try to tighten or loosen bolts. As a general rule, cheap tools are a false economy. If you want to save money, try to buy secondhand tools or buy good brands at sales or at discount suppliers.

Learn to make adjustments on your brakes and derailleurs right away. On new bikes, cables can be expected to stretch during the first few weeks of use and will have to be tightened. The shop at which you purchased the bike probably will do the job free, but have the mechanic show you how. Derailleurs have stop screws that limit the range of travel so that the chain moves as far as it should to each side but no farther. Incorrect adjustment either makes it impossible for you to shift into some gears or permits the chain to shift right off the cluster or chainwheels. The worst maladjustment is one that allows the chain to shift off the largest rear cog into the spokes. Be sure this derailleur adjustment is made correctly!

Most of the difficulties you initially might

have in working on your bike are connected with parts that are hard to get at or work on without special tools. These are the sorts of items you have to become familiar with on your own bike before going out on long tours far from home. You may be able to walk to a gas station and borrow a large crescent wrench, but you won't be able to find a freewheel remover, crank extractor, or cone wrench anywhere but at a bike shop. Once you have done a thorough overhaul on your bike, you will know exactly what you need to work on each part.

Bearing Maintenance

In principle, working on bearings is really quite simple. The idea is to clean the parts completely with solvent, coat the bearings and races lightly with a good grease, and adjust the clearances as tightly as possible *without binding*. Proper adjustment usually is achieved by trial and error, making sure that when everything is tight the bearings turn effortlessly but with no play from side to side. The only difference between you and an expert is that it will take you a lot more trials.

All the primary bicycle bearings work in pretty much the same way (unless you have some sealed bearings). Ball bearings are used, usually loose but sometimes held in a small frame known as a bearing retainer. The balls roll around between two grooves called bearing races. Usually, one race either is a part of the particular bicycle component or is press-fitted into it. The other race either slips over the first as part of the second half of the component (as with the inside pedal bearings and the lower headset bearing) or screws in, thereby adjusting the tightness of the fit. Some sort of locking method has to be used to keep the adjustment from slipping. One of the most common

methods of locking the adjustment in place (and one
of the hardest to get just right) is to have a locking
nut or ring screw down on top of the second race.
The race has to be held in place with one wrench
while the locking nut or ring is tightened on top of it.
A special wrench with narrow jaws may be needed
to hold the flats of the race, as with many hubs.

Whenever you take any bearing apart, position
the work so that the balls cannot fall on the floor and
roll off into a crack somewhere. Put a cupped
paper towel or something similar on your work-
table to catch them. As soon as you remove each
set of balls, *count them and write the number
down.* This is simpler than trying to figure out
later whether you have lost any or whether the two
sets in a headset or a pedal are supposed to have
the same number. After cleaning all the parts of a
bearing, set it vertically in a place where the balls
cannot get lost or covered with dirt if you drop
them. Pack a little grease in the lowest race, stick
the set of balls in it, put the next race on or screw it
down, and proceed upward until everything is
assembled. The same basic procedure applies
whether you are putting together a pedal, hub,
headset, or bottom bracket.

Mounting Tires
and Fixing Flats

In addition to brake and cable adjustment and
replacement procedures, you should learn to fix a
flat before you venture very far from home. Some
people seem to think that this involves some major
effort or mystery, but fixing a tire is not difficult and
really doesn't take very long. A little care and
patience can have you back on the road in a
relatively short time.

This section deals only with clincher tires. Sew-

ups require more time and effort to repair, though
there is no great mystery involved. Directions
for fixing sew-ups are readily available in many
catalogues and bike shops, if you are sufficiently rich and dedicated to using them for touring.
Clinchers are much easier to repair, though they
take more time to *change* than sew-ups. Directions given here also include installation of a
tire on a new wheel.

The first step in fixing a flat is to take off the
wheel, which is quite simple once you get used to
the procedure. If the brake mechanisms have quick
releases, they should be opened first. If your bike
is not equipped with quick releases, either at the
brakes or the levers, loosen the cables as much as
possible with the adjusting screws so that you can
avoid having to undo the cable clamp if possible.
(Closely adjusted brakes often will not clear the tire
without being loosened. Quick releases allow the
calipers to be opened wide without changing the
brake adjustment.) If the wheel barely makes it
out, remember to put it back on before inflating the
tire.

You should practice removing the rear wheel at
home with the bike hanging in a convenient
position. First shift the chain onto the smallest rear
sprocket. Then it usually is necessary to lift the
chain off the sprocket while sliding the wheel
forward. (Use a tire iron to lift the chain to keep
from getting any more grease than necessary on
your hands.) You may have some difficulty getting
the wheel past the derailleur, but rarely is it
necessary to take anything else off the bike once
you have worked out the sequence of manipulation.

Before you take the tire off the rim, check the
tread to see whether you can find the cause of the
puncture. Mark the spot if you remove a nail,

thorn, or piece of glass so that you can locate the corresponding spot on the tube later on. You may have to improvise to find something that can mark the tire visibly. I carry a white grease-pencil lead for this purpose, stored in my patch kit in a small metal tube from a Listo marking pencil. You also should mark the tire with an arrow pointing down at the valve stem and one pointing to one side for orientation. By making similar marks on the rim and on the tube when you remove it, you will be able to match up all the places that were in contact. This can be helpful in finding the original cause of the leak later on, when the tire has shifted around and the tube has been turned over several times. You should always check the tire after patching a hole, since the puncturing object may still be there and can be hard to find. It is a common error to pull a piece of debris out of a tire, assuming it caused the leak, only to have the real culprit punch another hole in the tube a few miles down the road.

If you are dealing with a slow leak, it is a good idea to pour a little water around the stem to see if the valve is leaky. A leak showing between the stem and the rim hole may indicate a problem there or may result from air leaking from a hole somewhere else and migrating around.

Deflate the tire completely and push one sidewall toward the center of the rim with your thumbs; this enables the wire to stretch over the edge of the rim more easily. Then pry part of one edge of the tire over the rim, being careful not to catch the tube or to pick up both edges of the tire at once. *Use a bicycle tire iron or the equivalent to pry off the bead.* (The bead is the wire-stiffened edge of the tire.) Never use screwdrivers for this purpose; they damage both the tire and the rim.

Tire irons or levers can be bought at bike shops and from mail-order houses. The better ones are notched at one end so that you can hook them on the spokes, making the job of removal a little easier. Once you have gotten the first twelve inches of the bead off, the rest slips off easily.

At this point you are ready to remove the tube, but before you do, mark it on the same side of the valve as you did the tire and rim so that you can match all three after finding the leak in order to locate whatever caused the puncture. If you already have pulled a nail or some other sharp object from the tire, the mark enables you to pinpoint the corresponding spot on the tube. If there is a nut fixing the valve stem in its hole, remove that and then take the tube out of the tire. Pump up the tube and find the leak; usually this is a simple enough matter, especially if you overinflate the tube somewhat. Just turn the inflated tube slowly and examine it. You probably will feel air on your face or hear it escaping when you reach the leak. A little water or saliva applied on the spot will show it clearly.

Next, clean the area around the hole to remove talcum, oil, and grit. Using sandpaper or the serrated tool from your patch kit, rough an area a little larger than the size of the patch you plan to use. Be sure the rubber is clean and dry and apply an even layer of cement from your kit. Wait until the cement is no longer shiny or sticky to a light touch; then peel the covering from the patch and press it on the tube, pushing it firmly with a smooth, rounded object. Whenever possible, I prefer to apply the patch with the tube inflated to its normal diameter, so that the glue bond won't be stretched. Dust the patch with a little talcum if you have it; soap dust or tooth powder also work. Let the patch cure while you check the tire and rim.

Using the marks you put on the inner tube and the tire, match the leak with the corresponding point on the tire and try to find the cause of the puncture. In many cases the object still will be imbedded in the tire casing. Once you have removed it, feel around the rest of the inside and outside of the tire for any other sharp objects that could cause leaks later on. Single bits of glass and sharp gravel rarely are found on the highway. Usually there is a patch of such fragments, and you could have picked up more than one. If the hole in the tube was on the inside, you probably will find a sharp spoke end protruding inside the rim. This has to be filed off, but if you aren't carrying a file, you may have to make do by covering it with a couple of layers of tape under the rim strip and putting the tube and tire back on the rim until you can fix it properly.

Before putting the tube back in the tire, overinflate it and go over the entire surface for leaks. If the cause of the original leak was a piece of glass or a thorn, there may have been several picked up at the same time. Thorns often break off when the tube is removed, and they may not be found during your inspection of the tire. A single nail may go through the tube in more than one place. It is distressing to find that there is another leak after you have put the entire tire back together. After letting the air out of the tube again, check the rim strip to see that it covers all the spoke nipples and that the valve hole is correctly positioned.

(Note: before using a new or retrued wheel, check the spoke nipples to make sure there are no sharp spoke ends protruding. Any that do eventually will rub holes through the rim strip and puncture the tube, so they must be filed flush with the nipple heads. A rubber rim strip or layer of tape must then be used to cover the nipple heads and keep them from abrading the tube. Some people use a length of twine running along each side of the row of nipples, covered with a strip of tape. The twine reduces the pressure of the tube against the nipples and spoke ends. [I believe this idea originated with John Forester.])

If you have taken the tire completely off the rim, push one side back on and over past the center. Put the valve stem through the hole, screw on the retaining nut a couple of turns, if there is one, and insert the tube all the way around the rim. (If the tube is new, inflating it slightly makes the job easier and prevents folds from being pinched off as the tire is blown up.) Begin pushing the second bead of the tire over the rim edge, starting at the valve stem and working around in opposite directions with your two hands. Work slowly and be careful not to pinch the tube between the bead and the rim. After you have gotten about three-quarters of the way around, go back and be sure that there is no pinching near the valve stem. There is a stiffened section around the stem to prevent the tube from bulging into the hole, and this can easily be pinched at the edges. Pushing on the end of the valve stem enables you to push the raised section into the tire. Also be sure that the valve is still centered in the hole rather than pushed to one side. Next, push the portion of the bead that is already over the rim to the center of the rim, so that the rest of the wire can stretch over the edge more easily. Go back and push the remaining one-quarter of the bead over the edge a little at a time, working from both sides with your two thumbs. Don't use a tire iron if you can help it since it is easy to damage the tube if you do. Lubrication with a soap solution or saliva may make it easier to get the last few inches on.

Using your pump, inflate the tire to a low pressure and then stop. Check all the way around both sides of the tire to make sure that an equal amount of sidewall is showing. The new, high-pressure clinchers have wires that are strong and tight-fitting, and they do not always seat all the way against the edge of the rim over the entire circumference. If one portion of the bead is pushed in toward the center, less of the tire sidewall will show. Leaving the tire this way and then inflating it completely creates high and low points that will cause vibration during high-speed descents. In extreme cases, it is even possible to blow the tire off the rim. If you are putting on the tire at home, a solution of soap and water can be spread all the way around the rim edges to permit the beads to slide into their proper positions more easily. In the field, however, you may have to work any low spots over with your thumbs or with extremely careful use of a tire iron. When the sidewall shows evenly all the way around, inflate the tire to full pressure. A Presta pump head should be pressed directly onto the valve and pulled directly off; jiggling it around causes leakage and wears the seals quickly.

Threading and Adjusting Cables

The methods of threading and adjusting the derailleur and brake cables are fairly obvious on inspection and won't be considered in detail here. Be sure both the cable connections and any fixing screws on levers and cable stops are tight when you install cables, since tension can easily pull a cable and loose or slide a clamp along the tube of your bike, flaking off paint all the way. Housing should be cut carefully so that there are no sharp, mashed ends. Cables should be threaded through the housing before cutting to length. I like to solder a cable in the area I plan to cut so that the end does not fray. This way, if it is ever necessary, the end can be rethreaded through small openings.

It is a good idea to carry one spare for each of the cables used on your bike, at least on long tours. In case of difficulties, various improvisations often can get you through. For example, if the rear derailleur cable breaks, the spring will shift the chain onto the smallest sprocket, an unattractive prospect if you have many uphill stretches on the way home. You can quickly adjust the stop screw controlling the travel of the derailleur, however, to keep it positioned at one of the larger sprockets, and this may be the quickest solution if you are racing to get to your house, motel, or campsite before dark.

Replacing your cables and housing when they begin to show signs of fraying and wear is the best way to avoid breakage. Broken cables nearly always are the result of neglecting routine maintenance. Grease any new cables as you install them to reduce friction and corrosion. If you ride a lot in wet weather, it is a good idea to occasionally spray LPS or a similar moisture displacer into the housings.

Replacing Broken Spokes

Some replacement spokes should be carried as part of your standard repair kit for touring. Depending on the cross pattern and the number of broken spokes, breakage can throw a wheel so far out of alignment that the bike cannot be ridden. The subject of broken spokes always is given a good deal of attention because the most likely breaks occur on the freewheel side of the rear wheel. The spokes there have to be pulled tighter because of the dishing of the wheel, yet replacement on the road can be a problem because of the difficulty of removing the freewheel. There are a number of ways to deal with this situation, some of which are discussed below.

It should be emphasized that too much attention often is paid to fixing broken spokes and not enough to preventing them in the first place. A high incidence of broken spokes usually indicates that your wheels have not been built properly. Wheels with well-chosen components and evenly tensioned spokes should hold up to a lot of hard use without requiring either frequent retruing or replacement of broken spokes. Good riding technique also is helpful. If you hit a lot of chuckholes and railroad tracks at full tilt with your weight on the saddle, you are naturally more likely to break spokes than is a rider who slows down, takes the bumps lightly, and knows how to jump the bike when a bad bump comes up unexpectedly.

The standard method of getting at the spokes on the freewheel side is to remove the freewheel, and a remover that fits your particular freewheel is an essential tool for general work on your bike. However, to use a conventional remover, you need either a very large wrench or a vise to hold the tool. A lot of leverage is required to remove the freewheel, even if you properly greased the threads before installing it, because it is screwed in with the full force of your forward pedaling. It should be possible to make a lightweight tool that could be used on the road, perhaps using part of the bike as a

lever arm. Another possibility is a freewheel body
that could be locked with a pin, so that you could
remove the freewheel by pulling the chain backward with the pedals. Unfortunately, no tools or
modifications of this sort are available, unless you
want to design your own. The same drawbacks
apply to tools for dismantling a freewheel, which
is an alternate approach to the problem of broken
spokes on the freewheel side of the rear wheel,
because on many hubs, removing the cogs from the
freewheel body gives you enough space to replace
the spokes.

My own solution to the problem is a tool
weighing about three ounces that enables me to
remove the cogs from my freewheel. Since this tool
weighs about the same as most freewheel removers
alone, does not require a wrench, and can be used
anywhere, it solves the dilemma for me. It works
only with those freewheels that have the outer two
or three cogs screwed on and the inner ones
installed by slipping them over splines. Most
modern freewheels are put together this way (see
page 111 for exceptions). The device consists of six
inches salvaged from a worn-out or shortened
length of bicycle chain. This is attached to a loop of
cable or a cable with loops swaged in each end. The
cable goes through the final rivet of one end of the
piece of chain and is just the right length to loop
over the seat post and reach down so that the chain
engages the front teeth of any of the smaller
freewheel cogs. To use the cog remover, you put
your bike in low gear and position the right pedal
near the top of its stroke without taking anything
off the bike. Then put the loop over the seat post and
engage the chain on the front of the smallest cog.
When you push hard on the pedal you turn the
freewheel in the forward direction, but the small

cog is held in place by the segment of chain, so it unscrews a couple of turns. The process is repeated to loosen the other screwed-on cogs. The wheel then can be removed in the normal fashion and the cogs unscrewed from the freewheel body by hand.

In making and using the tool, it is important that most of the stretch be taken out of the system before you push on the pedal; otherwise you will just stretch everything instead of exerting a lot of force on the sprocket. For this reason, the cable length has to be just right to avoid the need for a longer (and heavier) length of chain. I use Kevlar cable that is 1/8 inch in diameter; it is lightweight and does not mar the paint on the bike. This type of cable can be hard to find, however, so I suggest a loop of 3/64-inch stainless-steel aircraft cable swaged to the right length with a foot-long piece of heavy vinyl tubing put on before swaging. The vinyl protects the paint at the point where you put the loop over the seat post. You can purchase the cable and have it swaged at a machine shop. The cable does not have to be stainless, and the diameter is not critical. Carefully measure the length needed beforehand, however. It is simplest to take the chain with you, though you can drive the rivet over the cable later using a chain tool.

You should learn to use this gadget and a freewheel remover at home. Toothed removers should be held tight to the freewheel with the quick release or axle bolt so that they cannot slip and strip the freewheel notches when you are exerting a lot of force to loosen the threads. Most cyclists like to insert the remover in the jaws of a vise and turn the bicycle wheel by hand. A large crescent or monkey wrench can be used on the remover instead. If the notches are stripped accidentally, taking off the freewheel becomes a ticklish job that you probably should leave to a bike shop.

If you take the cogs off a freewheel, it is important to note the orientation of each one and of the spacers in between them. The teeth often are beveled in one direction, and shifting will be impaired if you put things back the wrong way.

The freewheel body usually is lubricated with light oil through an access hole. Dismantling the body itself for maintenance is fun if you enjoy esoteric mechanical work, but even bike shops rarely repair freewheels anymore.

Chain Maintenance

The chain gets dirtier than any other part of the bike, and because of the number of moving parts, it can create a tremendous amount of drag if it is not kept clean and lubricated. Even a tiny amount of friction occurring as each link pivots can result in a lot of work for your legs as the miles add up. Each joint pivots eight times for each complete circuit of the chain. When it is positioned on a front cog having the standard 52 teeth, the chain goes around about 40 or 50 times a minute. With something like 35,000 to 45,000 tiny oscillations per minute, you are well advised to make sure that each one is as smooth as possible.

There are quite a few ways to clean and lubricate a chain. The easiest, most effective way is to use a mechanical agitator that vibrates the chain slightly while it soaks in a solvent. (Use kerosene, diesel fuel, or the solvent sold by automobile supply houses.) You can simulate the same action by soaking the coiled chain in a coffee can with solvent in the bottom, wiggling the can back and forth lightly by hand. It is best to put a few layers of wire mesh on the bottom so that the dirt can fall away from the chain. Then take the chain out of the solvent, hold the ends near one another, and let one drop. Repeat several times, letting alternate sides drop. The whipping action sprays a lot of dirty cleaner, so don't do this over the living room rug. If the chain is extremely dirty, you should repeat the operation with clean solvent. Most of the fluid can be saved by allowing the dirt to settle out and pouring the clean solvent off the top.

Although a very dirty chain must be soaked in solvent, one that has picked up only a little surface dirt can be cleaned with a rag lightly coated with 10-weight oil. This method does not remove the lubricant inside the chain rollers.

Once the chain has been thoroughly cleaned it should be lubricated to prevent rusting and en- sure smooth operation. Of the many chain lubri- cants currently available, I prefer the ones with a molybdenum disulfide base. They penetrate and lubricate well with only a small application and have less of a tendency to pick up grit than conventional oils. For use on a tour, the non-aerosol type is preferable, though it is harder to find. You can carry an adequate amount in a small can, preferably with a pinpoint dropper that screws on to apply the lubricant.

Removal of the chain and reinstallation is quite simple with the use of a chain tool. A pin is screwed against one of the rivets in the chain, pressing it out through a slot in the other side of the tool. Be careful not to remove the rivet all the way since it is a nuisance to get back in. Push it past both the inside plates only. Don't be in too much of a hurry, and keep checking to see if you have pushed the pin far enough. The better chain tools have notches that enable you to press the rivet back in without compressing the outside plates together and making the joint stiff. If you have the other type of tool, you may have to pry the plates apart slightly with a screwdriver to eliminate binding.

An alternative to using a chain tool is to buy a Super Link, a special link that fastens the chain together and that can be removed and installed with a small screwdriver. You still need a chain tool to remove or install extra links, but if you have a Super Link in the chain, you probably can skip carrying a chain tool in the field. The manufacturer also claims the advantage of additional strength over rivets removed and pressed in with a chain tool, though breakage of a well-maintained chain is rather unlikely.

Getting Your Bike Ready for a Long Tour

There are major differences between taking off on a long tour (or a short one far from home) and making short trips near home, primarily because of the disappointment that a breakdown can cause. Safety considerations usually do not differ very much. Having a front tire blow out on a fast descent can be just as unpleasant ten miles from home as a thousand. There are a lot of other little problems that cyclists often ignore on day tours, however, that should be taken care of before heading off on a vacation tour you have planned for years. A tool kit for day tours can be kept very basic, if you are so inclined, including only the tools necessary to fix the most common problems, such as flat tires and broken cables. In the event of major mechanical difficulties, you always can hitchhike or have someone come to pick you up.

Before any lengthy tour, however, especially one far from home, you should make sure that your bike is in perfect shape by doing a thorough overhaul. In the process, you can check all the bearings to make sure that nothing has to be replaced, put on new cables and housing, be sure that the wheels are in top condition, and so on. This procedure is followed by most cyclists before they leave on special trips, but there is one rule you should make that is less commonly observed: *Do the overhaul a couple of weeks before you are scheduled to leave!* Standard operating procedure is to find yourself doing the final work at two o'clock in the morning just before you are planning to leave.

Aside from the usual arguments for doing something early, there are some additional reasons connected with overhauling a touring bike. One is that if you need any special parts at the last minute, all the local shops are sure to be sold out, an obvious corollary to Murphy's Law. A second point is that some adjustments are likely to cause problems after any major overhaul, and it is better to ride the bike a few hundred miles and find them all when you're near home. This is not a reflection on your competence as a mechanic. New cables are likely to stretch, for example, and housing to push into cable stops a bit. It is better to find that you cannot get the bike into low on a day trip without a heavy load on a steep grade. The same principle applies to a dozen other adjustments that need to be fine-tuned. Try to get all the work done on your bike far enough in advance so that you can test new parts and tighten loose bolts close to home and iron out any problems.

Two adjustments that often are neglected deserve special attention, particularly with a new bike or after an overhaul. The tightness of the headset bearings must be adjusted correctly or the bearing races are likely to be ruined, particularly if they are of the round instead of the V type. A loose headset permits vibration and impact when the bike is ridden on a rough surface, and the bearings are likely to make tiny indentations in the races. Once the indentations are formed, the balls tend to stick in them, bang them deeper, and stick still more, so steering soon becomes erratic. Check your headset adjustment from time to time, especially after an overhaul. The bearings should turn smoothly and easily but should have no play.

Cotterless cranks are essentially trouble-free, but only if the cranks are tightened properly and kept that way. Check occasionally to make sure they are tight, and be careful to check the tightness frequently with a new bike or after an overhaul. If you feel any looseness, stop and correct it immediately. Any play allows the hard steel of the axle to bite into the aluminum crank and ruin it. If you have a fancy bike with light alloy bolts securing the cranks, you should have a set of steel ones as well. Use the steel bolts to tighten the cranks, remove them, and then tighten the alloy bolts.

A Tool Kit for Touring

The tools you need on a particular trip depend upon many factors, ranging from the type of bike you own to the remoteness of the tour and your talents at improvisation. The ideal is to have a kit that is light in weight and that permits you to do anything necessary to fix your bike. You need to consider obvious work, such as flat tires, broken spokes, brake and derailleur adjustments, and the tight-ening of virtually any component on the bike. It also is important to consider the possibility of major problems and how you would take care of them. If your bike has unusual components that require special tools, you may not be able to assume that a bike shop could make the repairs. When touring with a group whose bikes have inter-changeable components, it often is worthwhile to carry special tools or replacement parts even for problems that are quite unlikely to occur, because one tool or part serves as insurance for everyone.

Similarly, when touring with two or more people, it often is possible to save weight by carrying only one of a particular tool to serve the entire group. Two people who cycle together may carry only one tool kit. It is important to consider how much you really ride together, though. If the rider with the patch kit is five miles up the road waiting for lunch, both that person and the cyclist walking the bike with the flat tire are likely to become rather irri-tated by the time they finally get back together. The acrimonious discussion that follows may consume a lot more energy than would have been expended in carrying an extra patch kit. On the other hand, the need to dismantle a hub is not likely to arise with nearly as much urgency, so there would be little point in carrying an extra set of cone wrenches. You have to balance the value of particular tools against their weight both for the group and for the individual rider.

Every experienced rider is likely to have a different opinion about the best tool kit to carry, depending on personality and past experience. Just as an army always prepares to fight the preceding war rather than the next one, touring cyclists design their tool kits to handle the mechanical problems they had on their last tour. In evaluating each item you are considering for the kit, you should ask four questions: How likely is it that I will need this particular tool? What would be the consequences if I needed it and it wasn't available? Is some other tool also required for this one to be of any use? Is there something else lighter that can do the same job?

When assembling your tool kit, you should pay as much attention to weight as you do when considering components for the bike itself. It often is cheaper to shave ounces in the tool kit than on the bike, and it is just as effective when you are climbing a hill, except in comparison to parts of the wheels. Unfortunately, many tools that have to be carried are rather heavy unless you have special modifications made. Even so, there are many easy ways to save weight if you give a little thought to your tools. My crankset dust caps require a hex key, for example, but only minimal torque is required to put them on or take them off. Instead of carrying a whole hex key, I cut off a ½-inch length of one and carry that instead. It can be turned with the crescent wrench I have to carry anyway. Some cyclists who have replaced most of the common bolts on their bikes with Allen-head bolts can carry hex keys and perhaps a small, three-way socket wrench, dispensing with the heavy crescent altogether.

Go over your entire bike and determine exactly what tools you really need on the road. Don't try to save weight by carrying tools of inferior quality, though. Badly made tools are likely to ruin a bolt or break just when you need them the most. A stripped bolt head is more trouble on a lonely road than it is at home.

The following checklist includes the items you should *consider* for your tool kit. You should not take them all! The ones you need depend on the factors already discussed and on your bike. On recent tours my tool kit has weighed 14 ounces (400 grams), and I feel I was carrying everything I needed. It is possible to go still lighter using modified tools and aluminum alloys wherever possible. (The 14 ounces does not include such items as the pump and pocket knife, which are carried elsewhere.)

TOURING KIT CHECKLIST

Tools	Comments
parachute cord (nylon line with a braided sheath)	Very useful in many situations. You can wrap it around the brakes to hold them in position while adjusting them, replacing the "third hand" tools used in shops. You can use the line to hang the bike from a billboard or tree branch to work on it or to make a dozen improvised repairs. I carry mine with my camping gear, but it is an essential tool.
tape	Another indispensable tool usually carried elsewhere. There are many good tapes, but I carry a good-quality cloth adhesive tape in my first-aid kit and use it for everything.
pocket knife	Carry one on all tours. I keep mine in my pocket.
wire	A couple of feet of easily bent solid wire, such as baling wire, can be very helpful for improvised repairs. I take a couple of extra feet on longer trips.
hand cleaner	Small, plastic tube of the hand cleaner mechanics use to remove grease from their hands. It won't help you fix the bike, but it makes you feel a lot better afterward.
6-inch crescent wrench	One of the two or three standard tools. Most bikes have many hex-headed bolts and screws. The wrench handle can be drilled to save weight.

4-inch crescent wrench	Much lighter and fits most small nuts and bolts, such as those on derailleurs. Usually a supplement to the 6-inch wrench rather than a replacement.
screwdriver	Try to find one that is light and that fits all your screws well. If you also need a Phillips bit or several sizes of regular bits, get one of the holders with interchangeable bits. The top part of the handle on many screwdrivers can be cut off to save weight.
Allen wrenches (hex keys) to fit your bike	The most common sizes are 3, 5, 6, and 7 millimeters. You can have a T-handled screwdriver or socket tool made in a shop using two sizes of hex keys brazed together for a handle. Campy makes a T-tool with a 6-mm hex key as a handle and an 8-mm socket. You easily can have another socket brazed onto one end of the hex key, adding a 9- or 10-mm size.
tire irons	Two are enough; try to find the aluminum-alloy type.
patch kit	Get the European or Japanese brands with thin patches made for lightweight bikes. The small kits are adequate, but once the tube of cement has been opened it has limited life, since the solvent evaporates; don't assume, therefore, that an old one is good. Include a piece of casing from an old tubular tire to repair tire casing rips.
pump	High-pressure model with the correct attachment(s) for the valves on your tires.
tire gauge	Most people go by feel on tour, but you should at least check the pressure at home so that you know what the correct pressure feels like.

freewheel remover	The correct one for your freewheel. Usable only with a large wrench or vise.
freewheel cog remover	Special tool explained on pages 218–21.
crank pulling and tightening tools	Some models fit a number of brands of cranks so that only one needs to be carried for several bikes. Check for interchangeability in advance.
pliers	Small, offset-type ignition pliers are handy and weigh very little. The jaws are offset at an angle and adjust to three different widths.
open-end, box, or socket wrenches for particular bolts	These can replace at least one and perhaps both crescent wrenches. May be combined with other tools (see "Allen wrenches").
chain tool	Can be replaced with a drift or a nail if you've practiced in advance. The nail or drift is used to drive a rivet out and in with wrench jaws as an anvil.
cone wrenches for hubs, bottom bracket tools, special tools for pedals, chainwheel tools, spoke wrench	Not usually necessary. For touring situations a crescent can serve as a spoke wrench. Improvisations likewise will do for most pedal, hub, and bottom bracket needs, depending on your bike.

Spare Parts	**Comments**
inner tube	I have carried one on a number of long trips, as do many tourists, but have never needed it. If you are traveling in a group with similar tires, one probably is enough.
tire	For users of clincher tires, the same comments apply as noted under "Inner tube," unless you are trying to get the last few miles out of old tires.

	Worthwhile if you are using ultralight clinchers. Spares are mandatory for users of sew-ups.
extra spokes	Usually should be carried, just in case. The number depends on the trip and your past experience. Four to six are plenty, except on extended tours, unless you are riding with cyclists who are badly prepared. They're usually also the people with poorly built wheels who break spokes constantly. If you have problems with broken spokes yourself, you'll naturally want to carry more.
derailleur cable, brake cable, yoke cable for center-pulls	Good spares to carry and quite light.
brake blocks	Some think these are a necessity. I don't carry them, but I replace them and tires at resupply points on very long tours. They don't wear out very fast.
brake nuts	Carry a spare one or two; they can fall off.
balls for bearings	If you take the tools to work on hubs, etc., you should carry some spare balls for each bearing, labeled as to their use.
strap for toe clip	With a large group it may be worth carrying one since pedaling without a strap is a nuisance. For solo riders or a couple, however, check the ones on your bike before leaving and plan on improvising with parachute cord if necessary.

On most trips my tool kit includes a 4-inch crescent wrench, a screwdriver, two aluminum tire irons, a patch kit, my freewheel cog remover, a drift for the chain, small tubes of hand cleaner and grease, a tiny can of chain lubricant, parachute cord, a small pair of ignition pliers, 3- and 5-mm Allen wrenches, and a Campy T-tool with a 6-mm hex key, 8-mm socket, and brazed-on 9-mm socket. I carry a pump on the frame with a few spare spokes taped onto it and take along a set of spare cables as well. On multi-day trips I generally carry a spare tube and tire, though I am not convinced they are necessary. On tours of more than three days I substitute a 6-inch crescent for the 4-inch one and carry tools for tightening and pulling the crank arms. (On my bike the need for a 6-inch crescent is mainly to work on the pedals; if you have hex-headed bolts instead of Allen-head bolts on your bike, you will want the larger wrench as a basic tool.) On much longer trips I take along a free-wheel remover and a remover for my sealed crank bearing. My hub bearings are sealed and don't require special tools. I always carry a few spare nuts and bearing balls in my patch kit, along with an adapter that permits me to use a gas station hose on my Presta valves.

The large nut on the headset usually can wait until you reach a gas station for work. In an emergency you can loosen or tighten it by putting the bit of a screwdriver against one of the points of the hub, angling it in the proper direction, and tapping the handle with a rock. This tactic can be used in emergencies with most large nuts and locking rings.

If you have the type of seat clamp that is tightened by nuts on both sides, you should make sure you have wrenches to fit. Two are required, and the nuts are fairly large. Usually a 6-inch crescent and a special spanner for the second nut can be used. The seat adjustment is one you are quite likely to need to make, and riding with a loose or incorrectly angled seat can be a real nuisance. Seats that adjust with Allen wrenches do not present this problem.

Finally, once you have assembled your tool kit and have checked your bike carefully, don't worry about mechanical problems. Most bike tours go by without a single adjustment necessary, much less a major repair. Even flat tires are relatively uncommon. A well-maintained bike is quite trouble-free, and the tool kit generally rides along for many tours without even being opened.

Part Three

Other
Equipment

Chapter 11

Seeing and Being Seen

LIGHTING IS ONE of the major problems for cyclists in general, but it presents special difficulties for touring cyclists. With a little time and ingenuity, the commuter can attach a bright motorcycle lighting system onto his or her bike and power it with a large, rechargeable battery pack, restoring the power supply every night with home current. For the tourist who is trying to pare every ounce, however, this is not a reasonable solution.

Most of the lighting systems currently sold for bicycles are junk. They put out very little light and often are unreliable, poorly thought out, and quite heavy considering their light output. Fortunately, more thought has been put into reflectors in the last few years, and these are generally of far better design.

Your touring plans determine your needs for

lighting and reflectors. If you are touring in midsummer in the northern latitudes and are not riding late into the day, you may be able to ignore lighting altogether, as most cyclists do on day trips. Even on day trips, however, it pays to think things out in advance. Always anticipate flat tires, mechanical problems, head winds, and the like, which can radically slow your progress. If you plan to reach your motel or get back home before dark, you ought to consider the consequences of getting off schedule.

On many of my own tours, by far the most dangerous part of the ride even in daylight is a fifteen-mile stretch of narrow, busy highway leading back to within a couple of miles of my house. Riding this road after dark without proper lights and reflectors is insane, so when I take a long tour or a late one that will bring me back along that road, I always go prepared in case I am caught in darkness. Late in the year, as the days get shorter, I take lights more often, since I have less time to get home before sunset.

Clearly, the items you need to carry "just in case" do not have to be as elaborate as those that might be necessary for a trip on which you actually plan to ride part of the time in the dark. On some fall trips, when the days are short, the ambitious cyclist may begin riding before dawn. Though the traffic usually is minimal at this hour, adequate lighting still is essential. Dusk and dawn are times when lighting is particularly important because dim lights and reflectors don't show up as well at this hour, yet visibility is still quite poor. A driver's eyes adjust to the light sky, while the road ahead still is rather dark.

If you are camping, your lighting needs in camp should be considered along with those on the road.

Often the same lights can do double duty, eliminating the need to carry extra equipment.

When you are choosing lights, keep in mind that there are two distinct functions you may want them to serve. The first is to make you stand out so that drivers approaching you can spot you from a long way off and won't run you down. The other is to light up the road ahead of you well enough so that you can stay on the pavement, avoid most of the worst obstructions, and steer clear of perambulating skunks. The two functions are quite different, and often it is most efficient to separate them completely rather than trying to make the same devices serve both purposes.

Daytime Visibility

For the cyclist, visibility is a necessity of life, like food and water. When you are touring on a bicycle, you find yourself constantly sharing the road with vehicles that could wipe you out instantly if they hit you. When purchasing lighting and reflectors, also give some thought to your visibility during the day. As noted earlier, motorists often do not see cyclists because they are not used to looking for them. The average driver watches for large objects, such as cars, and his or her brain simply doesn't register the presence of a bicycle. You can't help relying somewhat on drivers' skills and common sense; everyone on the road does that. The driver of one car coming down a highway at sixty miles per hour, for example, has to assume that a car coming the other way at the same speed will not suddenly swerve out into the wrong lane. On a bike, however, you must make sure that the driver sees you before you can take a reasonable gamble that he or she won't run you down. Anything you can do to make yourself more conspicuous is helpful.

Bright clothing and equipment is the cyclist's first line of defense. Whether the colors of bright jerseys, tee shirts, helmets, and panniers please you aesthetically or not, you should choose the brightest ones you can stand. Think in terms of drivers who are road-weary and inattentive, often with dirty windshields and the glare of the sun in their eyes. Wear anything you can to attract their attention. Bright yellow panniers and stuffsacks show up a lot better than navy blue ones, and garish clothing helps to attract attention. Pay particular heed to the colors of items that you wear during periods of poor visibility. Raingear, sweaters, and long pants are often the dullest items in cyclists' wardrobes, but they shouldn't be.

Special devices for daytime visibility also can be used. Large, brightly colored triangles of reflective material can be mounted on the back of your luggage. Personally, I don't like extra pieces there, but I sew strips of reflective material to the backs of my panniers and on the bottom of the stuffsack that I mount on my rear rack. The material has a bright, contrasting color so it improves daytime visibility as well as reflecting headlights at night. A lightweight, tie-on bib that shows to the front and the rear can be made using the same material and worn whenever the visibility is poor *for approaching drivers*. This can be in the evening, when the sun is low ahead of you on the road, or when it is raining or dusty. Always think of visibility from the driver's point of view; it is different from yours. You can look down at the road while a driver has to look into the sun. A windshield often can interfere with a driver's sight. A light shower on a dusty road may be worse than a downpour because it streaks a car's windshield without washing it clean.

Another device which is useful in some situations is a special safety pennant attached to a long fiberglass wand fixed to the rear of the bicycle. Besides contributing a certain amount to general visibility, a pennant allows a cyclist to be seen sooner by a motorist approaching over the crest of a hill. It also can call attention to a bike in many traffic situations in which the rider would otherwise be concealed. Safety flags do add air drag, however, and it becomes a personal decision as to whether they contribute enough to your safety to be worth using. This partly depends on the roads you are riding. A standard pole is rather unwieldy to carry for occasional use, but it is quite easy to make one from a fishing pole that can be broken down when it is not needed. Cyclists who fish regularly when touring can easily make flags and brackets that enable them to use their poles as safety pennants. Some tourists make pennant poles from collapsible radio antennas.

Reflectors

Modern reflective materials simplify the problem of making bicycles visible at night. You should make as much use of reflectors as you can since they require no batteries, using the bright lights of automobiles to achieve their luminosity. Reflectors weigh less than any light and are brighter than most practical bicycle lights. For most purposes, it makes far more sense to mount several large reflectors on the back of your bike, perhaps arranging them to be easily removable, than it does to fool with a small, red light shining to the rear. Bike lights are so weak that if they are fixed and shine steadily, few drivers even notice them among bright signs and road reflectors.

New bicycles now are required to have

reflectors on the front, rear, pedals, and wheels, but these usually are poorly designed for high-performance touring bikes and typically are removed after the bike is purchased to make room for touring gear. Such reflectors can be helpful in making the bike visible, however, and you should think seriously before just tossing them into the trash can; they can be remounted on your racks or bags. One reflector has to be removed from a pedal to permit the toe clip to be mounted. If you don't leave the other on, you might want to replace it with a piece of Scotch brand reflective tape. This useful material weighs virtually nothing. A strip on the heel of each shoe isn't a bad idea should you be caught in the dark. If you don't like to ride with reflectors on your bike, carry a roll of this tape in your repair kit to put on the machine and on your clothing if you are accidentally caught in the dark.

The reflectors that are placed on the spokes make you highly visible to a car approaching from the side, partly because of their eccentric motion. Most cyclists don't like either the weight on the wheels or the appearance, however. Your own evaluation may depend on how often you are likely to ride at night. If you get a pair of wheel reflectors that can be put on and taken off easily, they can be carried in your luggage and mounted on the spokes when you ride late, at the same time you put on your lights and other safety devices. An even lighter-weight alternative for those who occasionally ride at night is to carry two light but stiff plastic strips with reflective tape on either side. These can be laced into the spokes in a few seconds if you are caught out at dusk.

The 3M Company, which makes Scotch reflective tape, also manufactures a reflective fabric. A good combination for nighttime visibility is to sew strips of this fabric, perhaps in crosses or triangles, to the rear and side panels of your rear panniers and to the front of your front bag. Another pattern can be sewn on the bottom of any stuffsack you carry on top of your rear rack. This gives a good reflective surface with minimal cluttering of the bike. As mentioned earlier, if brightly colored reflective material is used, the same devices improve daytime visibility. The moving reflectors on pedals and wheels still should be used because they attract the motorist's eye better than fixed reflectors. If you use removable reflectors or strips on the wheels, the only reflectors that remain on the bike are the ones on the backs of the pedals. These can be made from strips of reflective tape. If you anticipate being caught out at night frequently, it also is a good idea to make or buy a bib of reflective material with panels that show to the front and rear. The large reflective area attracts the attention of a driver much better than small reflectors do, and a bib weighs only a couple of ounces.

White reflectors have much higher reflectivity than any colored materials, amber is next, and red reflects back much less light than either. Hence, in choosing reflectors, you should consider whether colored material in a particular place gives enough of an advantage to justify less brightness. The reflectors on your wheels almost certainly should be clear, since they can't be confused with anything else but bicycle wheels. If you want to use colors for other reflectors, amber probably is best.

Lighting the Cyclist

Reflectors do have limitations, and you should not rely solely on them to alert drivers to your presence. Motorists whose headlights are pointed away from you cannot see your reflectors, and at dusk, dawn, or in fog or rain, cars may not even have their lights on. Although their moving patterns are distinctive, wheel reflectors are rarely useful to an experienced cyclist on the open road, because if you see the headlights of a car approaching from the side, you should let it pull out before you go by. Wheel reflectors make you visible only when you allow yourself to become vulnerable. It usually is best not to gamble that a driver approaching from the side will see you and stop. Furthermore, your primary need is to be visible to cars overtaking from the rear. For dealing with these cars, the only moving spots available for reflectors are your pedals and shoes. Reflective cuffs also can be made or purchased, and they are helpful, but they still are not sufficient.

Flashing or moving lights are by far the most effective ways of attracting the motorist's attention from the monotony of the white line or the confusion of other lights. The leg light has long been used for this purpose and is strapped to the traffic-side leg at the ankle or the calf just below the knee (see Figure 20). Such a light can double as a flashlight in camp and makes you moderately visible to approaching cars. It also lights the road ahead slightly. A leg light requires two C cells, which don't last very long, so that spares usually have to be carried. All this weighs a significant amount for the cyclist trying to keep weight to a minimum, particularly one who is carrying the light only in the event of unexpected difficulties.

The best solution for attracting the attention of motorists is some kind of flashing light. The flash attracts the attention of an oncoming driver, and it also provides a brighter light with a much lower drain on the battery than can be achieved with a

20. A leg light; the light shows white to the front and red to the rear. Wear the light strapped to your ankle or calf, not to your arm as shown in manufacturers' ads.

light that burns steadily. Modern electronic circuits make it possible to manufacture such flashers cheaply and with minimal weight. The ideal type is probably a strobe-type light with a very bright bulb. A less expensive alternative that is quite effective employs a bulb such as those used in highway flashers. The Belt Beacon, made by Ampec, weighs less than 4 ounces (113 grams) with an alkaline battery and mounting hardware, 3 ounces less than a leg light with alkaline batteries. The Beacon's other advantages over the leg light are that its battery lasts longer, its flash is visible for a considerably greater distance, and it can be seen fairly well from the side. Its only disadvantages are that it cannot be used either as a camping light or to illuminate the road ahead. It can be mounted on the rear rack or on the panniers or it can be clipped to the waistband of your shorts. If you plan to ride a good deal at night, you might want to use one Belt Beacon on the rear of your bike and one on the front.

Lighting the Road

Lights to attract the attention of motorists are needed as soon as daylight starts to wane. If you have to start or finish a ride in complete darkness, however, you also need a lamp that lights the road ahead. This function of a lighting system usually is given first consideration, though it is far less important than making yourself visible to approaching vehicles. Depending on your situation, you may be able to ignore the matter of lighting the pavement ahead. You can see the road well enough to ride in surprisingly poor light, and often it is better to ride without a light if there is any visibility at all. This is because the light illuminates a small area ahead of the bike, and while you are looking at this bright spot you cannot discern much in the surrounding darker zone. Without a lamp, you actually may see more. This is especially true in marginal conditions, when your vision without a light still may be good enough to permit you to travel at a good speed and to pick out road hazards, while you must ride quite slowly when using most lights because of the limited area they make visible. Finally, if you are not actually planning to ride in the dark, but are carrying lights only in case of unforeseen delays, you may feel that ensuring your own visibility to cars is enough of a precaution. You always have a long period before complete darkness arrives.

There are a number of situations in which you really should have some kind of light to find your way, however. If you are traveling between lodging places without camping gear and are riding long distances every day, it is quite likely that at some time you will be caught with a considerable distance to travel after dark. A flat tire coupled with bad weather, for example, easily could delay you several hours. Moonless nights on back roads can be very dark indeed, so that it would be very dangerous to ride without a light to keep you on the road and to prevent you from wandering onto the wrong side. Reading maps and road signs also may be necessary unless you camp where you are. To handle these situations and others I usually carry a light, because I often ride late in the day, leaving little margin for error, particularly in the short days of fall.

Lighting the Camp

Those cyclists who are camping at night often need lights to do cooking and other chores, particularly during off-season trips when the days are relatively short. During midsummer, especially at northern latitudes, there is less of a need, unless you are on a high-mileage trip and are riding from dawn until dusk.

For low-key trips, when the likelihood of riding in the dark is minimal and when you expect to accomplish most of your chores before dark, a leg light can serve both as a camp light and as an emergency bicycle light. Leg lights also are inexpensive. A headlamp, discussed below, is more versatile and useful both on the road and in camp if you anticipate using a light very often. If you only need a camp light for occasional use, a small, plastic flashlight that runs on AA alkaline cells is versatile and relatively cheap.

Power Sources

The two sources of power available for lighting are generators and batteries. Generators have some merit for the commuter because they save the cost of continual battery replacement. They have a

number of major disadvantages, however, that
usually make them ill-suited to the tourist's
needs. The generators that operate with the least
friction are mounted in the hub, but these cannot
be disconnected mechanically when they are not in
use. The drag of a hub-mounted generator must be
tolerated all the time, whether the light is used or
not. While this does not present a major problem
on a utility bicycle, it generally is unacceptable
to the long-distance touring cyclist. The most
common type of generator is mounted on the fork or
seatstay near one of the wheels and is pushed
against the tire by a spring when it is needed. Such
generators are hard on lightweight tires and are
rather heavy. It should be possible to make more
suitable generators, perhaps using rubber rollers
contacting the tread of the tire rather than the
sidewall, but the types currently available are not
well suited to touring. If you do use this type of
generator, be sure to buy a rubber cover for the
roller to reduce tire wear.

There are several other problems with
generator systems. One is that they do not work
when the bike is stopped because the generator is
not being driven. This arrangement is unsafe when
the cyclist stops for traffic or signals, and it also
precludes using the generator as a power source in
camp or for reading a map or road sign. It is possible to wire a generator system with a rechargeable auxiliary battery which takes over when
you stop pedaling, but this entails extra weight
and expense. Besides, there is no commercially
available system of this type in the United
States at the moment, so you have to wire your
own. Finally, most generator lighting systems
have rather poor wiring and are notoriously un-

reliable. The simpler the lighting system, the easier it is to fix on the spot. Generator wiring systems are complex.

For the reasons just given, I do not recommend generator systems for most tourists. There are special circumstances for which such a system would be ideal, but for most cycle tourists, battery-operated lights are a more satisfactory alternative. If you use your touring bike for commuting long distances during the week and have to ride a lot in the dark, I think the best arrangement is to use a removable storage battery with a motorcycle lamp and to recharge it each night when you arrive home. This provides a lot of light, low operating cost, and good reliability.

A variety of batteries is available to the tourist for running a lighting system. The standard type sold in grocery and hardware stores is the carbon–zinc cell. Carbon–zinc batteries require a low initial investment, but you are likely to have to carry quite a few to provide good lighting for any length of time. This is especially true if the weather is chilly or if you have to use a light for hours at a time. They are very sensitive to cold, and they don't stand up well to heavy, continuous drains. Alkaline batteries, also widely available, are slightly heavier and more expensive, but they last much longer in use, have a better shelf life (which is particularly important when you buy batteries in small stores that may not have a high turnover), and perform better in cold weather and under a heavy, continuous load. A far better battery for the tourist, however, is the lithium cell. Lithium batteries are available only at specialty shops and are expensive, but they are cheaper to use because they last so much longer. They have the additional advantages of a much longer shelf life and better cold-weather performance, and they remain at full output for nearly their entire life (so your light stays bright instead of gradually dimming). A lithium cell produces 2.8 volts, approximately double the potential of carbon–zinc cells, so with most lights only a single lithium battery is used in place of two normal ones, saving on weight. Lithium cells can be used in standard lights by getting a dummy cell to fill the extra space or by substituting a special battery case.

Recommendations

Front lights on bicycles should be removable so that they can double as camp lights. There are a number of brands that serve the purpose, but I prefer a headlamp that straps around your forehead or helmet, pointing where you are looking (see Figure 21). A headlamp has several advantages over a light that clamps to the bike. It is very convenient for camping and for unloading your bike in the dark because the light moves with you but leaves your hands free. This feature is

21. *A lightweight headlamp, useful both to light your way on the road and to provide light in camp, leaving your hands free. The model pictured is made by MSR; it employs the lamp from a Wonder headlamp along with a lithium battery.*

especially welcome when you are digging in your panniers for small items, pitching a tent in the rain, or lifting the lid off a pot to stir the stew. It also is useful when you are reading road signs (usually at the wrong angle for conventional bicycle lamps), looking for chuckholes, or trying to attract the attention of a car approaching from the side. With a headlamp, you can wiggle your head in the direction of the driver and create a flashing effect. The battery case for a headlamp usually is carried in your pocket, where it stays warm, so the batteries operate at maximum efficiency. Finally, the headlamp receives a gentler ride than a light attached to the handlebars would. The only real disadvantage of a headlamp is the nuisance of arranging the wire running from the battery case to the lamp so that it stays out of your way.

Whether you use a headlamp or light that fixes to the bicycle or front bag, it is important that it be well constructed. Shake and bang it before you buy; if the light flickers with such treatment, it will do the same thing when you hit bumps on the road. Designs for bicycle lights must include cushioning for contacts so that they are not jarred by road shocks.

The actual light provided by any lamp depends on the quality of the reflector and on the voltage of the batteries and lamp chosen. It often is worthwhile to have more than one lamp size, so that you can use a bright bulb when you need good lighting and one that drains the batteries less when less light is needed. On a poor road or when you are searching for a campsite, for example, you may need good light output, but for cooking and other camp chores much less light is required. For the headlamp illustrated in Figure 21, a type 14 bulb provides twice as much light as a type 3502, but it also drains the battery more quickly. Thus, you might use a 3502 bulb and carry a couple of type 14's to use on those occasions when good visibility is required for safety. (The type 14's will burn out in a few hours. This generally is true when bulbs are used at a high level of output for their filament size; they put out more light for the power used, but they also burn out more quickly.) When using lights that take PR-type bulbs, again with a power source of about 3 volts (two carbon–zinc or alkaline cells; one lithium cell), a PR2 bulb gives the highest light output with the lowest lamp and battery life; a PR6 is somewhat less bright, with better lamp and battery life; and a PR9 gives much longer service with considerably less light.

On most trips I choose a combination of reflectors and a Belt Beacon for visibility, together with headlamp using a single lithium D cell. I carry spare bulbs and a spare 9-volt alkaline battery for the Belt Beacon. The lithium D cells are very long-lived. It is helpful to use black plastic tape to cover the transparent edges of Wonder brand headlamps to prevent light from shining down into your eyes. If you use a Belt Beacon on the front of your bike, tape also is useful to cover the top edge, again to prevent light from shining directly into your eyes and reducing your night vision.

Chapter 12

Clothing

CYCLISTS' CLOTHING TENDS to look a little silly to the beginning rider. However, although a few items may be as faddish as they seem, most are the result of considerable thought and experimentation over the years. What you wear when you are just getting started is not terribly important, but as you progress to touring long distances, you are likely to decide that specialized clothing is worth the cost.

The primary criteria for good bicycling garments are that they be easily adjustable to regulate the body's temperature, create no appreciable wind resistance, and permit free movement without chafing. Since the legs are in constant, rapid motion, any binding can cause a lot of unnecessary hardship over the miles. Similarly, any irritation in the area of the seat obviously causes problems; by nature, cycling subjects the crotch to more punishment than it was designed to take, and clothing should minimize abrasion rather than increase it. Wind resistance makes up most of the work load at normal touring speeds, so that everything you can do to lessen it is worthwhile.

Clothing to be carried on long tours needs to be as lightweight as possible. You have to carry some extra clothing on multi-day tours to enable you to wash your riding gear, keep warm at night and dry in the rain, go to fancy restaurants, and the like. Give a lot of thought to the additional clothes you take. If they are chosen with care, they add only a few pounds to your bike; if you simply throw them together, you easily can end up with ten or fifteen pounds of extra weight.

There are a few specialized items of clothing for the cyclist—shoes, gloves, and helmets—the design of which is quite unrelated to life away from the bicycle. Most touring cyclists buy these items soon after they take up the sport. Helmets and shoes are particularly important, the former for safety and the latter for efficiency, and they should be considered standard cycling equipment rather than frivolous accessories.

Helmets

A helmet is literally a pain in the neck. Its extra weight tires the neck muscles, and it is a nuisance to fiddle with. It eliminates the pleasant feeling of the wind blowing through your hair, reduces heat dissipation from your head, and tends to cause sweat to dribble into your eyes. There also is an excellent chance that it will save your life someday.

Your head is well designed by evolution to withstand minor knocks under natural conditions, i.e., in the countryside at foot-propelled speeds. It is poorly suited, however, for falling headfirst on-to concrete, smashing into cars, or sliding into a curbstone. Any of these can happen to a bicycle rider, and there is no question that one who is wearing a helmet is much more likely to survive the experience than one who is not. The better the helmet, the better your chances of living through a crash. The primary danger results from riding with your head five or six feet above the hard pavement in a position from which you can easily be knocked down without a chance to cushion your skull. If your head falls free for this distance, it will break on the asphalt due to the acceleration of gravity alone, quite apart from the additional velocity resulting from your motion on the bike, a car that has hit you, or whatever. Therefore it makes good sense to wear a helmet—*all* the time you are on your bike.

I will refrain from further preaching since wearing a helmet is basically a personal decision. Don't kid yourself with the rationalizations some people come up with, however. No matter how skilled a rider you are, some idiot in a car can come zooming out of a driveway and zap you. Brilliant riding technique on your part has nothing to do with it. If you don't want to wear a helmet, that's okay, but you should recognize that your failure to wear one increases the dangers of cycling.

If you decide to wear a helmet, you then have to decide what kind to buy. There are a number of helmets made specifically for bicyclists these days, as well as helmets borrowed from other sports. These provide varying degrees of protection and comfort. At one extreme is the traditional bicycle racer's crash hat, a network of padded leather bands which serve mainly to provide some protection from abrasion in a fall that sends the rider skidding across pavement and gravel. A secondary (or perhaps primary) purpose is to make the wearer look like a racer. About all that can be said for the protection such a hat offers in a crash is that it is better than nothing—but not much better.

There are several excellent helmets now made especially for cyclists which are designed to provide a good deal of protection against head injuries likely to be caused in bicycle accidents, while still allowing a reasonable amount of ventilation. Most notable are the helmets made by Bell and by Mountain Safety Research (MSR) (see Figure 22). Both employ very strong Lexan shells and have enough foam around the sides, where most of the impact in bicycle accidents occurs, to absorb considerable impact.

Some manufacturers and cyclists argue that such helmets are too heavy (a little over a pound) and provide too little ventilation. They make the incontestable point that the helmet is useless if it is not being worn and therefore maintain that a lighter helmet with better ventilation is far superior, even if the protection is somewhat reduced, since a rider is more likely to keep the more comfortable helmet on his or her head. One helmet made specifically for riders who agree with this theory is the Skid-Lid. It has a Lexan shell around the circumference of the head and tabs extending over the crown, so that large openings are left. Soft foam is used for padding. The helmet weighs eleven ounces. Other riders use hockey helmets or imported helmets with plastic shells and thin foam padding which are cheaper and lighter than the Bell or MSR models.

My own feeling is that the main difficulty in wearing a helmet is simply making up your mind to do so. Neither the MSR nor the Bell is sufficiently uncomfortable to cause any insurmountable problem, except perhaps in the most extreme heat

22. *The Mountain Safety Research helmet* (top) *and the model made by Bell* (bottom) *are the two best helmets currently made for cyclists. The ventilation scoops and the interior design of the Bell make it the more comfortable of the two.*

conditions. Once you make up your mind that the additional protection is worth the trouble of wearing a helmet, you might as well wear one that provides a reasonable amount of rigidity and shock absorbency. Also, once you have decided to wear a helmet, make up your mind to wear it whenever you are on your bike. Accidents tend to occur at the most unexpected times, so keep your helmet on all the time.

If you ever ride in conditions that present a genuine danger of heat stroke or exhaustion, it makes sense to switch to a white tennis hat, but such conditions are rare for a heat-acclimatized cyclist. I frequently have ridden with a helmet in temperatures well over 90° F with no particular problem. (See page 389 for a discussion of heat stroke.)

Shoes

Shoes made especially for bicycling ought to be one of your first investments after buying your bike. Standard bicycling shoes are made with lightweight leather uppers, perforated for ventilation, with thick leather soles that keep the edges of the pedals from digging into your feet after twenty miles or so. Stiff shanks relieve foot fatigue and permit better transfer of power to the pedals.

The thick leather soles on bicycling shoes also permit cleats to be nailed on. Each cleat has a groove that mates with the back edge of the pedal so that the foot is exactly positioned whenever the cleat and pedal are mated. The cleat also holds the foot in the toe clip when the strap is tightened, enabling the cyclist to transmit more power to the cranks at the top, bottom, and upward phases of the pedal stroke, particularly when honking up a hill.

Standard cleats are made of metal; they make a nice clicking sound when you walk and little scratches on wood floors. Racers use fragile plastic cleats to save weight. Many tourists use leather cleats so that they can walk into a building without attracting attention or scarring any polished oak floors.

The raised cleats at the balls of the feet and the stiff shanks found on regular cycling shoes make them poor for walking. There is, however, another type of shoe designed for touring cyclists who want to avoid the need for carrying extra shoes for walking. This shoe has a molded rubber sole with grooves that mate with the pedal and replace the cleat, but which do not give quite so positive a grip. Some shoes of this kind do not give enough protection to the foot because the sole is not stiff enough at the ball. This type also lacks a stiff shank, which is nice for walking but not so good for riding. The kind made by Avocet does provide adequate sole protection and the shanks seem stiff enough, but it remains to be seen whether the shanks will hold up to a lot of walking. They may break under the stress, as do the stiff shanks of many mountaineering boots.

You must decide whether the weight saved by not having to carry a second pair of shoes is worth sacrificing some cycling efficiency. Personally, I prefer to use standard cycling shoes with metal cleats and to carry a light pair of running shoes to wear when I'm off the bike. This also gives me dry shoes to change into after a ride in the rain, and I don't have to worry about wearing the grooves off my soles when walking.

On traditional cycling shoes, cleats are installed after you have cycled a few miles with the straps of the toe clips pulled tight. By this time the soles will show indentations from the pedals. A cleat and shoe can be inserted in each pedal and a tracing of the proper position for the cleat drawn, making sure that the shoe is lined up straight with the frame. The cleats are then nailed or screwed to the soles of the shoes. People whose feet point severely inward or outward may find that an angled position is better. This can be determined only with a lot of experimentation. Start with the shoes exactly parallel to the center line of the frame (see Figure 23). Adjustable cleats, such as the ones made by Pavarin, permit you to fine-tune the positioning without starting over.

When purchasing shoes, wear the socks you intend to use when cycling. Medium-weight soft wool socks usually are best. Don't get shoes that are too tight, particularly at the toe. The straps from the toe clip cut circulation somewhat, anyway, so the shoes should be as comfortable as possible. Insoles of nylon-backed neoprene foam or a fine mesh material often improve comfort and help eliminate numbness in the soles of the feet.

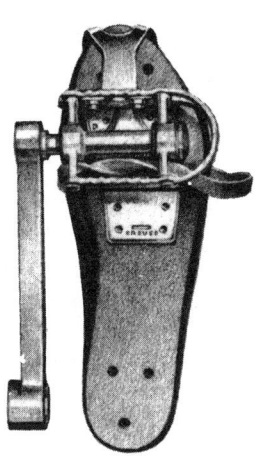

23. Proper positioning for mounting a cleat on the sole of a cycling shoe. The cleat should hold the shoe parallel to the crank and just short of rubbing on the end of the toe clip. In case of knee pain, some toe-in or toe-out may be needed (see page 386).

Cycling Shorts and Pants

When you start riding, you probably will want to wear just a normal pair of shorts or, if the weather is cold, long pants. Close-fitting warm-up pants are best if the weather is cold enough to require them. With both shorts and pants, try to avoid those that are cut with bulky seams in the crotch. These begin to wear on the delicate skin of that area after you have ridden for a couple of hours. One fairly satisfactory and inexpensive alternative is to make cutoffs from a pair of cheap sweat pants, which usually are cut so that there is no seam in the crotch. Leave the legs longer than those on regular shorts, though; otherwise they will ride up and chafe the insides of your thighs.

Men's underwear frequently is cut so that there are seams at the crotch that start feeling very bulky after twenty-five miles or so of riding. You may prefer seamless nylon briefs, though both women and men may find that the leg elastics rub or ride in. Women's underwear with legs that extend to mid-thigh often works better for both sexes.

Any alternative that works for you obviously is satisfactory. You have to expect to be a little saddle sore after a ride much longer than you are used to, particularly if you are breaking in a new saddle. (This expression is really a euphemism. More often than not, what actually happens is that you break in your posterior while the saddle stays pretty much the same. The exception is a good leather saddle, and the initial contest over whether you will break before the saddle does often is protracted.)

When you begin to take long enough rides—the length required varies with the individual—you are likely to find that the endurance of your rear end is more of a limiting factor than that of your legs. This is when you begin to realize that there is a reason for those funny looking cycling shorts after all, and you may even decide to buy yourself a pair.

Traditional bicycling shorts are tight-fitting, low at the waist, and rather long—altogether rather silly looking (see Figure 24). The design has been developed over the years as the most practical one, however. The low waist doesn't bunch when you are riding, nor does it interfere with your diaphragm when you are breathing hard. The legs extend to the lower thighs so that they won't ride up and chafe the insides of the legs. The fabric is cut so that there are no bulky seams at the crotch. A chamois crotch piece is sewn on the inside to provide maximum absorbency and to minimize friction in the crotch area. Usually there is a matching patch of fabric on the outside of the shorts to provide even more padding, improve wear, and further reduce friction. These shorts usually are worn without underwear. The chamois seat has yet to be

24. *Cycling shorts have legs that extend to the middle of the thighs so that the shorts do not ride up on the legs. A thick, soft chamois minimizes abrasion of the sensitive skin of the crotch. The chamois can be seen in the inside-out shorts pictured on the right.*

kind of weather. A good combination is a tee shirt, a long-sleeved wool jersey or undershirt, a wool sweater, and a lightweight nylon windbreaker. (Raingear is discussed later in the chapter.) Naturally, you wouldn't carry all these items on an afternoon ride in the summer, but appropriate combinations should be obvious depending on the ride. Just remember to allow for cool breezes, afternoon showers, and fatique at the end of the day when you pack your clothes.

Arm and Leg Warmers

Among the handiest accessories for cyclists are wool arm and leg warmers (see Figures 26 and 27), which can be worn along with conventional cycling shorts and short-sleeved jerseys, particularly in the early morning, when the air is cool and the muscles haven't yet warmed up, and in the evening, when temperatures dip and you are tired. It takes just a minute to put them on or take them off, and they are light and compact enough to be slipped into a pocket when not in use. Cyclists

26. Arm warmers can be put on or removed while you are riding and are useful on chilly mornings and afternoons.

27. *Leg warmers often eliminate the need to carry cumbersome and expensive long cycling pants.*

generate enough heat so that long pants and shirts are too hot when temperatures rise, so arm and leg warmers provide a convenient supplement to normal riding clothing. They can be obtained from some bicycle-supply outlets and from stores catering to dancers, who frequently use them for warm-ups.

Long Pants and Shirts

Long pants and shirts made specifically for cycling can be purchased, but since they are appropriate only for cold-weather riding, they are far less versatile than a combination of shorts, short-sleeved jersey, arm warmers, and leg warmers. Because of their lack of versatility, long cycling clothes rarely are carried on extended tours. It is better to carry several clothing layers instead; you can use all of them at once if necessary. Regular

warm-up clothes can be worn over cycling clothing, providing they fit closely enough to avoid flap-
ping. Tightly cut ankles with zippers are best.
Warm-up pants with bell bottoms can be held tight
with a clip or rubber band to prevent their getting
caught in the chain, but it is best to modify them so
that the ankles are tight, installing short zippers
for convenience in putting the pants on.

Windbreaker tops and bottoms also can be
used over cycling clothing when the weather turns
cool. My own preference is for a combination that
can serve as both a windbreaker and rain suit,
to avoid excessive weight and duplication of
function.

On lengthy tours, the long clothing normally
carried for evening use naturally can be pressed into
service for extra warmth and protection during
unusually severe weather, such as the conditions
often encountered when crossing mountain passes
in the spring.

Raingear

The ideal clothing for cycling in rainy weather
has yet to be developed, but the garments on the
market are getting better. The problem with raingear for all active sports is that any clothing which
covers your body and is completely waterproof
traps your perspiration inside as well as keeping
the rain out. If the air and rain outside are cool,
chilling the clothing, then the moisture evapo-
rating normally from your skin even when you
are not sweating condenses on the inside surface
of the raingear like dew, soaking you from the
inside. Therefore, any cycling raingear is bound to
be a compromise design, since it is impossible to
make a suit that sheds a downpour from outside
and also completely eliminates condensation and

perspiration problems. You will be a lot happier with the gear you choose if you realize that it cannot be perfect.

Riding into the rain creates additional difficulties for the cyclist, because rain will pour through any ventilation openings in the front of your protective clothing. Some protection is required even underneath, because water is often splashed from below as well as falling from above. Even if the bike is equipped with fenders and mudguards so that splash from your own wheels is minimized, you are likely to catch a lot of spray from cars, generally mixed with mud.

Most strong cyclists on day tours simply ignore the problem altogether, choosing to get wet if it starts to rain. They figure that they will either dry out if the shower is brief or return home, take a hot shower, and change to warm clothes if the rain continues. If the weather is fairly warm so that serious chilling of the body is not a problem, this often is a good solution for the long-distance cyclist as well. After you arrive at your accommodations or pitch your tent, you can change to a dry set of clothes and hang the wet ones to dry. If the weather is at all cool, however, you can lose a lot of body heat if you aren't wearing protective gear, draining your energy reserves and badly chilling your body. Furthermore, if you are cycling in prolonged rain, you may be a lot more comfortable if you can at least keep the amount of mud and precipitation hitting you to a minimum.

One special type of rain garment is the bi-cyclist's rain cape, which covers the upper body and hooks over the thumbs or handlebars to form a kind of rolling tent. The open bottom provides ventilation to help minimize condensation and permit some evaporation of perspiration. One problem with a rain cape is that it obscures your vision of the road directly beneath you, thereby distorting your perceptions and reactions at a time when they need to be most acute—when visibility is reduced for automobile drivers and they are least likely to notice you. Another problem is that in order for the cape to be any use at all, fenders must be used to cut the spray from below, and rain pants still may be necessary if you want protection for your legs and seat. Fenders add weight and a lot of rolling resistance, particularly in the rain. If you have equipped your bike with fenders, you might wish to consider a cape, but be sure to ride with it before it is needed so that you can get used to the change. Finally, the cape greatly increases wind resistance, flaps badly when you are riding fast, and acts like a sail to carry you in the direction of the wind whenever there is a gust due to a thunderstorm or a passing truck, thereby posing a severe hazard.

A rain suit is the other alternative; it covers most of the body and creates less wind resistance but increases condensation problems and the trapping of sweat. Rain suits can be made using several types of material and designs, and these are very important to their effectiveness. A rain parka above and full pants below are the most common combination for bicycling, though it is possible to wear a longer parka that comes well below your seat and rain chaps, which are tubes of waterproof fabric that cover the legs only. Garments that are cut fairly tight minimize wind resistance, bulk, and weight but provide poor ventilation. Baggier garments increase ventilation but also increase wind resistance as well as the bulk and weight that have to be carried.

A properly ventilated rain suit causes far less sweating and condensation than those without provision for the movement of air. The entire back of a parka can be ventilated by making the main back piece out of mesh and covering it with a large gusset of waterproof material left open at the bottom. The gusset is cut to overlap the lower part of the parka and acts like a shingle to shed the rain. Additional vents can be placed in the front of the parka and under the arms. It is handy to have the waist on the pants constructed so that it can be left open, since the pants are kept in place by the bicycle seat when you are riding and the extra ventilation is helpful. In fact, a good way to make rain pants for cycling is to have a seat piece attached to the legs and held up by a waistband; no piece is necessary in front, where the parka provides plenty of protection. No rain pants are currently made this way. The bottoms of rain pants should close tightly to keep them out of the chain.

The traditional hood used on parkas for mountaineering and backpacking generally should not be worn while cycling because it is difficult to take a quick glance over your shoulder while wearing one. The hood continues to face straight ahead while your head turns inside, and all you see are the inside seams of the parka instead of the truck bearing down on you from the rear. A sailor's sou'wester, a rain hat with a brim extending a couple of inches in front and much farther at the rear, provides good rain protection without interfering with visibility. Probably the best alternative is to make a brim for your helmet that serves the same purpose, as well as using tape or some other arrangement to keep water out of the vents. When the weather isn't too cold, it usually is better to close the parka at the neck and just allow your head to get wet.

Raingear for bicycle touring should be of the lightest possible weight since it is not subjected to much abrasion. Unlike the backpacker or mountaineer, the cyclist rarely bushwhacks through the brush or rubs against rough rock. A lightweight nylon fabric is the logical choice. For absolute waterproofing, a heavier fabric with double coating generally is necessary, but lightweight coated nylon with a good-quality coating passes very little water. Leakage is negligible compared with condensation.

A laminated construction recently was introduced as an alternative to fabric coatings. A film of Gore-tex® is sandwiched in between a lightweight nylon fabric and an inner material, usually a light, non-woven mesh. The film, made of a material similar to Teflon®, has billions of pores so small that liquid water droplets cannot pass through in most circumstances, but molecules of water vapor can. The material is thus waterproof but allows water vapor evaporated from the skin to pass though, so that condensation and perspiration build-up are far less than with conventional coated nylon. A Gore-tex parka thus can double as a rain garment and windbreaker with no more perspiration build-up than would occur with an uncoated nylon or cotton material.

Gore-tex rainwear is considerably more effective than ordinary coated-nylon gear, though it is a little heavier and bulkier to pack. It cannot work miracles, however. If you cycle hard while wearing your rain suit, you sweat inside much faster than evaporation can occur, particularly since less wind can get through the material to evaporate the perspiration. In a heavy downpour, the fabric exposed to the rain cannot breathe because the layer of liquid water on the outside traps the water vapor inside. Gore-tex is a great improvement over other materials, however.

Gore-tex also is expensive, and it requires greater care than other types of raingear since dirt can act as a wetting agent, reducing the surface tension of water droplets and allowing them to leak through the pores. Fairly frequent washing of Gore-tex equipment therefore is necessary. Whether raingear made of Gore-tex is worth the considerable additional cost depends on your budget and on how often you actually expect to use the rain suit as opposed to just carrying it along with you.

Booties made to slip over cycling shoes serve both in the rain and in cold weather. They also are easy enough to make from either coated nylon or Gore-tex scraps. Small cutouts in the soles allow the cleats to engage the pedals.

Any rainwear leaks at the seams wherever needle holes have been punched through, unless the seams have been sealed. Seam-sealing compounds usually can be purchased with your raingear. Just spread the sealant in a thin coat along each seam while holding the seam under slight tension. Resealing usually is necessary every season or so. Sealing on the inside alone keeps the garment looking neat; sealing both sides usually proves more effective.

Gloves

Cycling gloves (see Figure 28) are a bit of luxury, but a worthwhile one. They are fingerless and have mesh backs for cooling. The padding is designed to reduce pressure on the nerves in the hands during long rides. Leather palms provide some protection against abrasion in a minor spill.

28. Typical cycling gloves.

Clothing to Wear
at the End of the Day

For the cyclist on a day trip or on a tour supported by an automobile, extra clothing for wear at the end of the day can be chosen according to taste, but for the long-distance cyclist carrying everything on the bike, careless selection can add many unnecessary pounds to the load. It is important to anticipate the weather conditions you may encounter and to decide exactly what you *need* to be presentable at any hotels, restaurants, or museums you plan to visit. Choose your clothes to serve as many purposes as possible. Try to find items that are light, compact, and require little care.

Unless you plan to visit some rather formal establishments, your cycling jersey normally is suitable to wear in town. One jersey usually is enough, supplemented by a tee shirt that can be worn when the jersey is being washed or on days when you want it to remain fresh for an evening out.

A pair or two of underwear should be enough if you are using chamois-lined cycling shorts, three or four pairs if you wear them while riding. Underwear can be washed before you leave your camp or accommodations in the morning and can dry while you are riding. For use after the ride, nylon underwear that dries quickly is best. Women who wear bras should try to choose a type that has no abrasive hardware, since long periods of riding in hot weather can result in a good deal of skin irritation.

Your choice of long pants probably depends on the tour you are taking, since you will want them to double for any town use. For camping trips and tours on which you feel no need to dress up, warm-up pants probably are best. They look decent even after being stuffed in panniers all day and serve well for riding when a little extra warmth is needed. They can be put on right over your regular cycling shorts for this purpose. For men, some sort of double-knit polyester slacks seem to be the best solution for wear at the end of the day on tours during which you are spending some time in town. A dark pattern is less likely to show stains and snags than any solid color. Avoid light, solid colors as they show stains easily. Women may want to carry polyester slacks, too, or may choose to take a light pair of warm-up pants and carry a skirt for city wear. There are some handy pleated wraparound skirts that fold into a small package; these are ideal for carrying on a bike trip because they are so easy to care for.

The additional clothing you may need for warmth depends on the temperatures you expect on your tour. A jersey, tee shirt, shorts, and long pants may be more than adequate on warm-weather trips at low elevations. On most tours you probably want at least another sweater. If you take a decent-looking wool one, it can be worn for warmth during cold, wet weather and for casual but presentable dress in town. A jacket or pullover insulated with synthetic pile serves the same purposes and is even warmer; you can buy one at a mountaineering store.

On tours where some cool weather can be expected in the evenings, a light down jacket is a good addition. It keeps you warm during cool evenings in camp or on walks in town and can serve as a supplement to a lightweight sleeping bag if necessary. On spring tours over high mountains, where snow on the passes is a definite possibility, an insulated jacket is important for safety since your body cools off very quickly when you stop to rest in cold weather. Good-quality down provides more warmth for the weight than any other insulator and packs into a smaller space. If you are on a budget, a jacket insulated with polyester batting is a good substitute, better than low-quality down.

If your bicycling shoes are unsuited to walking around, as most are, some sort of extra shoes are needed. Many bicycle campers who don't plan to do much walking or city sightseeing just carry a pair of beach thongs. I take a lightweight pair of running shoes, weighing about a pound, which I can use for hikes, camp wear, or walking in town. Such shoes are presentable enough for most purposes if you wash them before the trip. If you want to keep them dry during wet weather, you might take a light, cheap pair of plastic overshoes. I don't bother.

A wool stocking cap provides a lot of extra warmth with minimal weight. Your head dissipates a great deal of heat because it has an excellent blood supply, a lot of surface area, and generally is uncovered. When you are chilled, the blood supply to most of your skin is reduced to cut down heat losses, but the supply to most of your head remains the same. Unless you wear a hat, therefore, you are going to lose much of the heat your body produces through your head. If your hat is fairly light it also can be worn under your helmet for cold-weather riding, and you can wear it at night if you are cold in your sleeping bag.

Sunglasses and Mirrors

Buy a good pair of sunglasses if you don't already have one. Cyclists often ride for hours in glaring sun, and this is very hard on the eyes unless they are protected. Riding in bright sun without glasses probably will give you headaches, especially when combined with your raised neck position while cycling. Many touring cyclists whose eyes don't require correction or who wear contact lenses make a practice of wearing sunglasses all the time simply as protection from flying road grit, insects, and the like. A minor eye injury can be a real nuisance on a tour, and cyclists are quite vulnerable to sharp particles thrown into the air by passing vehicles or gusts of wind.

One handy touring gadget is a small mirror that attaches to the left-hand temple piece of your glasses or sunglasses so that you can glance at the road behind you without having to turn your head (see Figure 3). Once you become accustomed to using such a mirror, it can help you stay aware of any traffic approaching from behind. A glance at the mirror is faster and easier than turning or ducking your head, particularly when you are riding on the drops of a loaded bike. You must practice using the mirror, however, since it is small and its angle depends on the angle of your head. You should bend it so that you see over your shoulder when you are looking up with a full view of the road ahead. Several types of mirrors are available to fit different types of glasses frames. If you don't wear glasses or sunglasses much of the time, you can easily rig one of these mirrors to fit on your helmet by drilling two small holes and changing the bend of the wire. Models are also available that clip on a helmet.

Lightweight Clothes
for a Camping Tour

The point of paying such careful attention to clothing is to ensure that it is functional with an absolute minimum of weight. On a fairly long camping tour across the Continental Divide, the clothing in my panniers typically weighs just 6¾ pounds, yet I have everything I need to be comfortable in any weather conditions that may arise. Besides the cycling shorts, jersey, helmet, gloves, shoes, and socks that I normally wear while riding, I also carry the following items:

    extra cycling shorts
    tee shirt
    extra pair of socks
    pair of nylon underwear
    nylon swimsuit
    set of arm and leg warmers
    wool sweater or pile jacket
    wool hat
    warm-up pants
    Gore-tex parka and pants

wool mittens
down jacket
running shoes

Washing

It is fairly easy to keep your clothes clean on a bike trip by planning occasional days that allow time for doing your wash at a laundromat. Even small towns generally have such a facility. Soap or detergent usually can be purchased from a dispenser at the laundromat so that you don't have to carry any with you. Some people simply alternate washing their bike clothes and extras. Others carry a nylon bathing suit to wear while everything else is being washed. (You can wear your rain suit over the bathing suit to maintain decorum.)

If you are camping away from towns for any length of time, you can wash your laundry in one of your cooking pots, using a mild soap that serves for everything—body, dishes, and clothing. Pick a warm afternoon so that everything dries quickly.

Chapter 13

Luggage and How to Carry It

ONE OF THE great blessings of cycle touring compared with backpacking is that your dunnage can be fastened to your bicycle rather than to you, resulting in a far more comfortable and enjoyable journey. Your shoulders are not rubbed by pack straps, and your back can be cooled by the wind. Though you still have to provide the energy to lift your load over the hills, you don't have to actually carry it. All you need is a means of conveniently attaching everything to the bicycle that adds as little extra weight as possible. Remember that unnecessary pounds are far more tiring when you are cycling than when you are climbing or back-packing. You also travel much farther each day than the most intrepid and tireless hiker.

Most important of all, your system for carrying your clothing and equipment must be absolutely reliable. The backpacker whose pack frame falls apart on the trail may be faced with a problem that is quite distressing. If, on the other hand, your carrier does the same and falls into your spokes while you are descending from a pass at thirty-five miles an hour, your dismay will be more profound. After such a mishap, you are likely to find yourself hurtling briefly through the air without your bicycle, your velocity temporarily undiminished, contemplating your inevitable meeting with the terrain ahead. Luggage systems that sway back and forth at high speeds or that have loose straps or strings that can wrap in the spokes or drive chain are dangerous. Pick your bicycle packs and carriers carefully.

Backpacks

Wearing a backpack is a terrible way to carry touring gear on a bicycle. The center of gravity of the bike, rider, and load is dangerously high, leaning forward to properly control the bike is difficult, and the pressure on the hands and crotch soon becomes excruciating. If a backpack is worn while riding a bike, the modern, contoured, aluminum frame would be the worst conceivable choice, designed as it is to raise the center of gravity so that the wearer can stand more upright. A frame also extends well above the head, making it nearly impossible to look at the road while riding on the drops of the handlebars.

Backpacks are a convenient way to carry books and other paraphernalia around town on commuter trips, however. A very light pack also may be useful when picking up an evening's gro-ceries on a long tour, particularly if the panniers are full or if you are carrying a load for a num-ber of people. The pack also can be used to carry

water a few miles to your campsite. For regular
load-carrying, however, using a backpack on
long bicycle tours is a poor idea. It can be done,
but falls into the same category as making a
transcontinental ride on a fifty-pound, balloon-tire
utility bike—one can admire the fortitude of the
practitioner but not his or her perspicacity.

Distributing the Load

The lower the load is attached to the bicycle, the
more stable you and the bike are going to be. Skids
are less likely with a low center of gravity, and
braking is far more reliable. Braking a bicycle
which is loaded high causes the weight to try to pivot
over the front wheel, so that the rear wheel loses
traction and skids out as soon as it is even slightly
out of line. Stability on curves and other handling
characteristics are similarly affected. It also takes
more work to pedal a bike that is loaded high since
slight shifts in angle require greater corrective
action with either the steering or upper body lean,
necessitating a constant series of small extra efforts.
For these reasons, the bulk of the load carried on a
bike normally is packed in panniers attached on
either side of the rear wheel. This results in a
much lower center of gravity than if most of the load
is carried in a bag attached to the back of the
saddle or tied onto the top of a carrier.

Naturally, any luggage on a bike should be
balanced fairly carefully so that the weight is
distributed evenly on both sides of the machine;
otherwise the rider must lean to one particular side
all day long to redress the balance. What is less
obvious is that the load also should be balanced fore
and aft. As a rule, it is a good idea to have about
two-thirds of the load on the rear wheel and about
one-third on the front. Thus, if your panniers and

gear weigh thirty pounds, the ideal arrangement is to have twenty pounds on the back of the bike and ten in front.

The standard luggage arrangement used by experienced tourists is to mount a set of panniers on the rear carrier and a handlebar bag to carry things that may be needed during the day, including snack food, camera, raingear, and the like (see Figures 29 and 43). This is a practical system, though the racks available for handlebar bags leave something to be desired. It is not a good idea to carry too much weight in a handlebar bag, since it is mounted high and is positioned in front of the axis on which the wheel is turned when you steer the bike, making the cycle less responsive.

29. *Standard touring luggage—a set of rear panniers and a handlebar bag. The bags shown here are made by the Touring Cyclist Shop, the originator of the design now copied by most makers of quality bags.*

Front panniers, which are smaller than most rear panniers, make a good alternative to the handlebar bag. A combination of front and rear panniers provides plenty of space for everything needed on most tours, distributes the weight easily on each side and between the front and rear wheels, and makes the bike handle well (see Figure 1). With good carriers, the arrangement is very rigid and stable. Carrying excessive loads in front panniers makes steering sluggish, but you can load far more in front panniers and retain quick steering than you can with a handlebar bag. The reason is that the panniers are placed closer to the axis of the headset so that they exert less rotational leverage and therefore resist steering changes less. A larger capacity than that provided by two sets of panniers rarely is needed, but for very large loads a handlebar bag can be used as well, concentrating the lightweight equipment in the front panniers and bag and placing heavier items in the rear panniers.

The major advantages of the front and rear pannier system are larger capacity, better load distribution, and increased stability. The rear pannier and handlebar bag system offers easier access to one bag while riding, so it is simpler to get at your camera, snack food, sunglasses, and raingear.

Carriers

At the base of any luggage system are the carriers that are mounted to the frame. It is important that these carriers be as rigid as possible and that they be absolutely reliable structurally. The consequences of having a carrier self-destruct during a high-speed descent have been pointed out. Some otherwise excellent carriers have had

faulty welds at critical points which have failed
after a bike hit a minor bump at high speed.

   The best carriers are those designed for custom-built touring bikes and attached to brazed-
on frame fittings. Though such carriers vary
in weight, they can be made to be very strong
and still light in weight. Brazed-on fittings are
inherently more trouble-free and simpler than are
fittings designed to fasten to a standard frame, and
they make it possible to eliminate some crosspieces
on the carrier. For example, two fittings can be
brazed onto the upper seatstays to serve as
attachments both for the arms of center-pull
brakes and for attachment points for a rear carrier,
resulting in a rigid, two-point anchoring that
permits a fairly simple carrier design. Most of us,
however, cannot afford a custom-made touring bike
and have to buy carriers designed to fit standard
frames.

   There are two basic types of rear carrier which
bolt onto standard frames. The better one employs
a rigid, inverted triangular structure that attaches
at the lower apex to the rear dropouts and at the
front to the rear brake bridge (the frame tube that
links the two seatstays). This type of carrier does
not depend on the frame attachment points for any
of its basic strength, only for holding the carrier
and the frame together (see Figure 30).

   The second type of rear carrier essentially
consists of a platform which has a clamp that
attaches to the seatstays and two pivoted rods that
drop down at an angle to attach to the rear
dropouts. This type of carrier uses the seatstays of
the bike to complete the third side of a triangle.
Generally it is not very rigid, but it does have the
virtue of low cost. The clamping mechanism at the
seatstays always slips with repeated road shocks,

30. A rear carrier made from aluminum-alloy rod. This model, manufactured by Jim Blackburn, is the best design currently available; it is very light but extremely rigid due to its triangular bracing.

so if you use this type of carrier, you should place a stop between the carrier clamp and the rear brake bridge to prevent the clamp from slipping down. You can either buy a stop or make one easily with a small piece of wood.

It is best to buy carriers with a rigid structure if you can afford them. You should be suspicious of models which rely on a single weld to hold up either side of the carrier since failure of that weld may permit the carrier to fall into the wheel. The

best carriers are designed to make such catastrophic failure impossible. At the time of this writing, the best carriers, front (see Figure 31) and
rear, are made by Jim Blackburn Designs; these
carriers are constructed of aluminum alloy and are
very light and rigid. The best bargain racks, also
available for both front and rear, are the English-
made Karrimor racks; they, too, are very solid, but
are made of steel and are a good deal heavier. Steel
carriers do have the virtue of being less vulnerable
to damage from falls or rough treatment by baggage

*31. The companion front carrier to the Blackburn rack
shown in Figure 30.*

handlers. Eclipse makes an adequate rack that includes a specially designed mounting system for its own panniers, but the carrier is both heavier and more expensive than the Blackburn.

Panniers

The most important characteristics of panniers are not the ones typically advertised, such as their dimensions or features for attaching them to a carrier. What really matters is the way they support the load and the way they ride on the bicycle. In several respects, the panniers and carrier work together; therefore I recommend that you buy the carrier and panniers at the same time, if possible, so that you can check them as a system. It should be impossible for any part of the panniers to be pushed, blown, or vibrated into the wheel. Loose strings or straps blowing around inevitably will find their way into the spokes. The inside panels of the panniers must incorporate stiffeners to keep the load from pressing between the stays into the wheel. Depending on the construction of the carrier, the shape of the bags, and the position of the panniers on the carrier, the corners may be able to swing into the path of the spokes if the load starts oscillating. Be sure that the stiffeners are strong enough to prevent this possibility or that there are bars on the carrier that prevent it. Such oscillation occurs only during rapid descents, so any interference with the spokes happens at the worst possible time. If the carrier–pannier combination you are considering doesn't fulfill these requirements, look elsewhere.

Another basic requirement is that the panniers fit the carrier, bicycle, and you. Due to variations in frame dimensions, crank lengths, and foot sizes,

some pannier–carrier combinations do not permit
enough clearance between the front of the bag and
the heel of the rider's foot. You should check to see
that the panniers can be mounted solidly on the
carrier and still allow adequate clearance for the
heels of your shoes while you are pedaling. To get
this clearance, you should not have to mount the
panniers so far back that the rear corners tend to
swing into the spokes.

Panniers can be made in several shapes.
Rectangular bags are convenient for packing since
the shape of the bag doesn't govern where things
fit. They also sit upright on the ground or floor
while you are packing them. Teardrop-shaped panniers are less convenient in these ways, but they
generally fit the geometry of the bicycle better and
are less likely to have corners that either get in the
way of your heels or swing into the spokes. Large
rectangular models usually have cutoff corners at
the front bottom ends to provide heel clearance.
Large teardrop types generally project farther from
the bike to provide greater volume, so they present
a little more wind resistance than rectangular-
shaped models of comparable volume.

The suspension of the panniers provides the
vital connection between the load and the carrier.
You must examine the suspension system carefully,
since there are many poor designs on the market
created by people who don't know much about
bicycle touring. The system has to anchor the bags
firmly to the carrier. Any floppiness will be amplified
when you are riding by flexing in the carrier and
frame. Ties can work loose and get snagged in the
wheel and therefore are generally undesirable,
although some tie-on systems are functional and
inexpensive. If ties are used, they should come

back through grommets in the bags and tie on the *outside,* away from the wheel. Hooks should be strong and should provide a positive connection that can't be shaken loose.

There are a number of other desirable, though not critical, pannier features. The bags should be as lightweight and as weatherproof as possible. Coated-nylon fabric best fits both these requirements. Canvas is useful in that it has a good deal of inherent stiffness, but it is heavy, rots if exposed to much damp weather, and must be treated frequently to remain water-repellent. Sewing should be neat and rot-proof thread should be used. Any zippers should be covered with flaps to help keep moisture out of the bags.

Fittings that permit the panniers to be mounted and removed easily are a major convenience. It is a nuisance to go through an elaborate fastening procedure when you are attaching loaded panniers to the bike and balancing the bike at the same time. There are innumerable situations that arise on bike tours in which it is a great help to be able to get your panniers on and off the bike quickly and with a minimum of fuss. A number of manufacturers market panniers that are connected by a piece of fabric over the carrier; fastenings of some kind are used at the crosspiece and at the bottoms of the bags. If it is well designed, this system can work reasonably well. Eclipse makes a special carrier with grooves on both sides to hold its pannier bags. A fiberglass wand sewn into the top of each pannier slides into the groove. A rod mounted at the bottom of the carrier slips into the pocket in the bottom of each pannier. An adapter plate is available so that Eclipse panniers can be used with other carriers.

What is probably the most satisfactory system developed so far employs hooks mounted at the top of each pannier to slip over the top of the carrier and one or more springs attached to the back of each pannier. The spring is hooked to the bottom of the carrier and the pannier is pulled up and hooked on the top. This system, invented by Hartley Alley of the Touring Cyclist Shop, also is used by Kirtland and Cannondale with modifications. The pannier kits sold by Frostline employ this system, too, except that shock cord is used instead of springs. (If you use a Frostline kit, you should buy springs at a hardware store and use them instead of the inadequate shock cord.) Once it is properly adjusted, this system allows the bags to be mounted or taken off the bike in seconds, yet it is stable and reliable.

Outside pockets are a convenient extra feature on panniers because they enable you to carry small items separately, providing easy access to cameras, tool kits, spare tires, or wallets. They also offer a little extra storage space without enlarging the main bag too much. However, they are expensive to sew on and thus raise the cost of the panniers considerably. If you are on a budget, it is better to choose panniers with a good suspension system and good materials but without extra pockets in preference to those with lots of side compartments but with deficiencies in basic design. Many of the better panniers also have fastening systems designed to permit the bags to be made into one parcel with a carrying handle; this feature is quite helpful at times, but it is hardly essential.

In recent years dozens of manufacturers have introduced panniers of one sort or another. Some of the designs are superb and well thought out, while others demonstrate that their makers know little about cycle touring. It is impossible to describe all the models currently on the market, much less to anticipate those that will become available in the near future, but the considerations discussed above should help you to judge the various offerings. Good standards for comparison are the handlebar bags and panniers made by the Touring Cyclist Shop and by Kirtland. The latter offers an economy line with fewer frills as well as their more elaborate designs.

Other Bicycle Bags

Besides handlebar bags and panniers designed to be mounted beside the wheels, there are a number of other types of bicycle bags. The saddlebag strapped to the rear of the seat is an old standard; it has the advantage of mounting easily over the rear wheel. Small saddlebags require no supporting carrier, and even large models can be used without a carrier on bikes with fenders. Saddlebags are handy for carrying small items around town, and many people like to use them to hold lunch and tools on day tours. If a rear carrier is mounted, however, a saddlebag takes up part of the space on top of the carrier, adding no real luggage capacity. Large saddlebags loaded with heavy items raise the bike's center of gravity, so they are not as satisfactory as panniers. They also are likely to hit the legs and to shift excessively.

Carrier-top bags which either are part of a pannier system or are mounted separately in addition to panniers can provide extra room if you aren't already using the space for your sleeping bag (see Figure 32). Bags that mount separately on top of the rack also are useful on day trips and for trips around town. They should be used for lightweight

32. A well-designed bag for the top of the carrier which you can use either with or without panniers. The bag is made by the Touring Cycling Shop and employs Velcro tightening straps. It can be used to carry a sleeping bag, but has a stiffener that also makes it useful for carrying small items on day trips.

items so as not to raise the load too high. I find them unnecessary for long tours because on camping trips I prefer to strap my sleeping bag and pad on top of the carrier and on non-camping trips I don't need the extra carrying capacity. On day trips, however, I prefer to use one of these bags instead of a handlebar bag. It is more rigid and adds less wind resistance.

Bags which hang in the center of the bicycle frame are widely available, but they generally are useless. Unless you plan an unusual tour requiring that you be away from supplies for weeks at a time, you don't need the extra carrying capacity.

Furthermore, the center space tends to be taken up in large part by your tire pump and water bottles. The legs pass so close to the frame of the bike that only a very narrow space can be used without interference, and it is nearly impossible to pack anything in a bag that will not bulge out too far. I have never seen an experienced bicycle tourist use one of these bags. A few small, lightweight stuffsacks provide a handy means of keeping things in order and of simplifying both packing and finding the things you want. The stuffsacks can be color-coded or labeled with an indelible marker so that you can find the particular sack you want more easily.

Loading the Bike

The best combinations of bags, then, seem to be based on a set of rear panniers. Additional luggage space should come from either a handlebar bag or a set of front panniers. Some lightweight equipment can be carried on top of the rear carrier, either with or without a special bag to contain it. If a large load is to be carried, first ask yourself whether everything you plan to take is really necessary. If it is, use front and rear panniers and a handlebar bag and pack some equipment on top of the rear carrier.

When actually loading your gear on the bike, try to put heavier items low in the bags and as close to the frame as possible. Each of the rear panniers should weigh about the same amount and be packed similarly, as should the front panniers if you are using any. If you have front and rear panniers, I advise packing about one-third of the load on the front of the bike and two-thirds at the rear. With a light load, the same plan can be followed for the pannier–handlebar bag combination, but a handlebar bag should not be loaded very heavily or it will tend to bounce a good deal on bumpy roads. You have to determine the limit of your own handlebar bag and support by experimentation, but ten pounds usually is the upper limit and I like to keep well under that.

It usually is convenient for the bicycle camper, who naturally has to carry more equipment, to fasten a stuffsack containing a sleeping bag and pad or air mattress to the top of the rear carrier. If this scheme is used, the stuffsack should be made of a coated-nylon material and have sealed seams and a flap over the opening so that the bag does not get soaked in a shower. Alternatively, a plastic bag can be carried to line the stuffsack. Food items, fuel, stove, and other heavy items should be packed in a systematic way on the inside of the panniers, with lighter gear, such as clothing, on the outside. Outside pockets and handlebar bags usually are reserved for things you may want to get at without opening the main bags. If you are using a gasoline stove, be sure to pack the fuel in a different pannier than you pack the food, to prevent any possibility of contamination. An alternative is to carry the fuel bottle in a water-bottle cage on the frame.

Most touring cyclists who are not camping should be able to get by without even needing to strap gear to the top of the rear carrier. Many campers can do so as well, if they are traveling with light, compact equipment. If this is the case, you might want to take along a carrier-top bag to use for shopping chores. Another way to avoid having to rearrange the items in your panniers to accommodate groceries or water supplies is to use a very light backpack. If your panniers have enough extra room, of course, the pack is unnecessary. Don't try to use a pack for heavy groceries if you

simply be called off in the event of truly freakish weather.

The approach taken to bicycle camping is likely to vary a good deal with the experience of the rider. Experienced backpackers, kayakers, and climbers will have little trouble applying their experience and some of their equipment to camping by bike. Beginning campers will have a somewhat different view. They run the risk of a little more discomfort because of their lack of experience, but are able to acquire their equipment with cycle camping specifically in mind.

Camping gear is expensive these days, and there is a good deal of poorly made equipment on the market. Well-made equipment lasts a long time and is fairly versatile if chosen carefully; however, it may be out of the price range of the beginning touring cyclist. If so, it often is better to make do for a while with the most inexpensive expedient, rather than buying medium-priced gear that is not really satisfactory. In the discussions that follow, I have attempted to suggest both the equipment that seems best for the purpose and the least costly items that will permit the beginner to get by without too much discomfort.

Camping styles vary in every outdoor pursuit. It is quite possible to ride across the country and sleep outside with no camping equipment of any kind. One can bed down in barns and culverts, spending some good nights and some bad ones. During the milder seasons in most of the United States and Canada, no one is likely to suffer anything worse than discomfort from exposure to the elements. If this is your cup of tea, you can skip most of the rest of this chapter. The camping style advocated here strives for reasonable comfort and flexibility without adding much weight to your panniers.

I like to be able to camp at a mountain lake without worrying about being kept awake all night by the cold. I prefer the convenience and economy of being able to cook enjoyable meals in camp, rather than having to rely on restaurants or being forced to eat cold food. If an afternoon thunderstorm comes up, I want to be able to pitch camp in the first secluded spot, rather than having to ride in the rain or huddle under an overpass or in a dilapidated barn. Since cycling is far more enjoyable if the load on the bike is light, the goal for me, then, is to be able to camp comfortably while carrying the least possible weight on the bicycle.

Shelter

There are several possible solutions to the problem of finding shelter while bicycle camping, and the best choice for you depends on the size of the group you normally travel with, your budget, the area you visit, and the season during which you plan to do most of your camping.

Tents

In general, the bicycle camper should avoid like the plague those heavy, cramped, expensive mountaineering tents that are typically recommended. Look at the weight first; if a two-person tent weighs 7, 8, or 9 pounds, forget it. It is quite possible to buy a roomy and comfortable bicycle camping tent that weighs 1½ pounds or less per occupant, and there is no need to go over 2½ pounds apiece.

The best tents for bicycle touring are those made by Warmlite (see Figure 33) and the some-

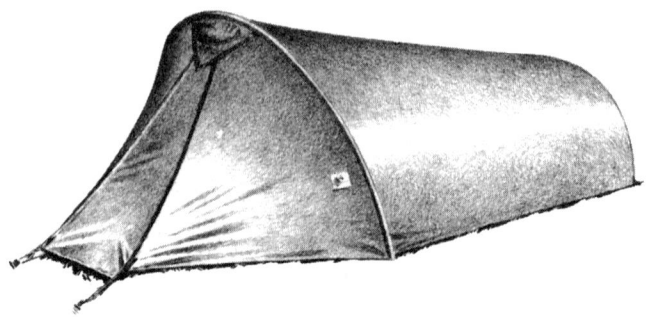

33. An excellent bicycle-camping tent made by Warmlite. It is a roomy, two-person model that weighs less than three pounds.

what modified copy made by Early Winters. The Warmlite tents developed by Jack Stephenson are shaped like a sloping half-cylinder, are made from a very lightweight coated nylon, and have two walls, one suspended from the other. The two walls reduce condensation, and strategically placed vents provide good air flow in most weather conditions, even when the air outside is still. Condensation in these tents is minimal for the conditions encountered when bicycle camping. The tents pitch very easily with just three stakes each and are very stable in wind. By current standards they are relatively cheap, less expensive than most high-quality mountaineering tents of similar size. They also are excellent tents for most backpacking situations, with the reservations about durability noted below.

The main deficiency of Warmlite tents is that they are not as durable as they might be. They are not reinforced at points of high stress, and the coating develops leaks after a lot of use. Ultra-violet radiation eventually weakens the light nylon.

My own experience and that of friends suggest that the useful life of a Warmlite is about 200 days in the field, given reasonable care but not pampering. Hence, if you use your tent quite a lot, it may last only a few years; if you make just one week-long trip and a couple of overnights each season, a Warmlite might be a lifetime investment.

For larger groups, Warmlite makes bigger tents of a similar design. These are particularly appropriate for families who tour together. A couple wanting lots of room could carry a Warmlite three-person tent and still carry only 2 pounds per person. Warmlite also makes ultralight tents with single walls; these weigh 1¾ pounds for a two-person size and 2¼ pounds for a three-person size. They should be excellent for cycle camping, though I have not tried them myself. All of these tents are much roomier than their conventional counterparts.

Early Winters makes a tent similar to the Warmlite two-person model except that it employs a single wall made of Gore-tex rather than a double, coated-nylon wall. The Early Winters tent is made of heavier materials than the Warmlite original and is carefully reinforced at stress points; however, it also is somewhat smaller and more expensive than the Warmlite in addition to being heavier. The workmanship is excellent and the tent should be quite durable; it weighs about 3½ pounds. The Gore-tex material is permeable to water vapor but not to liquid water and performs well in temperatures typical in bicycle camping; it also requires frequent and careful laundering to remain waterproof (see page 271).

Other copies of the Warmlite tent undoubtedly will be introduced, though the ones I have seen so far do not employ the tilted arches that help to make the tent self-supporting. For bicycle camping, in which light weight is important and ultraviolet exposure is less than at high altitudes, it is worth considering Warmlite tents first. They also are cheaper than any of their imitators, and for really luxurious bicycle camping they are hard to beat.

Somewhat less expensive (and less roomy) tents are made by using a high peak at one end of the tent dropping to either a lower peak or a guyed wall at the other. Such tents are basically lightweight versions of the old explorer tent. For lighter weight and less expense, a single pole may be used at the peak in front. If an A-frame of two poles is used, the peak should be moved back so that it is over the living space of the tent, where the full height is usable. If the poles are tilted forward, the walls of the tent can be used to tension it, requiring fewer guylines and therefore fewer stakes. A good example of this type of tent is the Sierra Designs Starflight, a two-person tent that weighs about 4¾ to 5 pounds with stakes (see Figure 34). Such tents can be built to weigh about 3¾ pounds with stakes, using lighter materials. My homemade tent of a similar design weighs 3½ pounds plus the weight of the stakes.

Conventionally designed tents like the Starflight usually are built with a double-wall construction to reduce condensation, as are Warmlite tents. Instead of having the inner wall suspended from the outer one, however, a second canopy is pitched a few inches over the main tent. The upper walls of the tent generally are uncoated so that water vapor can pass through, while the second canopy—called the flysheet, or fly—is

34. *Sierra Designs' Starflight, a good bicycle-camping tent in a conventional design. The fitted flysheet that pitches over the main tent is not shown.*

coated to shed the rain. Vents also may be incorporated, both for cooling in hot weather and to further reduce condensation. These tents also are made with single walls of coated material, but if you want a simple tent made with a single layer of coated fabric, I recommend that you pick one of the modified tube tents discussed below. In a conventional single-walled, coated tent with close-hanging walls, condensation is more of a problem than rain blowing in the ends, so you might as well save the weight and expense of the closures and buy an open-ended tent.

Conventional tents have both advantages and disadvantages when compared with arched tents, such as the Warmlite. The entire tent is bound to be heavier for the amount of space it provides since the modified half-cylinder is a more efficient way to enclose space. The tent takes longer to pitch and requires more stakes. The separate fly also requires extra stakes and therefore extra weight. On the other hand, these conventional designs are cheaper, easier to make at home, and more versatile. The versatility is due to the fact that poles can be left at home when you know that you will be able to suspend the tent from a tree branch. The fly alone also makes an excellent one- or two-person shelter on those occasions when you don't feel you need the entire tent. On many trips when I don't really expect rain, don't feel the need for mosquito protection, or just want to carry a minimal shelter, I carry the fly alone and suspend the apex from the branch of a tree. I then have a pleasant but effective shelter for two that weighs less than a pound. The half-cylinder tents are self-contained and more efficient when used in whole, but all the components have to be taken every time.

In judging the overall quality of a tent, there are a number of factors you should consider. Pitch the tent and see how many stakes are required. Though you may decide to improvise with rocks or sticks, it usually is a good idea to carry lightweight aluminum-alloy stakes, and these add to the weight of the tent. The tent should pitch easily and should hang smoothly. A lot of wrinkles indicates that the tent is badly cut and will flap a lot in the wind. All the pullouts and stake loops should be sewn to the body of the tent using some method that distributes the stress over a large area of fabric; otherwise they can tear out easily.

The seams in any tent should be well sewn and neat. There should be at least eight stitches per inch, and most of the seams should be felled (see Figure 35), with the laps on the outside facing downward so as to shed moisture rather than collecting it. The tent should have a waterproof floor. If a fly is used with an uncoated canopy, the waterproof fabric should extend up the sidewalls six inches or more so that there is no leakage at the bottom of the walls. Mosquito netting and doors should have reliable and smooth-running closures.

*35. A lap-felled seam.
With this type of seam,
the fabric ends are
folded in on one
another so that each
row of stitching
penetrates three layers.
It is used for
constructing tents
because it is strong,
helps to prevent
unraveling, and sheds
water when lapped
downward on the tent
surface.*

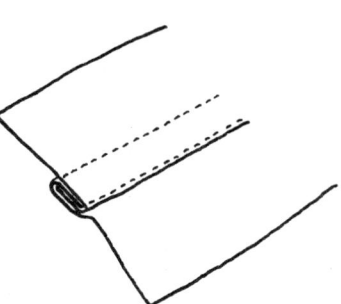

Tube Tents

Tube tents are among the best types of shelter for
the bicycle camper, particularly one who is trying
to save money and weight at the same time. In its
simplest form, the tube tent is merely a length of
tubular plastic sheeting that can be suspended on a
piece of line strung about a yard above the ground.
What results is a shelter with a triangular cross
section and a built-in floor that is held down by the
weight of the cyclist and his or her equipment (see
Figure 36). More elaborate and durable tube tents
may be made of coated fabric, and these may be cut
with eaves over the ends and have mosquito bars
installed. Tube tents are simple, light, and cheap.

Tube tents are not suitable for camping at
high altitudes, in exposed campgrounds, or in very
cold weather. Their open ends and simple pitching
system make them less than ideal in high winds.
Because they consist of a single layer of plastic or
coated fabric, they rely on ventilation through their
open ends to reduce condensation on the walls.
This system is less than adequate in severe cold or
when heavy, wind-driven rain requires the ends to

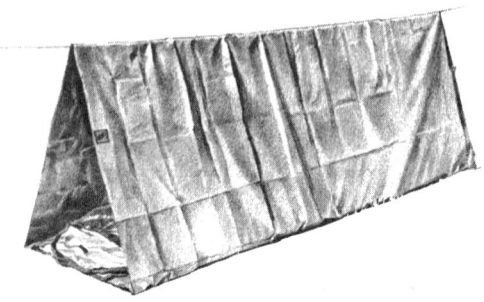

36. A plastic tube tent provides an adequate, inexpensive shelter for the bicycle camper.

be closed off as much as possible. Thus, a tube tent cannot provide as much protection against the elements as a well-designed double-walled tent that can be completely closed against the weather. For cycle campers, however, these limitations may not be of much consequence. Bicyclists generally camp in fairly protected areas during the warmer seasons, and a couple of nights of more severe weather is not a major cause for concern. You are not likely to get into a situation where you have to sit out a three-day snowstorm on most bicycle camping trips.

Usually it is not too difficult to find a site with suitable anchors for a tube tent. You normally ride in places with a fair amount of vegetation, and the bikes themselves can be used to support guylines (see page 396). In areas where there are few natural supports, you can either carry a single tent pole or pick up a suitable stick as the time approaches to make camp.

For the beginner who wants to start touring with a minimum outlay of money, a plastic tube tent is the logical choice for shelter. It usually is made from plastic 3 or 4 mils thick and 9 or 10 feet long. The tube should be about 10 feet in circumference for a single person, while a tube 12 or 14 feet in circumference can serve for two people. The single-person tent weighs a little more than a pound and the two-person tent is about 2 pounds. Carry a long piece of parachute cord (nylon line with a woven sheath, about ⅛ inch in diameter), a couple of aluminum-alloy stakes, and a few spring clothespins to aid in pitching. The clothespins can be used either to anchor the tent on the line or to partially close off the ends in case of wind-driven rain. These items increase the weight of your shelter to about 1½ pounds for one person and 1¼ pounds each for two people.

The main disadvantage of the plastic tube tent is its lack of durability. With a little care, however, you can make one last for quite a few nights, so it is an excellent choice while you are deciding whether you enjoy camping by bike or are struggling to pay for your initial set of equipment. Those who bike camp only a few weekends a year might be well-advised to use plastic tubes all the time, rather than paying a lot of money for a fancy tent that rarely will be used.

A much more durable alternative is a fabric tube tent. It retains the simplicity of the plastic tube and still is relatively inexpensive. Fabric tube tents are made with varying degrees of sophistication, the simplest being a mere copy of the plastic tube sewn from coated-nylon fabric. Refinements of the basic design include sloping one end down to save weight, since your feet need less room than your head and shoulders, adding mosquito netting and stake loops, and making provisions for pitching with simple poles. It is best to retain the open ends to minimize condensation. A tent of this type can be made at home easily if

you want to save money. A good example of a sophisticated and comfortable tube tent is the Trail-
wise Wind River Tent, a two-person model that
weighs about 2½ pounds without the poles that
are included. With stakes and parachute cord, the
weight still should be less than 1½ pounds per
person, and the tent is far less expensive than more
elaborate alternatives.

Tarps

Still another simple and inexpensive alternative,
preferred by many experienced bicycle campers, is
a tarpaulin. A simple tarp may be made of plastic 4
to 6 mils thick, but a coated-nylon tarp is far more
durable. In the case of plastic tarps, lines are tied
where they are needed either by using a special
fastener or by placing a small, round stone at the
point you want to tie off and cinching a loop of
parachute cord to hold the tarp around the stone.

Well-made nylon tarps usually have many
grommets or tie tapes installed so that it is easy to
pitch the tarp in many different configurations.
One advantage to a tarp is that you can use your
bike as a front support, protecting it from the rain
at the same time (see Figure 47). A tarp does not
provide nearly as much protection as a good tent,
but with good camping technique it usually proves
quite adequate. The advantages are low cost and
versatility.

Bivouac Sacks

Mountaineers often carry lightweight waterproof
sacks so that they can get some protection from
the weather without the weight of a tent or a
suitable location to pitch one. In cold, damp
weather, much of the moisture that evaporates from
the body condenses on the inside of such a sack,

however, gradually soaking the occupant and his or her insulation. For this reason, bivouac sacks were not very suitable for anyone to use for general camping purposes. With the development of Gore-tex, however, bivy sacks have become far more useful. There are a number of Gore-tex sacks now being made which are reasonably waterproof, and heavy condensation does not occur on the inside unless you are sleeping in a downpour.

A Gore-tex bivy sack makes a workable shelter for cyclists with a fair amount of camping experience on trips when rain is unlikely. They are far from ideal shelters in a real downpour, and I don't recommend them as the only shelter to be carried by most people. They can be an excellent supplement to a tarp or tube tent, however, since they also add a good deal of warmth to a light sleeping bag. The extra layer provides some extra insulation, and the very windproof surface of the Gore-tex greatly reduces convective cooling. A ground cloth is not needed with a bivy sack since its bottom is made from a durable coated fabric (only the top is Gore-tex). Such a sack weighs about a pound. A typical Gore-tex bivouac sack is illustrated in Figure 37.

Gore-tex is not cheap, however, so whether a bivy sack is worthwhile for you depends on your own circumstances. If you are camping with another person, two bivy sacks alone are likely to cost about half as much as a Warmlite tent, and they weigh as much without providing nearly as much shelter. The bivy sack is most advantageous for the lone cyclist who likes to travel with an absolute minimum of weight. By taking advantage of natural shelters whenever you can, you can use a bivy sack and a very light sleeping bag even in fairly nasty weather and remain dry.

37. A Gore-tex bivouac sack. This one is made by Early Winters.

Sleeping Bags

A warm sleeping bag probably is the most important and most expensive purchase for the bicycle
camper. You can get by without a fancy tent by
using a plastic tube, and many other items can be
improvised, but a snug bag is likely to be essential
for an enjoyable trip. After a long day of riding, a
comfortable night's sleep is important.

There is no one ideal sleeping bag for all
purposes, and your choice should depend on the
areas and seasons in which you plan to do most of
your camping. Any bag for bicycle camping should
be on the light side, however, since cycling always
is done in relatively mild weather; you do not need a
bag designed to keep someone warm at high
altitudes in the winter. If you are going to do nearly
all your camping in the summer in one of the
warmer parts of the country, you should buy a very
light bag designed for temperatures down to 40° F.
Otherwise, you probably want one that still will be
comfortable when nighttime temperatures hover

around freezing. Bags at the lighter end of the range made for backpackers usually are about right for an all-around bike-camping bag.

You have to take your own idiosyncrasies into account when you are buying a sleeping bag. Some people always tend to feel colder than others. If you always need two blankets when everyone else is comfortable with only a sheet, then you will want a warmer than average bag. A person who is comfortable in a tee shirt while others are piling on sweaters and jackets can get by with a lighter bag than normally is required.

The sleeping bags sold in stores and through backpacking catalogues usually are marked with temperature ratings, and these should be helpful in giving you a rough idea of what you need. When comparing bags, however, it is important to realize that different manufacturers' ratings vary by as much as twenty degrees for virtually identical bags. The ratings, therefore, are a good basis for comparing bags within a particular company's line, but they should be used with care in comparing different manufacturers' offerings.

Good-quality sleeping bags employ nylon fabric with the insulation sandwiched between inner and outer fabric layers. The warmth of the bag primarily depends on the thickness and uniformity of the insulation layer, providing that your shelter protects you from the wind. Since most of the actual insulation in the bag is provided by the air that is trapped by the insulating material, thickness is a fairly good indication of warmth. There are no major differences in the warmth provided by a three-inch layer of wool, polyester batting, or down.

High-quality down is the most efficient insulator for sleeping bags because it provides a thicker layer for a given weight. It also is ideal for cyclists because it compresses to a smaller package than any other insulator providing the same amount of warmth. Down is very expensive, however. Furthermore, a complicated system of baffles must be sewn into a down bag in order to distribute the down evenly. Sewing the baffles raises the cost of a down bag still higher. For this reason, some bicycle campers prefer to buy a less expensive bag insulated with a polyester fiber, such as Polarguard® (Celanese) or Hollofil II® (Dupont). Assuming equivalent design and craftsmanship, a polyester-insulated bag weighs about half again as much as a comparable down bag and takes up half again as much space. It cushions you and insulates you better from the ground, not requiring quite as thick a sleeping pad, but does not drape quite so well to fill in cold air spaces above. A polyester bag also is easier to clean and loses far less of its insulating capability if it gets wet, but it is not nearly as durable as a down bag. At the time this is written, a good down bag costs at least one-and-a-half times as much as a comparable polyester bag.

Regardless of the insulating material used, a sleeping bag that is cut close to the body is more efficient than one that is roomier. Thus, a larger bag of the same thickness not only is heavier and bulkier than a closer-cut bag, it is not as warm. Large, rectangular bags definitely should be avoided by bicycle campers. The choice is between very close-cut bags and those with a "modified mummy" cut that provides a little more room. Most people feel constricted in narrow bags when they first try them, but it is not hard to become accustomed to them. It comes down to a personal choice between saving a little more weight with a narrower bag or feeling more comfortable in a wider bag. A closer-cut bag should be a little less expensive than an equally warm one with a wider cut. The actual dimensions of the bag vary with the individual, but for a person with a normal build, a reasonably close-cut bag should have an inside girth at the hips and shoulders of about 55 inches, tapering to a smaller girth at the feet.

A sleeping bag used for bicycle camping should have a zipper that extends all the way down one side to provide ventilation on warmer nights. You are bound to encounter fairly warm temperatures some of the time when you are cycle touring, and a bag with no zipper or a zipper that extends only halfway down the bag is less versatile when the weather gets warm.

Polyester Bags

Sleeping bags with synthetic insulators make sense for bicycle campers traveling in relatively warm climates. If the evening temperatures in the places you tour never drop anywhere close to freezing during the bicycling season, there really is no need to pay for or carry a bag that is designed for cold temperatures.

The weight that can be saved by using down is far less in sleeping bags designed for warmer weather. Using a lightweight fabric and high-quality down, you can make a bag that is comfortable for most people down to 40° F which weighs 1½ pounds. An equivalent synthetic bag weighs 2 pounds or a bit more. The difference is not as significant as it is with warmer bags, and it is virtually impossible these days to find a down bag of this type.

Polyester insulation for sleeping bags comes in batts or rolls of batting, which are composed of millions of polyester fibers bonded together. Most types, including Hollofil, consist of relatively short fibers. Because Polarguard is made of long, continuous fibers, constructing bags with it is slightly easier, and most manufacturers of quality synthetic bags use Polarguard, even though Hollofil has slightly better lofting characteristics.

There are several methods of constructing polyester bags, but the most common is to cut a piece of batting the same size as the shell material and sew the pieces together at selected intervals with seams that run perpendicular to the direction of the fibers in the batting; this way the fibers are anchored at each line of stitching. The lightest bags usually use one layer of insulation sewn to either the inside or the outside shell. The stitching does not penetrate the other shell layer, thus avoiding some "cold seam" effect (seams insulate very little because the insulation material is compressed along the line of stitching). When two layers of insulation are used, one usually is sewn to the inside of the bag and one to the outside, with the stitching offset to prevent cold seams. With three layers, two usually are quilted and one sandwiched between and anchored at the sides. Since batting is available in different thicknesses, a bag designer can get almost any desired thickness by varying the number of layers and the thickness of each.

For the warm-weather cyclist, a close-cut bag with a single layer of polyester batting usually is a good choice. It can be made to weigh about 2 pounds and is comfortable down to 40° to 45° F for most people. Such a bag also can be used in somewhat colder temperatures if you wear a few extra clothes or add a sleeping-bag cover, making it the base of an inexpensive and versatile system. Heavier polyester bags weighing 3½ to 4 pounds work well in almost any conditions met by the cyclist if they are closely cut and well designed. For bicycle campers on a budget who need capacities down to freezing, the savings in cost over down may be worth the extra weight and bulk. Such bags should have a loft of 4½ to 6 inches. Sleeping bags any heavier than this really are not suited for lightweight touring.

Good examples of efficient synthetic bags in the 2-pound range are the Chinook and Pioneer made by Camp 7, though they lack the full-length zippers that are best for the cyclist. A slightly heavier bag with a full-length zipper is Moor & Mountain's Ultralight Bike/Canoe bag. Good Polarguard bags weighing 3 to 3½ pounds include the North Face Cat's Meow, the Snow Lion Small Sack, and the EMS Berkshire.

Down Bags

Down is an ideal insulating material for the bicycle camper because of its light weight and compressibility. Down also is very durable and tends to be comfortable over a wider temperature range than most other insulators are. The main disadvantage is its high initial cost. It also is important to note that down must be kept dry, because when it gets wet it becomes a soggy lump. Generally this is not a serious problem for the cyclist, since good camping technique should keep the down dry and since the bicycle camper rarely is trapped by storms deep in the wilderness. If you make a mistake as a beginner and get your bag damp, you can stop at a laundromat and dry it out.

Down comes in many grades, and you have to rely on your own inspection and the integrity of the manufacturer to obtain good quality. Federal regulations require only that 80 percent of the insulation in a bag labeled as down actually be down or down fragments, and there are no standards as to the quality of that percentage. (Only 72 percent of "goose down" has to be goose down, and a description such as "100 percent Grade AAA Northern Goose Down" is considered a trade name, not requiring any higher percentage.) The loft and weight of the bag tell you a good deal, and the workmanship is an important clue to the quality of the materials, but even the most careful inspection on your part won't tell you everything. Buy your bag from a good supplier who specializes in lightweight camping gear and values his or her reputation.

Down is the undercoating layer from the plumage of waterfowl. Each pod or plumule consists of a small nucleus with many fibers radiating from it. There are no quills in true down, but any batch of down contains small feathers as well. These are more likely to work through the fabric because of their quills, creating the impression that down is made of small feathers. The best down comes from mature geese raised in a cold climate. Mature ducks produce better down than immature geese do. Since most down comes from animals killed at an early age for meat, very little of it is of the highest quality. Down works through an elaborate market of brokers; it is mixed and then shipped all over depending on the fluctuations of the market. Manufacturers hardly ever know the origin of their down, though they can measure the filling power. Most of the better makers use or claim to use down that fills 550 cubic inches per ounce in a standard test. A few use a slightly better grade of down. Because of the scarcity of good down, however, a number of manufacturers actually use down that doesn't meet the standards claimed.

For the above reasons, it is best to stick to fairly reputable makers and then compare bags yourself as carefully as you can. It is quite easy to lay out two bags side by side and see which one has more loft after a given amount of fluffing. You also should weigh a bag before buying it, rather than assuming that the advertised weight is correct. Sometimes there are major discrepancies. If you buy a mail-order bag, check it carefully before using it. Most reputable suppliers of lightweight gear offer a money-back guarantee if you aren't satisfied.

Since down is a loose-fill material, the bag must be split into many compartments so that the down is distributed evenly around your body rather than sliding off to the sides. This normally is done by sewing baffles between the inner and outer shells at selected intervals to form a series of tubes that run circumferentially around the bag. The tubes may run all the way around or each may have a block opposite the zipper to maintain a particular distribution of down between the top and the bottom of the bag. Typical construction is shown in Figure 38.

Clearly, sewing baffles into a bag and filling it with down is a labor-intensive operation, expensive, and hard to control. Take a good look at all the stitching on the bag. It should be impeccable, with at least eight stitches to the inch and reinforcements at all stress points. Sloppy sewing results in a bag that falls apart quickly and usually is a clue that low-quality materials have been used as well. The outer fabric should not be prone to catch and snag.

All closely fit down bags should have a differential cut; that is, the inner shell should be tailored so that it has a smaller circumference than the outer shell. This reduces the tendency of the

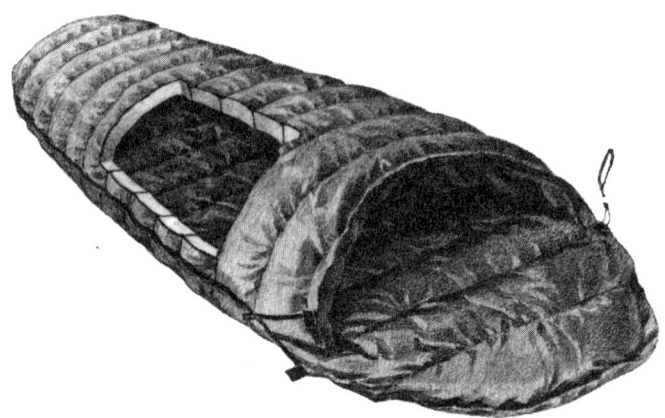

38. Down-bag construction. Inner and outer shells of nylon are used; in close-cut bags, the inner shell has a smaller circumference so that the sleeper is less likely to push this shell against the outer shell, compressing the insulation. Baffles made of a lightweight fabric or netting are sewn between the inner and outer shells to form a series of tubes that keep the down evenly distributed throughout the bag.

occupant to squash the insulation by pressing the inner shell against the outer shell while moving around. The amount of differential cut should be designed to conform to the cut and the amount of insulation in a particular bag. Although it is debatable whether a differential cut is better in a roomier bag, it is essential in a close-cut bag.

Down bags for bicycle campers should be in the range of 2 to 3 pounds, unless you decide that you need a bag that is both warmer and roomier than usual. North Face's Blue Kazoo is a good example of a baffled, 2-pound bag. Somewhat warmer close-cut bags are the Camp 7 Arete, Holubar Trimlite, Snow Lion Limited Edition, Sierra Designs Cirrus, Marmot Pocket Gopher, and Trail-wise Slimline.

Pads, Air Mattresses, and Ground Sheets

It is both more comfortable and more logical to carry a pad or air mattress to place under your sleeping bag as a ground bed. Even when you are used to sleeping on the ground, you are bound to encounter at least a few campgrounds where you have to sleep on hard, rough gravel, which feels a lot more comfortable if you pad it a little. The insulator used in sleeping bags has to be quite compressible or it would take up too much space and add too much wind drag to the bike. Your ground bed needs to be a little more resistant to being squashed if it is to provide any padding against bits of gravel and tree roots. You also can lose a lot of heat to the cold ground unless you are insulated from it, so a pad and a light sleeping bag make a lighter and more comfortable combination than a bag warm enough to be used directly on the ground. A few sleeping bags, such as those made by Warmlite, have a built-in pad or air mattress, but most require a separate one. Polyester bags don't squash underneath you quite as much as down bags do, but a pad or air mattress is still needed.

With pads and air mattresses, you can choose among a variety of compromises between padding, insulation, bulk, and weight. The easiest way to save weight is to cut the length and width to a minimum. Most people find they can sleep quite comfortably with a mat that is just long enough to reach from the hips to the shoulders, the areas which bear most of your weight when you are lying down. You can put your panniers under your feet and legs and use a stuffsack with a few clothes for a pillow. The pad I usually carry is 16½ inches by 31 inches, and it is generously sized.

Closed-cell foam pads are the cheapest and

lightest type of ground bed, as well as being
relatively low in bulk. They also provide the best
insulation, but they are less luxurious in padding
than are the other alternatives. "Closed-cell"
refers to foam in which each bubble of air is closed
off and does not join with others. Closed-cell foam
is not as soft as open-cell foam and won't absorb
water, so it doesn't need a cover. Because the air
cannot move around inside, less thickness is needed
to provide good ground insulation. Foam that is ¼
inch thick is adequate for bike camping, but ⅜-inch
or ½-inch thicknesses do not add excessive weight
and provide better padding and more warmth.
Many varieties are available, but various brands of
ethafoam seem to be most efficient for their weight,
which is considerably less than that of Ensolite,
the standard type.

Open-cell foam pads are the usual variety
found in backpacking stores. Because the cells are
linked to one another, open-cell foam acts like a
sponge, so pads usually are covered with fabric to
keep them from getting wet. Some are covered
entirely with coated material while others have
uncoated fabric on top. Open-cell foam pads are
more luxurious than the closed-cell type and are
the favorite ground beds of most experienced
campers; however, for an equivalent amount of
insulation, you have to carry about two-and-a-half
times the weight of a closed-cell foam pad and pay
twice as much. Thicknesses range from 1 to 2 inches, with the thicker pads being more comfortable,
heavier, and bulkier. I prefer to cover my own
open-cell foam pads and to reduce weight and bulk
by using a smaller pad than the ones generally sold
in backpacking shops.

Air mattresses of the standard variety are
much too heavy for bicycle camping, but there are

very light ones made from coated nylon. (The vinyl types are worthless.) Air mattresses provide the greatest padding of any ground bed, and many people find them more comfortable than foam pads. They are poor insulators unless they are filled with down, but they are warm enough for the bicycle camper. Air mattresses are the most compact ground beds to carry because they fold flat when they are deflated. Their biggest disadvantage is that punctures occur sooner or later and have to be patched. The better air mattresses have weights between those of open- and closed-cell foam pads. The best design employs tubes that inflate individually, making deflation easier and avoiding the hiss of air between the tubes whenever you roll over. Two types are available: one with coated nylon forming the airtight tubes and the other with fabric encasing replaceable vinyl tubes. With the latter, you simply carry a spare tube in case of a puncture.

If you don't carry a tent with a floor, you need something to keep your sleeping bag clean and dry. Coated-nylon *ground sheets* can be used, or you simply can carry a light, plastic sheet that can be replaced inexpensively when it wears out.

Stoves

Both for practical and ecological reasons, it usually is best to carry a small camp stove with you. Unless wood is brought in, most designated campgrounds receive far too much use these days to produce sufficient wood for fires, as evidenced by all the trees disfigured by people in search of wood to burn. Fires are fine when there are existing fireplaces or rings, sufficient wood, and no fire danger, but on other occasions you should use a stove. From a practical point of view, the bicycle camper often stays in places that are not designated as campsites but are close to roads. It often is illegal to build fires in these places, and even if it is not, local residents are likely to become upset by smoke or a fire. In many forested regions people have had unpleasant experiences with fires set by careless campers. When in doubt, it is better to stick with your stove.

Unlike the winter camper, the bicycle camper generally does not need a large-capacity stove since he or she has no need to melt snow and requires fewer dehydrated foods than the backpacker. Dried foods are necessary only on trips during which you are several days removed from grocery stores. When choosing among lightweight backpacking stoves, therefore, your primary decision is which fuel to use.

The lightest stoves use cartridges of propane or butane (see Figures 39 and 41). These also have the virtues of convenience and easy adjustment of flame level. To light a cartridge stove you simply open the valve and light the escaping gas with a match or cigarette lighter. The flame can be adjusted easily to a simmer, which is important for the bicycle camper since the foods most commonly used need only to be heated and cooked slightly. The greatest disadvantage of the cartridge stoves is the cost of fuel, which is quite high compared to white gas. The situation of the long-distance cyclist is quite different from that of the backpacker, however, and on some trips cartridges may turn out to be cheaper. Cartridges also do not have to be kept far away from your food to prevent possible contamination as gasoline and kerosene do.

Small, self-pressurized stoves using "camping fuel," otherwise known as white gas or naphtha, probably are the most common backpacking stoves

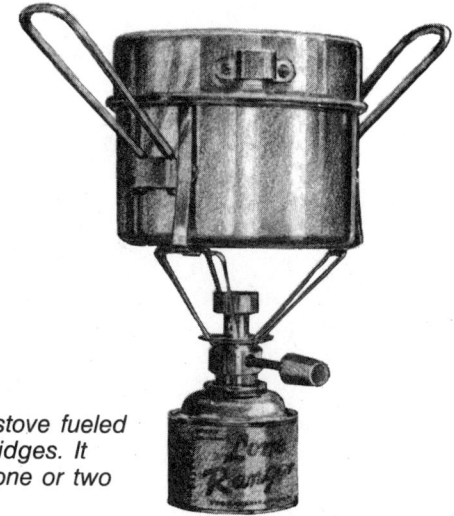

39. A very light stove fueled with butane cartridges. It cooks nicely for one or two people.

(see Figure 40). They are heavier than cartridge stoves and have more idiosyncrasies that you must learn to deal with when cooking with them. They must be primed to start vaporizing the gasoline: a little fuel must be burned to heat the generator so that the fuel is in a gaseous state when it comes out of the burner. This is easier to manage with a small accessory pump now available for these stoves, and it is no trouble once you are used to the routine. For the beginner, however, the ritual is often a trial. Furthermore, if you run out of fuel, you have to wait until the stove has cooled before refilling and relighting it.

One great advantage of a white-gas stove on short trips is that it can be filled completely at home and you can carry exactly as much fuel as you want in a fuel bottle. A half-empty cartridge cannot be filled up, so an extra has to be carried. On long trips, however, unless you are traveling with

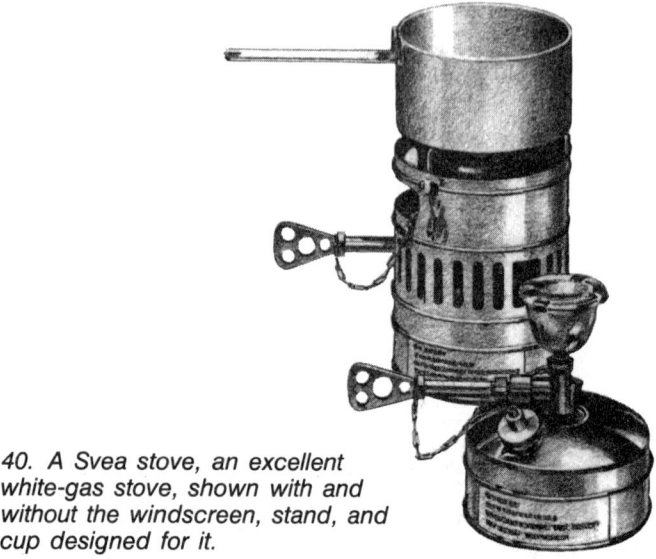

40. *A Svea stove, an excellent white-gas stove, shown with and without the windscreen, stand, and cup designed for it.*

a large group using white gas, having to buy some more fuel can be wasteful and expensive. White gas is cheap, but often it is impossible to buy in containers of less than a gallon—far too much to carry while touring. The only alternative to buying a lot and giving most of it away is to prowl around campgrounds and try to buy small quantities of white gas from car campers. (Automotive fuel should *never* be substituted for white gas, as it contains additives that make it dangerous to burn in a closed space and that will clog the burners of most white-gas stoves.)

Either small cartridge stoves or self-pressurized white-gas stoves satisfy most bicycle campers. The Svea 123 is the standard lightweight white gas stove, but good ones are also made by Primus, Optimus, and Phoebus. There are several cartridge models that can be recommended, depending on where you plan to travel and your own preferences. The lightest is the Lone Ranger model shown in Figure 39 (also sold under other brand names). The combined weight of the stove, cookset, and one cartridge is only a pound. This type does have small parts that can get lost and is not as stable as it might be, but for the solo light-traveling camper it is hard to beat. The EFI Mini-stove (see Figure 41) doesn't weigh too much more than the Lone Ranger and is easy to use. It is best to avoid those stoves that use "Gaz" cartridges, which cannot be removed from the stove until empty. As any cartridge nears the empty point, the stove's flame will drop, but with cartridges that are punctured when attached to the stove, it is unsafe to take them off until they have completely run out, a real nuisance when you are trying to boil water for tea.

If you are cooking regularly for four or more people, or if you are looking for a multi-purpose stove that is good for winter camping as well as bicycle camping, a white-gas stove with a pump usually is the best choice. The one that is simplest to use and that best satisfies the bicyclist's needs is the Coleman Peak 1 (see Figure 42). It weighs a little less than 2 pounds, which is relatively light for a pumped stove, and it adjusts easily to a low

41. The EFI Mini-stove, one of the best cartridge stoves available. It is a little heavier than the type shown in Figure 39 but has a more stable base.

42. A Coleman Peak 1 stove, fueled with white gas. It is a bit heavy for the solo cyclist but is excellent when cooking for three to six people.

flame for simmering. It is simpler to use than most gasoline stoves, has a high capacity, and lights without priming. By far the lightest pumped stove is the MSR, an excellent gadget that uses a fuel bottle for a tank and weighs less than most self-priming stoves. The MSR is a virtual blowtorch, ideal for winter camping and expedition use. It is too temperamental for most cycle campers, however, and does not adjust very readily to a simmer. In areas where white gas may not be available, though, as noted below, the MSR is by far the best solution.

One final consideration, particularly for those planning trips abroad, is the availability of different fuels. Some cartridges are widely available in certain countries but not in others. For bicycle tours in the United States, I suggest visiting a good hardware store to see if you can find the type of cartridge required for the stove you are thinking of buying. This gives you a good idea of current availability in the United States. One advantage to such stoves as the Bluet and Globe Trotter is that the cartridges for them are very widely available in Europe (Gaz C-200 and GT cannisters). In underdeveloped countries neither cartridges nor white gas usually are available. Since airline regulations generally prohibit carrying fuel, a stove that uses kerosene—or automobile fuel in an emergency—is the best alternative. The MSR multi-fuel stove is the best choice if you are traveling to South America, Asia, or Africa.

Cooking and Eating Utensils

Pots, pans, and other cooking and eating utensils are important items on which to save weight. It makes little sense to spend a lot of money on special titanium parts for your bike in order to shave a few ounces and then lug along three or four pounds of cookware. Buy functional, lightweight, aluminum pans, no more than you need to do your cooking. Two pots and a cover that can serve as a frying pan usually are more than enough. If you plan to do enough frying to make an easily cleaned Teflon surface worthwhile, try using one of the Teflon-coated pie pans you can get in any supermarket. They make good plates too. Don't get pots larger than you need. To cook for one or two people, I usually carry a single pot that holds five cups. To cook for four people, one pot that holds about two quarts and one smaller pot usually are sufficient. I normally take a plastic bowl and cup so that I can have a beverage and use the pot to heat water while I eat, but many campers carry only a cup. Use a cup that is tall and narrow, rather than shallow and wide, so that your tea, coffee, or soup won't get cold before you are halfway through with it.

Other utensils should be light as well. Ignition pliers from your tool kit can be used as a pot-gripper, as can an arm warmer pulled over your hand. Some people prefer to carry an aluminum gripper. If your pocket knife does not have a can opener, get a small GI can opener; it weighs a fraction of an ounce and costs very little. If you do much frying, a nylon spatula is relatively light. Early Winters distributes Lexan forks and spoons that are very light. Staple food supplies, such as oil, powdered milk, and honey, can be packed in plastic squeeze bottles.

Water Containers

Water may not be available at all campsites, so it is worth taking a separate container specifically for carrying water to your camp from the nearest source. Collapsible plastic containers well suited for this purpose are available at backpacking stores. I carry a gallon-sized container that weighs only a couple of ounces. If each member of the party carries one water container this size in addition to personal water bottles, you should have plenty of water to use in camp. Keep in mind that you must have room on your bike to carry the full container from the water source back to camp. If your luggage is full, it is a good idea to take along a very light backpack for carrying water or groceries, as suggested in Chapter 13.

Other camping necessities, such as lights and spare clothing, are discussed in earlier chapters. If you do not carry tape and parachute cord for other purposes, however, be sure to include them with your camping gear. They are invaluable in many situations.

Part Four

Hitting the Road

Chapter 15

Planning the Tour

BICYCLE TOURING is attractive in part because of the variety of trips that are possible, and the nature of any tour depends as much on the personality, style, and mood of the participants as it does on the route or on such external conditions as the weather. Some cyclists prefer to plan every day to the last detail, from motel reservations and the number of miles to be covered to departure time and rest stops. Others prefer a free-form trip, allowing for spur-of-the-moment changes in plans so that riders can explore an interesting place, take a day off when they feel like lying around, or push twice the normal distance one day just because everyone feels like riding hard.

Tours also vary according to whether you camp or stay in public accommodations, use a sag-wagon or not, and plan to cover sixty miles a day or two hundred. Some variations are dependent on the riders themselves; their physical condition, riding skill, and the loads they carry determine the general range between hard and easy days. For riders who can barely complete a 100-mile ride in twelve hours under good conditions and with no load on the bicycle, there is no chance of pushing for 150-mile days on the tour. For a hard-riding group, any 50- or 60-mile days on normal roads are certain to be easy ones. However, given the abilities of the group, some tours may be chosen deliberately as fairly tough ones, while others are consciously planned as easy trips. The degree of spontaneity also varies from one tour to the next, though a tour perceived as rigorously planned and regimented by one person may seem relaxed and casual to someone with different expectations.

The Touring Party

The most important single element of any bicycle tour is the group you are riding with, or the lack of it. A solo trip is a completely different experience from touring with other cyclists. The quality of any trip that you make with others is influenced more by your interactions with your companions than by the weather, traffic, or any other factor. It follows, therefore, that the most important single decision to be made in planning any bicycle tour is your choice of riding companions.

Go with people you like. Even a ride that is made miserable by heavy traffic, rain, and cold temperatures will linger pleasantly in your memory if you enjoy your companions. In fact, the bad days are one of the best reasons for riding with a group. Riding alone can be fun on the good days, but it is a lot easier to suffer through the ones that don't turn out so well if you have a friend with a good sense of humor along.

It is not usually a good idea to take a really long tour with people you don't know. On a tour of a thousand miles or more, you are guaranteed to have some rough times along with the smooth, and people who don't really get along can make each other's lives miserable. Try to get acquainted with your riding companions on weekend rides first. Then, if you don't enjoy one another's company, you can part amicably. After a very long tour together, people generally are either friends or enemies, with no neutral ground in between.

Touring companionships, however, are not really made in heaven, any more than marriages are. The primary ingredient in any successful tour has to be a mutual understanding of the general objectives and spirit of the trip. Even if you are riding with friends or lovers of long standing, things can go sour in a hurry if part of the group thinks the object of the trip is to sightsee at a leisurely pace while another contingent intends to *ride,* perhaps for twelve or fourteen hours a day. The situation is that much worse if there are major disparities in ability and experience: "Well, Mildred, you *knew* we were going to be riding a hundred miles a day, for crying out loud! You looked at the maps with me. So how come all you want to do now is sit around and complain about how sore your bottom is?" People of widely divergent ability and experience can tour together enjoyably, but only if everyone has roughly similar expectations and attitudes about the trip *in the context of their own capabilities*. The daily mileage covered may be tough for some members of the group, moderate for others, and very easy for still others. As long as people are prepared for the reality and are ready to enjoy it, a group whose abilities vary greatly can still have a good time.

People's expectations of a trip vary in many other ways. Attitudes about finances, accommodations, and meals need to be considered. Some cyclists prefer to stop at good restaurants for most of their meals. Others are content to buy some cottage cheese and fruit, either because they like to eat informally or because they can't afford to do anything else. A large group may split up for certain meals, but hard feelings can develop if one person feels pressed beyond his or her resources while another feels restricted.

Riders who have had a lot of outdoor experience are likely to feel far more comfortable camping in difficult conditions, even with minimal gear, than those who are less experienced. The members of the group should understand each other's background and attitudes. If there are people along who haven't done a lot of camping, it may be a good idea to spend a night at a motel and have a few meals in restaurants if the weather turns bad and morale starts to deteriorate.

The attitude of the group members is the most important factor in making a trip enjoyable. Keep your sense of humor, spend some time pedaling with the weaker riders in the group if you are among the stronger, and keep a rein on your temper in difficult situations. If you make it a point to enjoy your companions, you will like the tour, regardless of the scenery or the mileage you cover.

What Kind of Tour?

All the specifics of planning a tour depend on the overall concept you have of it. Planning and preparation vary quite a bit depending on whether you want to visit castles and museums in Germany or camp in Waterton-Glacier International Peace Park on the Canadian–United States border, and whether you envision riding forty miles a day or a hundred.

As suggested earlier, it is best to acquire some basic experience and conditioning on day tours before undertaking circuits of several weeks far from home. The transition also is easier if you make a lot of weekend trips before you undertake a long and elaborate journey. Tours with sag-wagons are an excellent means to gain experience; they permit a greater margin for error and more room for a diversity of experience and conditioning.

For people who lack a great deal of outdoor experience, the use of public accommodations is another good way to ease into long tours, since less equipment and weight need to be carried on the bike. It also is a psychological relief for many beginning tourists to be able to eat in a restaurant and sink into a normal bed after the day's activities. If you don't carry any camping gear, however, there is less freedom to stop whenever you get tired; thus more planning is required, especially if the group is not a strong one. Riding fifteen miles longer to the next motel may be inconsequential to a strong cyclist at four o'clock on a sunny afternoon, but it can be devastating to a weaker rider who is already tired and saddle sore from pedaling forty-five miles.

In considering the kind of tour you want to make, you must think about the circumstances in which you will be riding: terrain, type and condition of roads, availability of water, location of grocery stores, and both the probable and possible weather. You must decide whether to use a sag-wagon and, if so, what the arrangements need to be. Many questions need to be answered as your ideas for a tour begin to take shape. Where do you plan to spend your nights? Are reservations necessary if you are using public accommodations, and how soon do they need to be made? If transportation is required, how is it to be arranged? Do you need reservations for airline tickets? What are the possible complications in transporting your bike? You must begin planning well in advance for any tours that are long or require complicated arrangements.

Sag-Wagon Trips

Personally, I rarely go on trips with a sag-wagon. I prefer to be totally independent of the automobile on bicycle tours, and having a car along is aesthetically unappealing to me. However, there are a number of advantages to using a sag-wagon, not the least of which is that it can greatly simplify the planning of tours. You do not have to be nearly so careful in choosing equipment for camping trips or clothing on tours where you may want to dress up for eating in restaurants or for sightseeing. The sag-wagon provides support if someone's bike isn't in top shape. It adjusts for differences in the abilities of a group that varies widely in skills and conditioning. Beginners can go on trips with experienced riders without worrying about being a burden. People who haven't yet acquired specialized and expensive bicycle luggage and ultralight camping gear don't have to choose between pedaling overloaded and badly packed bikes and being ill-prepared for a cold, rainy night outdoors.

Of course, you can use a sag-wagon on virtually any tour. You can have one along whether you are camping or staying in fancy hotels, and whether you are riding in sparsely settled regions or in areas where there are quite a few towns. There seem to be two kinds of trips for which sag-wagons

are particularly useful, however. One is the highly
organized tour on which quite a few people may ride
who don't know each other at all. Clubs often
arrange such tours, and people from many parts of
the country may ride on them. Since the organizers
have no reasonable way to be sure of the competence, experience, and equipment of all the
participants, such tours can result in many headaches if they are self-contained. If one participant has an equipment malfunction for which
he or she is not prepared, the leaders may have to
go through all kinds of trouble to solve the problem,
inconveniencing the entire group. A sag-wagon
easily solves this sort of difficulty. A rider with
equipment problems or inadequate physical conditioning to handle the tour may even become
an asset rather than a liability if he or she takes
over as a willing driver of the sag-wagon. On such
highly organized tours with a sag-wagon, the cyclists also can ride farther and in greater comfort
since they don't have to carry touring gear on their
bikes. The loads are the same as on a normal day
tour.

A second type of trip for which sag-wagons are
particularly well suited is the loosely organized
tour among a group of friends. Here a certain
minimal level of competence is assumed, though
strength may vary widely. A rough trip plan can be
drawn up for a given weekend and arrangements
made to meet at a specific place and time on
Saturday morning. There is no need for elaborate
arrangements as to who is to bring what or for
long-term commitments on who is coming. Except
for setting up car pools to get to the start of the tour,
no real advance preparation is needed by the
group. People can come if things work out or skip
the tour if they don't, without creating problems

for anyone else. Sag-wagons are arranged at the
beginning of the ride on Saturday morning, with
everyone sharing driving responsibility. Here, too,
sag-wagons can help equalize abilities. If some
riders have more energy than they know what to do
with, they can always drive the cars twenty miles
ahead, ride back to the beginning, and then cycle
hard to catch up with the group. Later in the day,
weaker cyclists who might have felt reluctant to
come because of the stamina needed on a long
day's ride may quickly become the most popular
participants if they are willing to do more than
their share of driving.

Some friends of mine organized a fine version
of this sort of trip, a model for enjoyable tours
involving large numbers of cyclists with a
minimum of hassle. Every fall they send out a
xeroxed schedule of weekend jaunts billed as
"low-key, disorganized bike trips." The schedule
includes maps of the rides planned each weekend
for a period of a couple of months, together with a
definite meeting time and place for each trip and
phone numbers to call for those who need help with
car-pooling. It is sent out to all the friends of the
organizers who might be interested in the tours.
On some weekends there may be twenty riders and
on others seventy-five, but no elaborate planning
is required in any case. Some of the rides are
favorites that are repeated every year; others
are new routes that no one has tried before. A
campsite usually is chosen in advance, and some
indication is given as to the availability of restaurants, water, and so on. Those who wish to can
stay in motels, though everyone usually camps.
On some trips the touring party divides into those
who want to eat in restaurants and those who want
to cook in camp. On other tours the virtues of a

particular eatery are heralded in advance, and the place is taken over on Saturday night by a hoard of hungry cyclists. The availability of the sag-wagons simplifies the trip into town for eating and carousing, if that is the mood of the evening.

This sort of tour can be a superb introduction to multi-day trips for beginners, while still retaining attractions for experienced tourists. Large groups can be great fun on cycle tours. The pack spreads out and you usually ride with just a few people at a time, but you can ride with different people depending on your mood. The usual problem with large group trips is the trouble involved in organizing them. This type of trip is a lot of fun for everyone and doesn't require that any one person put out an inordinate amount of effort.

There are a few points to keep in mind when any sag-wagon trip is organized, both in the planning stages and during the ride itself. Some points are relevant to one type of trip and not to another, while others apply to all sag-wagon tours. By keeping these points in mind, you can manage to avoid a number of problems.

On highly organized trips with a large number of cyclists per sag-wagon, it is important to give people an idea of the amount of luggage that is reasonable. If one station wagon is carrying the gear of twenty people, everyone has to keep his or her duffel light and compact. If each participant shows up with an ice chest, a large tent, two suitcases, a lantern, and a stove, things are not going to work out. Even if they don't have an ideal selection of gear, bicyclists should be able to travel light, whether they are staying in motels or camping.

On carefully planned tours the driving of the sag-wagon should be arranged beforehand, too, and the participants should be informed, *in advance,* of their obligations and of what they can expect of the sag-wagon. Will it follow the last cyclist the entire way so that any rider can expect help in the event of any small mechanical problem, or is it to be primarily a luggage carrier that is available for support in case of serious problems only? In the latter case the sag-wagon might be driven ahead, perhaps from the lunch spot to the evening campground, whereupon the driver may ride back to meet the group or go out for a beer. The hard feelings harbored by someone left sitting at the side of the road with a disabled bike can be avoided by making everything crystal clear beforehand. Everyone should know whether the car can be expected within the half hour or will have to be driven back a couple of hours later.

There are many possible approaches to the way the sag-wagon should be used. Usually the choices are obvious and fairly arbitrary, but it is important to make the rules of the game clear from the beginning. The driver of the sag-wagon should know his or her responsibilities, and the cyclists should know what to expect. A person who has chosen to leave spare spokes in the car will be more philosophical about waiting two hours for help if he or she knows the sag-wagon isn't going to follow the riders all the way. If there is a misunder-standing about the arrangements, however, everyone can become unnecessarily annoyed.

It is important to decide lunch arrangements in advance. Are the lunches to be carried in the car or on the bikes? If carried in the car, is a lunch spot going to be set, whether the riders get there on time or not, or is the car going to be shuttled in such a way as to be sure it isn't too far ahead? Again, the specific decisions made are less important than everyone's understanding of them. A certain amount of friction is guaranteed if some hotshot, without checking with anyone, shuttles the car (with lunch) up to the top of the pass, and half the party doesn't make it until two or three in the afternoon. Rank beginners, of course, have to be counseled on such matters as taking enough food, not letting the sag-wagon get too far ahead when they may not be able to finish a stretch, and so on.

On some occasions a group may be lucky enough to have a volunteer sag-wagon driver who genuinely does not mind doing all the driving, but the job is not one that many people enjoy, and normally it should be shared. Doing a little of the driving can be pleasant; doing it all is extremely boring. Everyone should take a turn, and the slower riders should not be stuck with longer driving shifts unless they really want them.

Some precautions should be taken to be sure that no one is accidentally dropped behind the group and the sag-wagon. This can happen easily if someone gets a little behind or is passed while he or she is off the road for a few minutes. Subsequent mechanical or physical problems can then leave the straggler far to the rear of the group. You should have some method of checking, formal or informal, to ensure that you don't discover at suppertime that someone has been missing since mid-morning.

When sag-wagons are used on point-to-point trips with most of the cars left at the beginning of the ride, some thought should be given in advance to the mechanics of getting everyone back from the finish. A lot of driving may be saved if the cars used as sag-wagons are chosen carefully so that a maximum number of bikes and people can be stuffed in at the end of the ride. Otherwise it may be prudent to shuttle the remaining cars to the end point before starting the ride. Shuttling is less onerous early Saturday morning than late Sunday night. The shuttle sometimes can be done by faster riders in the group while the slower ones start off. The stronger cyclists then can work off a little steam catching up.

Self-Contained Tours

Though sag-wagons are handy and make certain types of enjoyable touring possible, they also get in the way of the primary experiences associated with bicycle touring. A long tour loses its continuity, becoming a series of short two-hour or half-day jaunts, and the trip becomes centered around the car rather than the bicycling. The special advantages of sag-wagon-supported trips make them worthwhile some of the time, but my own feeling is that the best touring is experienced on self-contained trips. The self-contained rider may camp or stop at motels, eat at picnic grounds or at restaurants, but whatever the style of the trip, everything needed is carried on the bike. The rhythm of the trip comes from the interaction between the cyclist and his or her surroundings: the little towns along the way, the wind, the hills, and the bends in the road.

A self-contained trip clearly requires more thorough planning than one supported by a sag-wagon. You must get out of the habit of taking something "because it might come in handy." Every ounce and pound on the bike should be functional because it all has to be pedaled over every hill and against every head wind that you encounter on the tour. If you forget to buy something for dinner and have to ride ten miles back into town, you won't be able to hop into the car to do it. This sort of approach isn't particularly inconvenient; it simply demands that you get into the habit of thinking as a touring cyclist rather than a motorist.

It is important to develop some kind of system to be sure you remember everything you need. Much bicycling gear is fairly specialized, and it is difficult to replace things on the spot if you forget them. One way to handle this problem is to make up a checklist of all the things you sometimes need when touring. Then each time you are preparing for a tour, you can go through the list, checking things off as you pack them or crossing them out if you decide you don't need them on that particular trip. I like to repack my panniers as soon as I have cleaned up after a tour and then hang a list on them of those items that have to be packed just before leaving, such as food and down-filled gear that I don't want to leave compressed in stuffsacks. Then, when I am getting ready for my next tour, I take out the items I don't need rather than having to round up the ones I do. When I go on a day trip, I simply get my tool kit and the other items I need from the panniers, carry them with me for the day, and put them back in the panniers when I get home. This way I can leave for a weekend tour on short notice without the risk of forgetting something essential. The list on the panniers also includes items that serve multiple purposes and that might be stuffed in a pack for a climbing, backpacking, or kayaking trip.

The items you carry must be carefully chosen for the conditions of a particular tour. On a desert trip with long stretches of highway between locations where water is available, you have to carry containers for extra water. I clamp additional bottle cages to the bike frame and also carry a large, collapsible container for camp use. For a ride in the mountains in the fall or spring, your clothing and sleeping bag must be warm enough to allow for the possibility of very cold weather. If you are planning to stop and visit museums while your bike stays outside, you may need to carry a good lock. There is an endless variety of special situations and needs because of the many different kinds of tours that are possible.

Specific items that you may need to carry are discussed in the preceding chapters—usually in the context of their suitability for different types of tours—and are summarized in the checklist at the end of the book. It should be emphasized once again that light weight is the key to enjoyable bicycle touring. The trick is to take everything you need and not an ounce more. Once you have pared down the weight, then you can concentrate on having items serve more than one purpose and on becoming more efficient so that you can carry even less weight with each succeeding trip you take. On any given tour, plan to satisfy a few special interests that require extra equipment rather than taking everything. Don't try to haul cameras, fishing gear, and binoculars along with bird, flower, tree, and geology guidebooks all on one tour.

Mapping Out the Tour

Planning tours shouldn't be a chore. Sitting down with a pile of maps and dreaming up new trips is one of the more pleasant ways to spend part of an evening. The amount of time required, of course, varies with the trip. With a little practice, weekend tours can be planned completely in a very short time, but longer tours far from home may take months of research, planning, letter-writing, and juggling of possible routes and schedules. This is as it should be, since half the pleasure of long tours is in the anticipation.

Before you start to map out a tour, particularly a long one, you need to have a precise idea of your capabilities and those of everyone else on the trip. The amount of ground that you plan to cover must be decided with the weakest member of the party in mind. Unless you want the trip to turn into a disaster, this means planning for the distance everyone can *enjoy* riding, not the distance the slower riders can survive before totally collapsing. If you aren't satisfied with that mileage, ride with other cyclists; don't try to push people beyond their capacities. Allowing your ambitions to override the ability of someone in the group is going to spoil the tour for everyone.

A rider who is in poorer physical condition than the rest of the group doesn't just have to ride more slowly and take more frequent rests. A weaker person also is not able to enjoy pushing as close to the fatigue point as a person in better shape. Thus, with a group of strong riders, you may find that everyone likes to ride hard for long days, day after day. You do not find this with a less powerful rider, whose capacity to recuperate after a hard day is not nearly as great.

In figuring mileages, it is important to allow for the fact that you will be touring day after day and are not simply out for a one-day push. A hundred miles a day on a tour requires a lot more effort than it does on a day trip. You also have to do your daily chores, get yourself fed and ready for bed in the evening, and off on the road in the morning. You are carrying a load, and if your bottom gets sore, you don't have a week to let it heal. Until you have a good feel for the exact mileage you can cover on the road during a tour of a particular length, you should probably figure on riding about half the distance that the weakest rider can manage on a local day tour.

You have to make additional allowances for bad weather and for exceptionally difficult riding conditions, such as mountain crossings, poor roads, and severe head winds. Most people taking day trips near home tend to ride on the good days and do something else when conditions aren't propitious. On a tour, however, you take the bad days with the good. On a weekend tour, you can be reasonably sure of the weather, but if you misjudge the riding conditions and the tour turns out to be hard, at least the difficulties only last two days, rather than dragging on for a week or more. You still should be careful not to push the slow people in the party too hard, however, if you want them to have a good time.

Pay some attention to the length of daylight during the period in which you will be riding. This can be particularly critical if you are planning a hard tour for a group of strong riders. If you are planning well in advance for an extended tour during the fall, it is easy to forget that the days will be much shorter then. Riding from dawn until dusk in early October will not get you nearly as far as it does in mid-June.

Consider special objectives and difficulties when planning your touring schedule. If you are going to stop and see the sights in an interesting town, you have to allow for time by subtracting from the day's mileage. If you have a section of dirt road to ride or if severe head winds can be expected, you must allow for them also. Examine the route carefully and try to anticipate delays. Very strong riders can ride mountain roads as fast as the flats, making up for the time lost in climbing with faster descents, but most cyclists slow down a lot in the mountains. Picking one's way through any large city or around it nearly always takes at least a couple of extra hours because of traffic lights, congestion, and wrong turns. The signs in all such areas are designed for automobiles, and a route suitable for cyclists can be very hard to locate. All the routes marked by signs are likely to lead to freeways closed to bike traffic, and many other possible routes may be blocked by them. Unless you are following a well-marked bicycle route, you are likely to have problems even if you have a good map or directions.

Maps, too, are drawn for motorists. The difficulty encountered in finding suitable maps depends on the tour and on the part of the country. It naturally is a lot easier to find maps for areas near your home. A good, up-to-date road map is the first requisite. Oil companies distribute maps that vary widely in detail and quality. Check each company's maps to determine which ones are relatively suitable. Most state highway departments send maps of their states free of charge to anyone who asks, and these usually are adequate for all the main highways in the state. Auto clubs also provide maps for their members, but these often are less detailed than those distributed by highway departments and gas stations. The situation varies with the club and the state, however; the AAA publishes some excellent local maps for different parts of California.

The greatest problem is finding maps with good coverage of secondary roads, which usually are the ones that the cyclist wants to use. If you want to head straight across the North American continent using Trans-Canada Route 1, you won't have much of a problem getting maps for the trip. However, if you want to tour on back roads, getting suitable maps can be quite difficult. State tourist bureaus sometimes can provide helpful maps, particularly if you describe your needs. If a particular bureau doesn't have them, ask for information about commercial map companies that publish maps of secondary roads in the state.

Sometimes you can obtain good maps of secondary roads in a particular area by writing to individual county governments, though this varies with each state. Some eastern states divide the responsibility for roads mainly between the state government and individual towns, so that it is not always possible to get road maps from counties. Another drawback is that on long tours a stack of county road maps quickly becomes unmanageable. Such maps can be useful in planning trips within a limited area, however, and in working out routing problems on long tours in which superhighways or natural obstacles make it difficult to link up two portions of a route. To obtain information from state agencies, either look up the addresses at your local library or write to the tourist bureau in care of the governor's office at the appropriate state capital.

Sometimes it is useful to have topographic maps covering all or part of a tour if you want to know how hilly a route is. In addition to showing roads, buildings, rivers, lakes, and high points of land, topographic maps show elevations with contour lines drawn along profiles of constant elevation. To determine how high the climb is up a pass, you simply count the number of contour lines crossed on the way up and multiply by the contour interval shown at the bottom of the map. (For more information see the backpacking references listed in Appendix V.)

Topographic maps issued by the United States

Geological Survey are available for the entire
United States. The ones familiar to wilderness
travelers are much too detailed and cover too little
ground for most cycling purposes, but topographic
maps of individual states and the 1:250,000-scale
maps can be used in conjunction with road maps to
answer specific questions. The 1:250,000-scale
maps each cover an area approximately 70 miles by
110 miles, a reasonably useful size. The manmade
features typically are quite out-of-date, so you have
to correlate the topo maps carefully with an
up-to-date road map. Index maps showing the topo
maps available for each state can be obtained free
of charge from the United States Geological Survey
(see Appendix V for addresses).

Once you have found decent maps covering
the roads you may want to take, you need a
convenient way to carry and use the maps while
riding. Most good handlebar bags include a waterproof map pocket, though seam sealer must be
used to fill stitching holes. A well-designed handlebar bag with map pocket is shown in Figure
43. A Zip-lock plastic bag taped to your carrier
or luggage also serves the purpose.

Two-Lane Roads
vs. Superhighways

In picking out the best bicycle route between two
points, you can tell a lot just from a good road map.
Old U.S. highways and primary state roads tend to
be narrower and to have less of a shoulder than
newer highways, but they can be excellent bike
routes if they don't carry too much traffic. In
general, if this type of road parallels a superhighway between two large towns, the traffic will
be concentrated on the superhighway. On the
other hand, these narrower roads can be quite

43. A well-designed handlebar bag with a waterproof map pocket. This particular model is made by Kirtland and includes a rack with prongs that slip into specially designed pockets on the sides of the bag, along with Velcro fasteners to help hold the bag on the rack. A compass can be handy on confusing back roads.

harrowing if they are the primary transportation corridors between good-sized towns; truck traffic on such roads poses the greatest threat to cyclists.

If you have time and want to make the effort to obtain and analyze them, state highway departments maintain figures for the relative concentration of traffic on the various highways of their states. You can write and ask for these figures. If you have to choose between two roads with heavy, high-speed traffic, a superhighway generally is less hazardous than an old, two-lane U.S. highway. The speed of the traffic doesn't vary a whit, and you are a lot safer on the wide shoulders of an interstate than on the often non-existent edges and narrow lanes of the older road.

The most dangerous superhighways are those with tunnels that have no place where bicycles can get out of the main lane of traffic. Also dangerous are freeways through urban areas that have frequent exits, entrances, and merging roads that are difficult to cross safely. Sections of interstates with many miles between exits generally are fairly safe, though they leave a good deal to be desired from an aesthetic point of view. Some of the older throughways in the northeastern United States also are much too narrow to be safely ridden on a bike, but the alternatives are not always any better.

From a practical point of view, one of the biggest problems with any of the superhighways is the legal one. According to federal regulations, the decision as to whether bicycles are allowed on interstates is up to the individual states. Most states opt for the easy, irrational solution of banning bicycles from the interstate system altogether, even in those cases in which the interstate has replaced the existing road and no alternative exists. This attitude has been modified somewhat by a number of court rulings that bicycles cannot be banned where there is no alternate route. What constitutes an alternate route then becomes a matter of interpretation. Since standard highway maps do not show legal routes for bicycles, much less safe ones, it often is difficult to figure out how to get from one place to another. Some of the worst problem areas are bridges over large bodies of water, especially along the eastern coast of the United States. Mountain passes in the West also frequently present problems. One solution is to write to the appropriate state highway patrol and ask what the legal bicycle route is between the points you are interested in. If interstates are involved, it may be a good idea to take any reply you receive with you. State police are not always consistent in their interpretations.

Most of the time, of course, it is best to avoid main highways as much as possible. Try to follow secondary roads, to cross large bodies of water by ferry whenever possible, and to follow roads over higher passes than the ones used by interstates. The length of the route between two points will be longer, but the touring will be more enjoyable.

Organizations and Clubs

Some fine routes have been carefully mapped out by cycling organizations, which publish maps and guides to particular tours. The best examples are the ones published by the Bikecentennial organization, which organized the transcontinental bicycle tour of the United States undertaken to celebrate the Bicentennial. The route worked out by Bikecentennial is longer than most, but takes a fine line across the country using secondary roads. The guidebooks and detailed maps for the 4250-mile trip are divided into five sets. Bikecentennial currently is producing similar guides for a number of other long routes. A portion of any of these routes naturally can be used for a shorter tour, with most of the planning already done for you.

Bicycling clubs are another good source of information when you are planning a tour far

from home. Writing to local clubs along the way
or to local members of the League of American
Wheelmen often is a good way to obtain information,
especially concerning problem portions of a tour.
The names and addresses of a number of bicycling
organizations are listed in Appendix IV.

Daily Mileages

Once you have planned out your basic route, divide
it into daily segments, figuring the appropriate
distance for each day. If you are planning a very
loosely organized trip, this may require only that
you make sure the mileage comports with your
abilities and that you develop an idea of how far
you have to go each day to be on schedule. On a
two-week trip, for example, you may plan to cover
an average of 50 miles a day and allow two days for
rest or bad weather, for a total of 600 miles. By
breaking the trip into 50-mile legs, you can keep
track of how well you are doing and make
adjustments along the way.

If you want to make specific stops each day,
you need to plan a little more carefully, making
allowances for particularly difficult stretches or
attractions that may take a lot of your time. On a
day when you plan to do a lot of sightseeing or to
climb several long passes, you have to plan either to
cover less mileage or make up the time by starting
early or finishing late.

Groups that have reservations for specific
dates at hotels, motels, or hostels also have to meet
a rigorous schedule, so they must plan mileages
carefully and make specific allowances for rest days.
Since they generally have to plan to move on regardless of the weather, such groups should figure
daily mileages conservatively to allow for difficulties. It is not enough to gauge the average
daily mileage correctly; if you have to be at a

certain place each night, you must be sure that you can manage each day's allotment. In this situatioɪ, it usually is best to plan on covering a little less distance each day and to start riding early so that you are sure of arriving at your destination. Any members of the group who haven't had enough riding at the end of each leg can always make some afternoon side trips.

For very long tours, unless you simply want to relax and take things as they come, it is best to map out the entire trip fairly thoroughly in advance. You can mail maps home as you finish various legs of the tour and periodically pick up new ones and other local information at resupply points along your route. (Resupply methods are discussed later in the chapter.)

Where to Sleep?

Public Accommodations

There are a number of ways to arrange for accommodations at hotels, motels, and the like, depending on your circumstances and preferences. With a very large group on a tightly planned schedule, it is mandatory to make firm reservations in advance. You can't depend on being able to find rooms if you roll into a small town one evening with fifty cyclists. It is a good idea to pay for your rooms in advance and to have itemized receipts from the hotels (not travel agents) so that you can be reasonably sure the rooms actually will be available. If you want your rooms saved no matter when you get in, make it clear that you will pay for them whether you show up or not. Motels and hotels take a lot of reservations from people who never arrive, and many have a reasonable policy of canceling the reservations of those people who don't check in by a certain time. In busy places and seasons, some hotels also use the more unsavory technique of overbooking, so that rooms may not be available even though they have been reserved. The precautionary measures just suggested should improve your chances of avoiding such a problem. If you do come up against this shady practice, however, make a scene. Don't be afraid to escalate the conflict to any point short of getting yourself thrown in jail; the noisiest victims get the remaining rooms in such situations, while those who are polite are left with nowhere to sleep.

Except in resort areas during the busiest season or in a town filled with conventioneers, a small group of cyclists usually can gamble on finding rooms as they go along. You should plan to be on the road early and to stop early if you want to be sure of finding space. This sort of riding schedule is the best one for bicyclists anyway, since it usually affords the best chance of avoiding afternoon winds and thundershowers.

The greatest advantage to picking your shelter as you go along is that it gives you the flexibility to rearrange your tour as you go. You can ride up a canyon road just to see where it leads or accept an overnight invitation from people you meet on the way. If you are caught up in the rhythm of the tour and feel like going past the planned stopping point, you aren't inhibited by room reservations. Finally, you usually pay less at small motels you come across that are not affiliated with chains.

The disadvantage, of course, is that you occasionally may run into difficulty finding a place to stay. In the rare instances that this does happen, however, you usually can camp or find someone who will take mercy on you and give you a place to bed down. Cyclists have found shelter in churches, jails, police stations, doctors' lounges in hospitals, fire stations, laundromats, and many private homes. People are extremely nice if you give them a chance. If you explain your situation, you'll be amazed at how often you'll be taken in. Encounters of this kind often turn out to be the most memorable events of your tour.

Hostels

Hostels often require reservations just as hotels do. Since they generally are closed from late morning until five o'clock in the evening, there is no way to check in or even to find out whether space is available unless you have an advance reservation. If you wait until the office opens, it already is rather late to start looking for something else if the hostel is full. For this reason, it usually is impractical to use hostels for a loosely planned trip unless you are equipped to camp as an alternative. Staying at hostels works out best when you know in advance which specific nights you need to use them.

Hostels are designed to provide dormitory-type accommodations at a reasonable price. A few have family rooms, but couples should plan to separate for the evening at most hostels. You are expected to help with a few chores. There may be meals available, and there may be cooking facilities where you can cook your own food. "Lights out" typically is at eleven. Hostels usually have hot showers, but not always enough hot water to supply them, and there are always safe places to store bikes. The clientele naturally is on the young side, though hostels are used by people of all ages. Be prepared to make allowances at hostels so that you won't be disappointed when things aren't perfect. The people who operate hostels are generally very dedicated, but they have to make do with limited resources and always have five times more work than can be accomplished by a single human being.

Hostels naturally are a good deal cheaper than motels, at least for a single cyclist. If you have a group of four to share a room, however, you may be able to do better at some motels than at hostels. Hostels can be alternated with commercial accommodations to gain some of the benefits of each. You can have enjoyable experiences at hostels if you use them with a relaxed attitude, being prepared for occasional inconveniences and foul-ups.

To stay at American Youth Hostels you must have either an individual or family membership card, which can be obtained at any hostel or by writing to the address listed in Appendix IV. You can buy directories of United States hostels from these same sources. Lists of affiliated hostels in other countries are available by mail and at some local hostels. United States family memberships are not valid abroad; each person must have an individual card. The directory lists the accommodations, facilities, and other information for each hostel. When you make reservations at any hostel, you should ask for a map or directions, if they are not included in the current handbook. The addresses listed for many hostels are mailing addresses, and they don't do a bit of good when you are riding around the rainy streets looking for the building. (This problem has been largely corrected in the current United States handbook but is still a problem in other countries.)

The original hostel rules called for all guests to arrive under their own power: on foot, by bike, etc. This rule is often ignored these days, and in Europe especially you may find yourself bumped by a busload of members of a club. To stay in hostels you are required to have a fabric sleeping sack that

substitutes for sheets, though sleeping bags are
sometimes allowed instead, particularly in Europe.

Camping

For some cycle tourists camping is the only way to
travel; for others it is an anathema. Still other
riders like to camp out most nights, but take a
break and stay at a motel every few nights to get in
out of the weather, do their laundry and take a
shower, or just to relax and experience a change of
pace. The cyclist equipped with camping gear
obviously has considerably more freedom of
movement than one who is dependent on public
accommodations. When camping, you don't have
to keep to a schedule determined by reservations or
stop at a particular town for fear all the rooms may
be taken by the time you reach the next one. There
is a great deal of freedom to stop when you want
to and to ride when you want to. If it is more
convenient to stop at a motel on a particular night,
you can do so. The disadvantages of camping trips
are the cost, weight, and wind resistance of the
equipment that must be carried.

   The primary planning for a camping trip
consists of choosing the right equipment, allocating
enough money for food, and mapping out the route
you want to travel. You can plan to use regular
campgrounds along the way or to camp wherever
you can find a place. The choice depends on your
attitude and the part of the country you tour.
Chapter 18 includes suggestions on finding campsites. If you expect to use public campgrounds,
you naturally need to map your route with that
in mind, using one of the many campground
guides sold at bookstores and newsstands and
available through automobile clubs. Either transfer the information to your map or tear out

the appropriate pages and take them along.
At commercial campgrounds you can make reservations, though for cycle tourists this rarely is essential. Campgrounds do fill up, however, especially in some parts of the country at the height of the season. If you want to be sure of a picnic table and a standard site, it is a good idea to stop early. Regulations at campsites operated by government agencies often prohibit camping except at marked sites to avoid overcrowding and damage to the surroundings. If you practice low-impact camping methods, however, carrying a stove for cooking and treading easily wherever you stay, you nearly always can find an inconspicuous spot to spend the night outside of regulated areas, leaving no evidence of your stay after you depart in the morning. This method is particularly suitable for hard-riding cyclists who ride most of the daylight hours. Naturally, you should not camp in restricted parks, national or state, where camping is regulated to prevent overuse. In some areas, such as Hawaii and places in California, heavy camping pressure has caused camping to be regulated everywhere, and advance campground reservations are needed.

Remember to consider the conditions in the region you want to tour at the time of year you plan to go. Shelter that is adequate for occasional rain in the Rocky Mountain region may not do for the heavy downpours of Ireland or Washington's Olympic peninsula. A sleeping bag that is comfortably warm for spring tours in the mid-Atlantic states may not keep you from lying awake shivering at the same time of year in the Canadian Rockies.

Experience is another important factor in planning equipment for a camping trip. If you already are a veteran backpacker, kayaker, or climber, you can probably get by with considerably less reserve gear than someone who has done only a little camping. There are dozens of little techniques that help the camper keep equipment dry, stay warm at night, and cook efficiently, and most are applicable to any style of lightweight travel. The beginner requires a larger margin for error.

Physical conditioning is also a factor. A cyclist who is in relatively poor shape needs warmer clothing and a warmer sleeping bag to stay comfortable at the end of the day because his or her energy reserves are often exhausted from the day's ride. Someone in better condition needs extra warmth much less frequently. The best way to learn your needs for warm clothing and the like is to take weekend trips and experiment. When planning equipment, try to make everything serve as many purposes as possible. Carrying a greater reserve of warm clothing should not add more than a couple of pounds to the panniers. The less experienced or weaker rider may need to carry more than the skilled tourist, but the difference should be less than five pounds.

For those inexperienced in cooking on bicycle trips, it is a good idea to write out a series of menus with associated shopping lists. You should do this at home, when you have plenty of time to figure out just what you need for particular meals and can work without the distraction of having to keep an eye on your bike. For the novice camp cook, it is altogether too easy to forget something essential at the store and to discover the error after reaching camp twenty miles down the road. Menus should be worked out to utilize foods that are readily available in convenient portions, so that you don't have to deal with leftovers. Don't develop a recipe, for example, that requires half a can of tuna or corn. On trips that may take you away from stores for several days at a time, prepare some menus using foods that don't add a lot of extra weight and bulk to your panniers. These are the days to use rice, spaghetti, Parmesan cheese, chipped beef, and other foods with little water content.

Of course, one advantage to bicycle touring is that you don't have to stick to menus, but having them available makes shopping easier. If you are on a budget, take this into account when devising menus. Don't forget to allow for the fact that small, low-volume stores along secondary roads are not known for their low prices. If you are touring with friends, you might agree to share the responsibility for cooking and menu preparation in advance. This way, no one person has to cook all the time and you can put together less expensive meals, since larger, more economical quantities can be purchased. Remember to bring larger pans than when you are touring with only one companion, though; cooking for four or six people requires a larger pot than for one or two. If four are cooking together, probably only one stove and two pots are necessary.

Money Matters

On any extended bike trip, you almost certainly are going to buy most of your food along the way, so unlike the backpacker or other wilderness traveler, you won't be escaping the world of monetary transactions. Be sure to take along enough money to travel in whatever style you plan to go. If you want to eat in restaurants on your tour and do not go out to eat much at home, be sure to take a look at prevailing prices before you project your expenses. With the current rate of inflation, anyone who hasn't eaten out in the last year is bound to get a nasty surprise upon inspecting the right-hand side of the menu. The same comments apply to hotels and motels. Be sure to make allowances if you are planning a tour in one of the more expensive parts of the country, particularly if you expect to eat in restaurants or stay in hotels in a city or resort area.

If you are going abroad, try to get a realistic idea of current prices at your destination. The best source of information is a friend who has recently toured the area you plan to visit, but you can obtain information from up-to-date travel guides, articles in travel magazines, and newspapers with extensive travel coverage. Just before leaving, you need to make further adjustments for changes in the rate of exchange between U.S. dollars and other currencies since the time you received your initial information. At the time this is being written, the dollar is losing value daily against Japanese and most European currencies. This situation, combined with the high cost of living in Japan and in many European countries, makes all purchases in those countries quite expensive. If you choose to camp most of the time and to shop in markets, you can travel fairly cheaply by bike, taking advantage of lowered air fares. If you plan to spend much time in hotels and restaurants, however, you will find your money disappearing fast in many foreign countries. Be sure to plan for this fact so that you don't run out of funds halfway through the trip.

Credit cards can be handy if you don't want to carry a lot of extra cash or travelers' checks. The credit cards can be a costly nuisance if you use them exclusively, however. A lot of small restaurants on secondary roads don't accept these cards and therefore don't charge as much as they would if they had to cover the fees levied on participating establishments by the credit-card companies. Food stores rarely accept them, and many bicycle shops don't either. Motels generally do, dependent as they are on salesmen who use company cards. A credit card is very useful if you want to call ahead for hotel or motel reservations, however, since you can pay for the rooms by giving your card number and thus make sure they are held. You should probably carry enough currency or travelers' checks to cover most of your needs, though, exclusive of motels and hotels.

Make sure you have some way of carrying your money, identification, credit cards, travelers' checks, and passport with you *at all times*. Take them with you whenever you leave your bike unattended, even for a few seconds. Some tourists carry these items and cameras in their handlebar bags, taking the bags with them whenever they leave their bikes, while others prefer to carry valuables in a secure pocket or somewhere else on their persons. Money, credit cards, and important papers should remain with you wherever you go, including stops at snack bars, rest rooms, grocery stores, etc. This is especially true of passports when you are abroad. It is a good idea to sew a pocket into your sleeping bag to keep these items safe at night. Unlikely as it may be for someone to steal from you while you are in camp or are momentarily away from your bike, taking precautions is easy and can prevent a lot of trouble.

Special Preparation for Long Trips

While there are as many styles of touring possible on long trips as on short ones, there are some special preparations and traveling techniques that can help you get the most out of any tours longer than ten days or two weeks. One important rule is to plan to start out slowly, whether you are trying to speed across the continent in a few weeks or are making a leisurely European museum tour. One cyclist's idea of a short day may be ten miles while another's is eighty or ninety, but it nearly always is best to work into the rhythm of your tour slowly. From a physical point of view, even those of us who do a lot of riding usually have to engage in activities other than cycling most of the time. Your body is not used to riding all day, every day, and it helps to build up the average mileage slowly, rather than finishing the first few days with a sore bottom and a generally overworked body. Psychologically, it is usually more enjoyable to relax during the first couple of days of a long tour, instead of pushing to your limits immediately and going stale before the trip has really begun.

Though I am a believer in traveling light on long rides as well as on short ones, most of us like to splurge and carry a few extra items on extensive tours. A few luxuries are worthwhile, and as long as you don't overdo things, the added weight may not be excessive. For trips lasting a month or two it is worth spending the money, if you can possibly afford it, for really light gear that is also comfortable. If you plan to spend six weeks touring Ireland, for example, a really light tent may be worth the extra cost rather than using a bivy sack, tarp, or tube tent. The weight is about the same, but the difference in comfort can be enormous. By trying to save the cost of a tent, you may end up spending a lot of expensive nights in hotels drying off.

On many long trips it is a good idea to plan on replacing certain items once or twice along the way. You may not need new tires, inner tubes, or brake blocks, but if you do, it is convenient to have them available rather than having to search around for them. The best method of replacing items is to ship things that you might need to a point along your route or have friends do so at specific times. Tires, for example, display enormous differences in durability. One brand may give good service one year but wear out quickly the next, so you can't be sure at the beginning of a trip how long a pair will last. Bad luck with punctures may also take its toll. In addition there are a number of other items that need to be replaced periodically. By having a series of packages waiting for you at specified points, you can simplify things, especially on a tour that bypasses large towns.

A typical resupply package might include a set of tires and tubes, a few spare spokes, a new paperback book, film, hand cleaner, soap, fuel for your stove (if you are using cartridges), Vaseline, a few first-aid supplies, suntan lotion, supplies for personal hygiene and grooming, spare cables, a new pair of shorts or chamois lining, seam sealer for your tent and raingear, batteries, spices and other condiments, maps and guidebooks for the next leg of the tour, and stationery. You also may want to include a clean, lubricated chain so that you can replace the one on your bike and ship it home for attention when you get back.

If you have friends along your route whom you plan to visit, the best resupply method is to ship your packages to these friends well in advance, requesting confirmation of their arrival. This way you *know* everything will be there when you arrive. Post office locations in most small communities in the United States and Canada can be used as convenient resupply points, but this method requires some care, the mails being what they are.

You simply ship the parcel to yourself in care of general delivery at whatever post office you want to receive it, or have a friend ship the package for you. You must pick a place that you can be fairly certain of reaching at a convenient time—during the week and during business hours. You must be sure that the package is shipped soon enough to reach the post office before you do, but that it doesn't get there too soon, as an unclaimed parcel will be returned to the sender after ten days. Have the package insured, and if you ship it yourself, carry the receipt. You must also show identification to pick up general-delivery mail.

It is a good idea to pack and open the packages in such a way that you can reseal them and send them back easily. If you include a return label and some tape in the packages, then you can use them to ship everything you no longer need back home. Mailing things home is a good way to get rid of items that turn out to be unnecessary and things that are required for only part of your trip, such as maps, guidebooks, or warm clothing for a mountain crossing.

Planning a Tour Abroad

For those who do not travel abroad regularly, probably the most important difference in trip planning is that you must begin your preparations much earlier. The least expensive transportation often requires booking and sometimes payment well in advance. You may find that there are major advantages in shifting your plans a few months, something you can't do if you haven't started planning soon enough.

Excellent maps of European countries are available, but it takes time to search them out, order them, and receive them. The same delays are bound to occur in making reservations, getting the guidebooks you want, and so on, unless you have a friend in the country you plan to visit who can help you out. You may want to learn another language before leaving, and you must begin doing so some time in advance.

If you need a passport, as you do except when traveling into Mexico or Canada, be sure to apply early. Waiting for a passport to arrive after everything else is set for you to go is not the most pleasant way to spend the final few days before your departure. If you are going to a country for which special immunizations are necessary, get these early too. You may have a reaction to the inoculations and feel ill for a day or two. Public-health doctors at your state health department are good sources of information concerning what shots are desirable for particular parts of the world.

Let your own interests guide you when choosing a place to visit on a foreign tour. The exploration of a culture and region different from your own is the important part of the experience, and you should go to a place that captures your imagination, not the country that is someone else's favorite. Once you have chosen your destination, however, it is important to do your groundwork early in the game, so that you can prepare realistically for the tour. Consult maps, travel guides, books about the country or region, and any other sources of information you can find. National tourist bureaus and the various transportation companies that serve an area can provide a tremendous amount of information. By starting early and writing to all the sources you can think of, it is easy to get the information you need. Inquire about cycling clubs in the country you want to visit; often they can provide a great deal of help.

Focus your trip on a small area. Don't try to see everything or to cover too much ground in one trip. The bicycle is an intimate vehicle, enabling you to become really familiar with places and people. It is well suited to traveling on the fine network of secondary roads lacing many countries and to viewing these countries close up. It also helps to break the barrier that normally exists between the resident and visitor. The best way to learn about another culture is to spend your time covering a small area, getting to know it well and becoming acquainted with some of the people. The bike is ideal for this sort of travel. If you try instead to rush from one place to another, covering the maximum ground possible, you will miss a lot of what you came to see in the first place. The temptation to try and see a lot of countries or a lot of places within a country is great, especially since foreign trips are far more costly than they used to be and most of us cannot afford to take them very often. Resist this siren, however; you can learn a lot more about Greece, England, or Guatemala by covering a few areas well than by experiencing bits and pieces of a great many places. Do your long, hard rides at home and take your time when you are away.

Europe is the most popular place for Americans to cycle abroad, except for neighboring Canada. Its culture, while diverse, is more familiar than that of many other parts of the world, and the visiting American doesn't have to deal with tremendous culture shock, poor roads, sanitation problems, and the like. Air fares have dropped to quite reasonable levels and are much cheaper than those to Asia or Latin America. Prices are high, however. The dollar is no longer king, and the days when visiting Americans had great buying power with modest sums of money are long gone. If you are frugal, however, traveling by bike still can enable you to get around fairly reasonably.

There are numerous travel guides and excellent maps available for European touring, and you should start out with these (see Appendix V). If you are unsuccessful in finding these publications, try writing to the airlines serving the country you plan to visit. Also write to that country's national tourist bureau, the address of which can be obtained from a guidebook, consular office, or the appropriate embassy in Washington, D.C. Many countries maintain at least one branch of their national tourist bureau in the United States.

Visiting developed countries outside Europe and North America is expensive because bargain air fares are hard to find and prices in these countries are high. Japan is particularly expensive, and you must carefully plan the finances of your trip so that you don't run short of money. As with travel anywhere, bicycle touring is the least expensive way to get around, but any time spent in public accommodations in large cities can drain your pocketbook rather quickly. Australia and New Zealand are not outrageously expensive, but getting to either place is costly.

Visiting less developed countries presents some of the most interesting and adventurous possibilities for the touring cyclist. The lower prices naturally are advantageous to someone on a budget, though transportation to most areas is likely to be expensive. Air fare to Latin America, for example, is quite high, and it remains to be seen whether competition among the airlines will result in lowering the cost of traveling to the Far East or South America. Air fare to Central America also is fairly high, though it is possible to use land transportation. Trains and buses in Mexico and parts of Central America are not very fast ways to travel, but they are unbelievably cheap. For the cyclist who has enough time, some very interesting and inexpensive trips can be arranged with the use of such ground transportation. If you consider taking an automobile past Mexico, you must leave a very high deposit on the car to ensure against its being sold without payment of duty.

The network of well-paved roads in most non-industrialized countries is usually far less extensive than it is in Europe or the United States. In many cases this is compensated for by the light traffic on them. If you plan to do any significant amount of riding on unpaved secondary roads, make sure that you adjust your choice of tires and rims to match. Extremely narrow and lightweight tires suffer a lot of punctures on gravel, and control is not good. The minimum width you should consider as a compromise is a 27-inch-by-1¼-inch tire with a beefy tread. Take spares no matter what type of tire you use, and don't count on being able to replace them or any other parts locally. For extensive riding on bad roads, steel rims and wider, heavier tires are best.

Buying a Bike Abroad

Since most decently made bikes are imported, it is tempting when you visit a country where fine bicycles are manufactured to try to arrange a purchase in conjunction with the trip. This method can work out quite well. If you have a bike waiting on your arrival, you can use it for your tour and then report it as a secondhand vehicle with a lower valuation when taking it through Customs into the United States. The bike's lower nominal value combined with your duty-free allowance may permit you to bring the bike into the country for little or no duty. If you also manage to get a good price on the bicycle, the arrangement works out very well indeed.

There are some serious pitfalls, however. You should expect to find good touring bikes that can be purchased off the shelf only in a few large cities in those countries where a lot of racing is done. Many European bike shops concentrate primarily on utility bicycles for commuting and shopping. You have to find a bike that suits your needs and fits you, and you have to get appropriate equipment changes and adjustments made. By the time you finish taking care of all this and waiting through the inevitable delays, you will have spent far more on lodging than you can possibly save on the bicycle. This sort of hassle is not most people's idea of a vacation, either, especially if time and money are limited. It is pretty hard to enjoy the city sights while you are wondering whether your entire trip will be spent waiting for your bike to be finished.

Another option is to have a custom bicycle made and waiting for you. This involves placing your order far in advance, but the savings and the bike may be well worth the effort if you are planning a European trip at least six months to a year ahead, so that the details and schedule can be worked out. You should make sure the bike is ready before you leave home and allow for extra time in the schedule you originally get from the builder, particularly if the frame is being con-structed to your measurements. I am sure that somewhere there are frame-builders who finish bikes when promised, but I haven't found anybody who actually knows one. Even if you make careful arrangements, however, you should plan on a few days' delay after you actually arrive. Unless you have ordered the racks you need as custom accessories for the bike, you should probably bring them with you, especially on the Continent. It may be impossible to find suitable ones on short notice; except in Britain, touring gear is less widely available in Europe than in the United States. Bring your old seat as well, since a long tour is no time to try out and break in a new one.

Because the pitfalls of buying a bike at your destination are many and can easily spoil your trip, I do not recommend it unless yours is a special situation: for instance, if you travel to an area frequently, know someone who has just had a good experience with a particular builder, or have an acquaintance in the country who is capable of handling things for you. Normally, though, the problems far outweigh the advantages. If you want to order a special bike, such as a tandem, while touring, it still may be best to take along a bike from the United States for your tour and have the new prize shipped home when it is ready.

If you do purchase a bike abroad, be sure to get a written receipt for possible use at Customs when you get home. There is no way to predict how much of an allowance United States Customs agents will make for wear and depreciation on the bike; they may make none at all. If you ride in rain and mud during the last few days of your tour, however, it might be prudent to put off the cleaning until after you have arrived home.

When traveling from the United States with a foreign-made bike, be sure to carry evidence that you brought the machine from home; otherwise you may be charged duty on re-entry.

Chapter 16

Getting to the Starting Point

OFTEN, THE GREATEST logistical problem of a
tour is arranging the transportation to and from
the beginning and end points. This is particularly
true of point-to-point tours, where you may finish
hundreds or even thousands of miles from the place
you started. Cherished weekend touring routes
are likely to be those that make a circuit ending
at or near the starting point, so that there is
no need for elaborate shuttling. Frequently, however, transportation needs are a major factor in
planning a tour. When deciding how to get a group
to the start of a tour and back home at the end,
conservation concerns and aesthetics also come into
play. It is rather hypocritical to be pious about
riding one's bike to work every day and then take
off for a drive of several hundred miles to a tour
each weekend.

The ideal way of getting to the beginning of a tour is by bike. I always have most enjoyed those tours that start and end at my doorstep, so that I don't have to worry about driving, taking the bus, or any of the irritations attendant on using other forms of transportation. Unfortunately, this method is not always feasible. In a society that caters to the automobile, it can be unpleasant, hazardous, illegal, or impossible to reach the beginning of a tour by riding your bike. Many people live in places where the only practical access routes out of town are superhighways on which bicycles are banned, while others find traffic dangers to be too much of a risk.

Public transportation can be an excellent way to get to or from a tour, if you can work out the logistics. It is unfortunate that very few buses, trains, and planes are set up for transporting bicycles, since a bike is so beautifully complementary to public transit. With a little perseverance, though, you can take your bike virtually anywhere. Some of the problems and techniques concerned with taking your bicycle on places, trains, and buses are discussed in this chapter.

You also can get to the start of a tour by car. With a full complement of passengers, even the automobile can be reasonably efficient. Automobile travel with bikes is simple once you have a rack to carry the bikes, and the rack itself is worth some attention.

Bike Racks

There are two basic types of racks made for carrying bikes on automobiles. One is designed to fit on the back of a car or the front of a van. It consists of some sort of frame that normally clamps to the bumper and includes a pair of hook-like bars that support the top tubes of one or two bikes, which are strapped to the rack in one fashion or another (see Figure 44). The other type of rack is mounted on the roof of the car, and the bikes are clamped to it in one of several ways so that they stick straight up in the air. Variations of both types are sold to fit on trunks, depending on the car model.

There are advantages and disadvantages to each type of rack, and the choice you make depends on your situation and on the automobile on which the rack is to be mounted. A convertible cannot take a roof rack, while bumper racks are difficult to mount on some cars. It also is very hard to fit a roof rack on a car without gutters at the sides of the roof.

In general, it is easier to load a bike on a bumper rack, especially for a short person with a tall car. On the other hand, bumper racks rarely can hold more than two bikes, and the cycles are

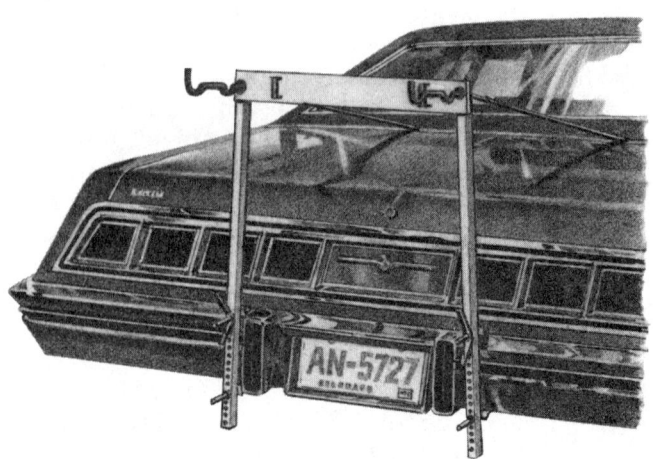

44. A bumper rack for carrying bicycles.

45. A typical commercially made roof rack.

more vulnerable to road grit and to damage in case of a minor accident. Furthermore, even though some bumper racks pivot, they can make access to the rear of the car difficult. Bumper racks have a lot of advantages for commuters, but if you plan to take three or more people in your car to the beginning of a tour, a roof rack is much more practical.

There are a number of commercially made roof racks available that have fixtures designed to hold bicycles (see Figure 45). Some of them also have accessory attachments for other uses. My own preference is for a cheaper, more versatile rack employing four cast aluminum brackets that are attached to the gutters and then bolted to a pair of two-by-four crossbeams. You can easily attach fittings to such a rack for skis, kayaks, canoes, and bicycles. The bicycle-carrying method that I like best is to remove the front wheels and either carry them in the car or attach them with shock cords to the bikes. A short length of aluminum channel is mounted on the edge of one of the two-by-fours for each bike with a length of threaded rod or an old axle running across it. Nuts on this axle are tightened on the fork ends so that the fork of the bike is clamped firmly to one crossbeam. An elastic band is used to hold the rear wheel on top of the other. If the bikes alternate back to front, six bikes can fit easily on the top of a small car, which is a big help when you are arranging shuttles. This type of rack is not quite as fast to use as some others, but it is very solid and is easy to make at home.

The most important feature of any roof rack is its attachment to the car. There are far too many racks made that are not strong enough. Racks that depend solely on hooks that pull against the gutters are not safe, either for bikes or for other users of the highway. Each support for the rack should have a sturdy leg that rests in the gutter and holds up the rack, with a hook that screws in from the side to hold the leg firmly in place. All the hardware should be very sturdy; wind and inertia can exert fairly large forces on a rack full of bikes.

When you drive a car with bicycles on the roof rack, it is important to take great care not to drive under low-hanging objects. This is easier to do than it might seem since we all drive largely by habit. Driving under a low carport roof or tree branch will not make you popular with the owners of the bikes on top of the car!

Air Travel

With the increasing number of air-fare bargains, air travel to the start of a major tour has become more practical even for less affluent bicycle tourists. It is fairly easy to take your bike on a plane, but there are a number of problems you should anticipate. Even though airlines are carrying more bikes all the time, they have not yet learned to deal with them as a matter of routine. If you call the same airline three times and talk to three clerks, you probably will be given three different stories about the regulations on carrying bicycles.

There are two theories concerning the best way to carry a bike on an airplane. The first is that it is best to package the bike in a protective box or bag to keep it from being damaged. The second is that if the bike is left uncovered, it is likely to be handled more carefully. Those advocating the latter theory contend that a baggage handler is less likely to pile a thousand pounds of air freight on your bike if he or she can see the beautiful paint job and the sparkling chrome—a deliberate act of vandalism would be required rather than merely an un-thinking slip. It used to be possible to persuade baggage clerks to let you wheel your uncrated bike out to the plane yourself, placing it gently in the baggage compartment. Security regulations established due to hijackings have eliminated this option altogether.

More and more airlines are requiring that bicycles be placed in cartons, and some of them actually provide the necessary boxes. There still are many experienced air-traveling cyclists who take their bikes without boxes and manage to have them accepted that way, even by airlines which theoretically require packaging. If you do plan to have your bike boxed, I suggest that you do it yourself if at all possible. It is a lot simpler to pack the bike beforehand, rather than trying to use a box supplied by the airline at the last minute. You can also do a lot better job of padding to ensure that your bike won't be damaged. However, if you are riding your bike to the airport, this approach may not be feasible unless you use a bike bag.

If you decide to pack the bike yourself, there are several alternatives. One is a bike bag, which is a large, nylon sack just the right size to accept a bicycle with the wheels removed and stuffed into padded side pockets. Such a bag probably gives as much protection as a box. It has less rigidity, but it isn't as likely to develop holes through which the bike can be scratched and is very fast to use. Best of all, it can be rolled up and tied to your carrier so that you can ride your bike to the airport, eliminating the need to worry about getting a ride or parking your car. I suggest that you make a block that can be bolted between the dropouts to prevent rear stays from being bent if anything is piled on top of the bike. The main disadvantage of a bike bag is that you have to find somewhere to store it at the other end of your plane ride, but on most trips this is quite easy. You can store the bag in a luggage room for a fee, or if you are staying part of the time at a hotel, you often can keep your bag there while you are off touring. Another disadvantage is that a bike bag costs quite a bit, even if you make it yourself.

A cheaper container that is even more rugged, compact in use, and easier to haul on buses and trains to and from the airport is a sturdy box like the one illustrated in Figure 46, made to the minimum dimensions necessary to hold a bike. The exact size depends on your bike frame. The inside

46. A carton specially made for packaging a bike to be carried on public transportation. A slightly larger box is used as a lid, and the two are strapped together with a nylon band that is worn over the shoulder.

height is 27 inches, just large enough to accept the wheels. When the cover is added, the outside height measures 27¾ inches. Mine is 41¾ inches long on the inside, just long enough to take my frame, and 42½ inches long on the outside. The depth is 9½ inches on the inside and 10 inches on the outside. Measure your bike carefully and then make a box just large enough to hold it; use heavy-duty, corrugated cardboard, preferably the kind that is treated to make it water-resistant. You can get large boxes from appliance stores that provide excellent raw material, or you can go to a local carton maker and either buy the material or have a container made to order. Make a box like the one illustrated and another just enough larger to be used as a cover.

Once you have made your box, puncture holes in it and pass nylon cords through to tie all the parts firmly in place, covering the chain with plastic and removing the right-hand crank with the chainwheels. If your handlebars are padded, you must pull the stem out instead of just loosening the stem bolt and turning the bar to the side. If you can fit one of your touring bags into the box, it provides extra padding. Strap the box closed or tie it tightly with parachute cord and attach a wide, nylon shoulder strap so that you can carry the bike comfortably over one shoulder while you hold the panniers in the opposite hand. (I first saw this type of arrangement suggested in an article by Jack Fields in the October 1973 issue of *Bicycling!* It has worked well for me.)

As with the bike bag, it is practical to use a semipermanent box such as this only if your circumstances allow you to store it somewhere while you are touring. Unlike the bike bag, you can't carry the box very conveniently if you ride your bike to the airport.

In circumstances that make storage impossible, you have to use a container that can be thrown away when you arrive at your destination. If you need a box that is disposable, you can pick up a bike carton at a local shop. I prefer this alternative to relying on the airlines to provide a box, since it permits me to pack my bike more carefully. The airlines often have a hard time just checking your baggage before the flight leaves without adding extra complications. When using a bike-shop box, buy a roll of reinforced tape to seal the carton effectively. I carry a long piece of nylon webbing to form a carrying harness and puncture two sets of holes through both sides of the carton so that the frame and wheels are supported directly by the webbing. The box is a lot easier to handle this way.

You usually have to pay an excess baggage fee on domestic flights because the bicycle is oversized according to current regulations. The largest size you are permitted to carry as luggage is 62 inches, adding the height, length, and thickness. It is impossible to fit a standard bike into a box this size and have it emerge in ridable condition. The excess baggage fee should not run more than ten to fifteen dollars, however. On international flights, the rules formerly required an excess baggage fee but this is no longer the case. Most clerks try to charge extra, but stand your ground. You don't have to pay the excess. If your trip is planned well in advance, it is a good idea to write the airline and ask for clarification of this point; then carry the reply with you for use at the check-in counter.

The major worry for the cycle tourist traveling by air is possible loss of the bike. With current security procedures at airports, it is usually impossible to make sure your bike is on the plane, though you can sometimes watch from the windows of the passenger waiting room and see the baggage being loaded. Unfortunately, by the time you are sure your bike has not been put on the plane, it is usually too late to do anything about it.

Some precautions can help reduce the likelihood of misrouting. Mark the container and bike with your name in several places. Get to the airport early so as to have plenty of time to check in. If you can book a direct flight, there is less chance of a mistake. Most misroutings seem to occur either with baggage coming in at the last minute or during changes from one plane to another. Precautionary measures do not always work, however.

The only time I have had my bike lost, I arrived at the airport two-and-a-half hours ahead of time and stood in line for two hours. Airlines are quite good about trying to get lost baggage to you once it has been found, so even a mistake in routing your bike is not always disastrous.

You should be aware of the fact that the airlines' liability for lost baggage does not begin to approach the value of a good touring bike, much less the cost of your trip if the loss of a bike ruins it. Travel insurance against such losses can be obtained through a travel agent and may be worthwhile.

Buses

Buses are wonderfully complementary to cycling because they travel to all sorts of interesting places from which you can begin bicycle tours. There are far more choices available than with airlines, and transportation to and from bus stations is far easier. Airports often are located on filled marshland with no access except by superhighways, tunnels, and bridges—none with bicycle access. Bus terminals are situated more conveniently, if not usually in the most genteel sections of town. On a bus, you don't have to worry as much about having your bike lost or having tons of freight dumped on it because you can take it to the luggage compartment yourself and keep an eye on things whenever the bus stops. Bus transportation is fairly inexpensive, though the major fare reductions have been on long-distance trips, which may not be the ones you want to take by bus.

Current regulations seem to call for excess baggage charges on bicycles carried on a bus, but representatives of both Trailways and Greyhound, the major United States bus companies, say that bicycles can be taken along as regular luggage at no extra charge. To protect your bike and other passengers' luggage, loosen the stem bolt and turn the handlebars around ninety degrees. Tighten the bolt again and fasten the handlebars to the frame with a shock cord or string. Either take the pedals off and put them in your panniers or screw them in from the insides of the cranks so that they don't project outward. If you reverse them, first pad them with newspaper and tape so that they can't mar the frame. Finally, wrap some newspaper around the chain, gears, and rear derailleur, tape the paper or tie it with string, and the bike is ready to go. With a little practice, the entire operation can be accomplished in a couple of minutes.

Buses are particularly useful in arranging point-to-point tours ending at your house, thus doubling the radius in which you can tour during a particular time period. You can take a bus to a stop several hundred miles away and ride home, avoiding a tiring drive at each end of a tour to place and pick up cars. It also isn't difficult to arrange weekend tours with bus transportation at both ends, enabling you to undertake weekend tours some distance from home with minimal trouble and expense.

Trains

Trains can be even better aids to the cycle tourist than buses, a fact that is clear from the ease with which one can mesh with them in many countries of the world. Europe provides an excellent example of how well train travel can be combined with bicycle touring. You can tour for a couple of days in one part of Europe, take your bicycle on a train (with no trouble) to another location, and resume your tour. This method also can be used to adjust your schedule if you find you have been too ambitious in your plans, have been caught by bad weather, or simply decide you want to spend more time in one spot than you had planned. You simply hop on a train and ride the number of miles necessary to get you back on schedule.

Unfortunately, train service in the United States has been allowed to deteriorate so much that in many parts of the country it has become nearly worthless, particularly in rural areas that are most likely to be of interest to the cyclist. You may still be able to work train travel into your trip, but doing so is more an act of faith in the concept of rail transportation than a practical expedient. Schedules are poor, trains run late, information is hard to obtain, and fares are frequently more expensive than either bus or plane fares. The number of communities served shrinks a little each month.

Regulations on the handling of bikes change from year to year, but at the time this is written cyclists are required to box their bikes on Amtrak trains and to pay a surcharge over the regular ticket price. Be sure to call in advance when planning a train trip, and write down the information you receive, including names and dates, in case of later problems. When you arrive at the station, do everything you can to ensure that the bike is actually put on the train. Amtrak is not nearly as efficient as the airlines in finding lost baggage or in delivering it once it has been found.

Chapter 17

Living on the Road

MOST TOURING TECHNIQUES have been
discussed in previous chapters, together with the
equipment you need to take with you. There are a
few aspects of longer tours that deserve special
consideration, however. Tours lasting more than two
or three days take on a different quality from day
trips and weekend tours. On a long tour you
actually live on the road, rather than taking off
from home for a day or a weekend, and your life
becomes more intimately entwined with your
style of travel and your experiences along the way
than it does on shorter rides. You find yourself far
more influenced by the mood of the trip, whether it is
good or bad.

Don't try to set any records on your first few
long trips. It is better to save your double-centuries
(200-mile days) for day trips close to home or for

weekend excursions, rather than squeezing them into long trips. On longer tours riding should be savored, along with the scenery, your companions, and the people you meet along the way. This doesn't mean that you can't cover a reasonable amount of ground, but if you keep the trip low-key you will enjoy it more. Racing to finish a specified mileage every day is a good way to cover spectacular distances, but it rarely results in memorable tours, at least not in the positive sense.

Special Riding Techniques

Spend some time warming up your muscles in the morning. Don't burn yourself out early in the day, particularly if you are in only moderately good condition. It takes a little while to get your circulation functioning efficiently, and your joints are not as well lubricated when you first start riding in the morning. It is best to start at a moderate pace with warm clothes on. It seems to be easier to hurt your knees or to strain a muscle if you start riding hard early in the morning or if your legs are chilled.

Long rests tend to convince your muscles that it is quitting time. It is better to take short breaks and then get back on the road, unless you want to do some sightseeing or really are finished for the day. On an easy day, of course, you can stop frequently and not worry about it, but on days when you are riding a long way, work into the rhythm of the ride and then try to keep it up.

Remember to keep up your cadence, but don't try to push too hard with each stroke. Especially on a long tour, you are likely to develop knee trouble from trying to push large gears. As the day rolls on and your legs get tired, there always is a tendency to slow your cadence and to make up for it by pushing harder. Don't.

Think about your technique occasionally. If you pay attention to moving your legs in circles rather than simply pushing down with the forward leg, you can make riding easier. It is amazing how easy afternoon riding can become if you begin to think about your pedaling technique and clean it up. The bike suddenly seems to be flying along again.

When riding with others, drafting can be a big help because it reduces the effort you must expend to cover a certain number of miles and speeds your pace (see pages 44–47). It isn't something you want to do all the time, however. You have to pay attention to your riding when you're drafting, and you aren't quite as free to look around at the scenery. It can be useful psychologically, though, when you feel you've seen enough corn fields for a while or when you're traveling through a seemingly endless sagebrush desert. Once you get into the rhythm of spinning out in front or drafting right behind a companion, the miles begin to speed by. Drafting also is a big help when you are fighting a head wind or are beginning to feel tired on a late-afternoon push into town or camp.

Riding out of the saddle for a few minutes every half hour ventilates your seat and allows the blood to circulate better to the pressure points where you sit. It also helps to reduce soreness over the pelvic bones during many days of riding and changes the stresses on your leg muscles, helping to prevent fatigue there. Don't spin too fast, though.

Aches, Pains, and Saddle Sores

Conditioning before the tour and properly breaking in your saddle are the best preventatives against saddle sores, but constant vigilance is needed.

Personal hygiene is critical to prevent infection of any chafing and bruises that occur. Wash thoroughly every night, and wash your shorts frequently, particularly if you are having trouble with sores. Vaseline helps to reduce abrasion, but it also traps bacteria next to the skin and prevents ventilation, so use it only as a last resort. Some people find that cornstarch reduces friction well while keeping the skin dry.

Changing shorts when one pair becomes soaked with sweat is helpful both for preventing sores and for treating those that already exist. Sewing a second chamois over the first or wearing two pairs of shorts, one over the other, also helps. Anything you can do to reduce friction is worthwhile. Sometimes when you develop painful sores in the course of a tour, switching saddles with a friend who has a different saddle style can change the pressure points and abrasion slightly and enable you to heal. As a last resort, a day or two off the bicycle often works wonders.

Irritation of the genitals in men is simply a matter of friction and usually is only sporadic. Vaseline is a big help. Numbness is caused by pressure against nerves in the crotch; tilting the saddle slightly forward often remedies this situation. Constant irritation of the genitals in women is due to their different pelvic structure and should be solved before a long tour. If saddles designed for women do not work, cut a hole the size of a half-dollar in a cheap nylon saddle at the point of irritation. If this saddle is comfortable, cover it with closed-cell foam and split leather glued down with contact cement.

Knee pain most commonly is the result of trying to push too large a gear. If this does not seem to be the problem and you do not wear shoes with cleats, these often can eliminate the difficulty. If you do wear cleats and have a pain or feel stress on the outside of the knee, try moving the cleat so that your shoes toe out *very slightly;* if you feel pain or stress on the inside of the knee, toe the shoes in a little bit.

Numbness in the soles of the feet is common after a day of cycling. The biggest help is to lift your feet slightly on the upstrokes so that you restore circulation with each rotation of the pedals. Cushioned insoles are also helpful.

Numbness in the hands is very common and is caused by the pressure of the handlebars against sensitive nerves in the hands. Well-padded handlebars (see Chapter 8) are the best solution. Cycling gloves and frequent changes in positioning the hands on the bars also help.

Numbness at the back of the shoulder blades usually is caused by longer periods on the bike than the rider is used to. It is not serious, and the remedy is to condition better before the tour, ride for shorter days, or grin and bear it. The same comments apply to assorted shoulder and neck pains. All this assumes that the bike fits. If your stem extension is too long, it can cause a lot of extra stress on your shoulders. Regular stretching and switching positions can relieve a lot of shoulder and neck aches.

Blisters on the feet should not occur if you have used your shoes on training rides. If they do, it is best not to break small ones. Use moleskin (an adhesive-backed felt available in drugstores) to surround the irritated area. Cut a hole the size of the blister in the center of a piece and apply the moleskin to the surrounding area. A better idea is to prevent blisters in the first place. If you feel any irritation on your foot, stop and take care of it immediately; otherwise you'll end up with a large blister that is much harder to manage.

Sunburn can ruin your tour, and if you are careless it is easy to get a bad one, particularly riding shirtless. Wear a jersey and a helmet or hat and make judicious use of a sunscreening lotion.

First Aid

It is my opinion that every cyclist who does much touring should take a first-aid course and carry a good first-aid kit. Since one is useless without the other, there is no point in going into detail concerning the first-aid kit here. You should construct your own. For the types of abrasions likely to be suffered from cycling spills, the treatment is to thoroughly cleanse the wound with soap and water. If there is grit embedded in the wound, this must be removed. The job is painful but necessary. I carry a fingernail brush for the purpose. Antiseptics are not really needed, but if you do use one, avoid the types with red dye or color, which mask the appearance of infection. Most wounds are best left exposed to the air, but if an abrasion occurs in a place that can be irritated by rubbing clothing, apply a clean, dry dressing. I carry a few large Telfa pads and a wide roll of gauze for this purpose.

Finally, if you carry any painkillers (or any other prescription medicines) in your first-aid kit (which is a good idea), it is wise to have copies of prescriptions for all of them. If you are crossing international borders, it is absolutely essential. Customs officials, especially United States Customs officials, can become completely irrational on the subject of drugs. Don't carry quantities beyond those that may be necessary for first aid. Those who engage in wilderness activities often have supplies designed for use in situations in which an evacuation may take a long time. Cyclists are never that far from civilization.

Heat Stroke and Exhaustion

Cyclists who maintain an adequate fluid intake rarely have problems with serious heat injury, but it can occur and you should learn to recognize the symptoms. The most dangerous condition is a combination of heat and humidity because humid air reduces the evaporation of sweat and therefore the cooling effect. The situation is made worse by a tail wind that neutralizes the breeze created by your forward motion. Direct sun makes you much hotter, particularly on your head.

Heat stroke is a breakdown of the body's cooling system. The victim's temperature rises rapidly and, if not lowered quickly, can cause death. Symptoms are a flushed face; hot, dry skin; a strong, rapid pulse; and sometimes unconsciousness. The victim's body temperature has to be lowered by the fastest available means, including water, undressing, shade, fanning, and ice. Once the person's temperature is back to normal, he or she should be taken to a hospital since the syndrome may recur.

Heat exhaustion is less serious, though it can turn into heat stroke. The victim of heat exhaustion feels tired, dizzy, and often disoriented. He or she may faint. The skin is pale and clammy, the temperature is normal or cool, and the pulse may be weak and fluttery. The victim is suffering from circulatory distress, so sit the person down in the shade before he or she falls down. Elevate the legs slightly and administer fluids when the person is conscious enough to take them. The heroic cooling measures used for heat stroke are not needed, but watch for signs of stroke.

Heat injuries are best avoided by keeping up your fluid intake and by beginning your hot-weather cycling in small doses until you have acclimatized to the heat. When you begin to feel the heat badly, find a shady place and sit down for a drink and a rest. Pay attention to the other members of your party in hot weather, and don't pressure the weaker riders to push beyond their limits. Watch for signs of heat distress among the tough guys; they often are the people who don't have the good sense to stop in time.

Chapter 18

Camping on the Tour

THE REAL DELIGHT of bicycle camping is that it frees you from worrying about finding a motel, getting to a hostel where you have a bed reserved, or discovering that your room reservation has been canceled by the time you reach your destination. Camping gear packed in your panniers guarantees that you always have a place to stay, at least once you have escaped heavily populated areas. It provides real freedom of the roads, especially in those parts of the country where motels are few and far between. You can ride until you feel like stopping, pick a campsite, and settle down for the night.

The most important ingredients for enjoyable touring are an adventurous spirit and an open mind, but next to these, minimal weight is the key. Choose your camping gear carefully and learn how to get along with the lightest gear that you can.

The trick to doing this is practice. If you have done a lot of backpacking or other lightweight camping, you won't have much trouble adjusting to cycle camping, except that you will want to trim down your gear a little more. For those who haven't done much camping, however, it makes sense to initiate yourself and your friends gently. Don't first attempt bicycle camping during a tour on which you are pedaling 150 miles a day. The weather probably will go along with the overambitious plans you have set and rain on you for good measure.

Try a few easy bicycle camping trips near home in the beginning, then work into the routines gradually. As your technique improves, you will be able to camp along the road luxuriously with a minimum of equipment. Though you always should try to keep your weight down, I don't recommend that you start with an absolute mini-mum. Anyone can get through an uncomfort-able night, at least in summer, with no equip-ment at all, and this may be appropriate for those who happen to enjoy spartan trips. The real art, however, lies in traveling *comfortably* with a minimum of equipment. Learn to cook enjoyable meals with a small stove and to stay dry with a tarp and a bivouac sack. For most people, the best method is to start out moderately. If there is a downpour your first night out, there is nothing wrong with getting a motel room. In fact, on long tours, one of the advantages of bicycle camping over many other forms of self-propelled travel is that you can take a break when you like, get a motel room, and take a hot shower.

Planning

One important difference between camping tours and those that rely on commercial accommodations is that you need to be better prepared. There are many important small items of equipment that can be forgotten, and unlike most standard touring gear, their absence won't be noticed until you get into camp. Also, if you are cooking in a campground some distance from the place you shop, you have to remember all the groceries. This is inherently more complicated until you get used to the routine than it is to just stop at motels and restaurants.

Checklists are particularly helpful for bicycle campers, both to prevent leaving anything behind and to help reduce weight. Work out the menus for meals before your trip, even if you revise them later, so that when you are shopping you can be sure to get everything you need. There are two ways you can use your checklists to reduce the weight of gear. The first is to mark the weight of each item beside its place on the list and then try to find ways to reduce the weight of each item. The second is to go through your checklist after you have returned from a tour to determine what you used and what you didn't so that you can eliminate some items on the next trip.

If you are going to stay at organized campgrounds, be sure to take along directions to get to the sites. Tearing out the relevant pages of a campground directory is one method. (See Appendix V for recommended directories.) Such campgrounds often are some distance off your route, and wrong turns can waste a lot of time. You also should keep in mind that popular state park, Forest Service, and national park campgrounds often are filled during the popular seasons. Check in advance to see whether reservations can be made and how long they will be held. It is much more difficult to find a camping place in some parks than it is along the superhighways.

Campsites

The desirable features of a campsite are fairly obvious. The most important requisite is a dry, flat, comfortable patch of ground on which to set up your shelter, either in an organized campground or in a spot that is secluded enough so that you aren't likely to be bothered. When bicycle touring I usually don't bother with conventional campgrounds. If you start looking early, it is amazing how many good campsites can be found along the highway.

It is best to avoid private land or make some attempt to locate the owner and obtain permission to camp. Farmers and other country people usually are very generous in allowing cyclists to camp on their property, but they do like to be asked. You might even end up being invited for dinner!

There is a surprising amount of wasted land, usually owned by the state, along the rights-of-way of many roads. You often can find an excellent spot just off the road that is concealed by a hill, a grove of trees, some bushes, or a dry wash. (Be careful of dry washes during thunderstorm season.) The possibilities are endless, and you will have little trouble finding them if you keep your eyes open. Don't wait until it is almost dark to start looking, though, if you want to find a good place. It is best to start riding early in the morning and stop well before dark, unless your objective is maximum mileage and you don't care where you sleep. Among the best prospects are areas along superhighways; these often have very large rights-of-way.

When you are near towns, maintain a low profile and try to avoid spots that are obvious hangouts. These usually are well marked by huge accumulations of beer cans. The most difficult places in which to find campsites are heavily populated areas where one suburb merges into the next. Try to plan your tour so that you don't get trapped in these places. If you do, you have to rely on your imagination (cemeteries, railroad or power-line rights-of-way?) or throw yourself on the mercy of a minister, the police, or a school janitor. You nearly always can find someone who will let you put up your tent or will give you a place to sleep. The limitations are more in our minds than they are real.

Around most of the pleasant places to tour, however, it is quite easy to find a campsite. The experience of bicycle camping is different from that of backpacking or canoeing on remote rivers. Pristine wilderness campsites naturally are rare, since you are riding the roads; yet peaceful farm country, friendly strangers, and little nooks thirty yards from the concrete can leave impressions as pleasant and as vivid in their own way as the wilderness can.

The weather and the equipment you carry also should be kept in mind when you are choosing a campsite. If your sleeping bag is barely warm enough for the temperatures you expect, try to find a place that is sheltered from the wind, particularly if you are sleeping without a tent. In hilly areas, canyon bottoms often harbor cold winds at night as cool air sinks down the hillsides. On the other hand, if insects are a problem, the breezier the spot the better. Sleeping under a clear sky is quite a bit colder and results in more condensation than sleeping under a tree or other shelter. This is because if you are in the open on a clear night, you radiate heat directly to the sky, which is very cold and returns little radiation. This can cause frost to accumulate on your bag even if air temperatures don't drop below freezing. If rain threatens, be sure the spot you choose has good drainage.

Try to clear a spot for your tent or sleeping space before dark, removing all the rough and sharp objects you can, both to protect your equipment and to ensure a good night's sleep. When you think you have everything smoothed out, lie down to test the spot. Sloping ground can bother you more than you think, but if it can't be avoided, set up your camp so that your head points uphill. Put up your shelter and lay out your bed first, especially if darkness is approaching. Other things are easier to accomplish without daylight. If you are cycling with a group, the chores can be divided, of course. Once your shelter is up, it is a good idea to lay out your sleeping bag and fluff it up, so that it regains its loft; leave it stuffed until bedtime only if the air is very damp.

In setting up your shelter, particularly in an organized campground, it is a good idea to try to incorporate your bike into the supports, particularly if you are not carrying a lock. The bike not only makes a good brace for your tarp or tent guyline, it is protected when used this way. If the bike is thoroughly tied into a line anchoring your tent a few feet from your head, it is extremely difficult for anyone to make off with it without waking you. With a tarp, as shown in Figure 47, it often is possible to keep the bike protected from the elements at the same time.

Cooking

Cooking in camp really is no harder than cooking at home. Simple meals should be planned, but it is pretty difficult to make supper taste bad to anyone who has been riding hard all day. Meal possibilities

47. A tarp can be used to create a shelter, with the tourist's bike serving as a support.

are limited chiefly by your imagination. Because you usually are within an hour or two of a grocery store, you can include a lot of fresh foods or nearly anything else you want, rather than relying heavily on dehydrated foods as most backpackers do. I like to eat a lot of fresh vegetables and salads on bicycle tours, but you can satisfy your own taste. Since cyclists tend to be somewhat dehydrated after a day of riding, soup almost always is welcome, and it is easy to put on a pot of soup for the first course when you first get to camp. The soup will be ready to eat by the time everyone has finished unpacking and setting up camp. Packaged or canned soups take very little time to cook, so they are handy to revive flagging spirits after a long ride. If you want to dress up a packaged soup, a few fresh vegetables tossed into the pot makes it very tasty. Some foods, such as celery, do not have to cook completely; they taste fine at almost any stage.

The camp stoves and lightweight pots carried by bicycle campers are best suited for frying or boiling such dishes as soups, stews, and moist, casserole-type meals. Recipes that require lengthy cooking burn too easily and should be avoided. There are many cold foods that also taste fine on bike trips, including salads, cottage cheese and fruit, and combinations of breads, cheeses, and cold meats. If you want to cook thick cuts of meat in a thin pan, the best way is to begin cooking the meat with a little water in a covered pan and then take off the cover, add oil, and brown the meat.

Tortillas make fine meals on a bicycle tour. Buy a package of ready-made tortillas at a grocery store, along with butter, cheese, sauce, and some vegetables, such as lettuce, bean sprouts, avocados, spinach, or whatever suits your fancy. To fry a tortilla, put some butter or oil in a pan, add the tortilla, cover with vegetables, and top with thinly sliced cheese. Cover the pan for a couple of minutes while the cheese melts and then serve, adding sauce to satisfy individual tastes. Members of the group can take turns cooking tortillas and eating them.

Hamburgers, hash, and similar dishes can be cooked just as easily over a camp stove as at home. So can Chinese-style, quick-fried vegetable dishes, either with or without meat. To serve these with rice using only one stove, slice the vegetables before you start cooking. Cook the rice first, set it aside in covered bowls, and quickly stir-fry the vegetables lightly with a little oil. Top the rice with the vegetables and serve with soy sauce. If you want meat, stir-fry a little ground beef just before adding the vegetables. If you like brown rice, the quick-cooking kind is fairly good and takes about as long to cook as regular white rice.

Most egg dishes make good suppers for bicycle camping, including scrambled eggs and all sorts of omelets. These also can be prepared for breakfast, of course, if you don't mind full-scale dishwashing before starting off in the morning. I prefer to have simple breakfasts, heating water for beverages and perhaps for instant hot cereal, but avoiding any real cooking. Granola and Grape Nuts cereals with fruit and milk also make good breakfasts.

It is best to shop so that all the items that are difficult to carry are used up at supper and breakfast. There is no sense in having a pint of milk or half a can of fruit cocktail left over when it is time to pack. Whenever there are fairly frequent stores along the route, I try to plan well enough so that I carry food only from the last store to the evening's camp, with nothing left over when I start off after breakfast the next morning except a little trash to be thrown in the first rubbish can I find. It is not hard to manage this with a little fore-thought, though the solo cyclist may have to use some of the same foods at supper and breakfast, perhaps eating half a can of fruit for dessert and the other half the next morning.

Cyclists can eat pretty much what they want on the road, but it is a good idea to emphasize carbohydrates, which provide the most readily available fuel for working muscles. The normal stores of glycogen in the muscles have to be replaced after a day of hard work if you want to have as much energy the next day, and this is done with carbohydrates. This is the reason cyclists often have a craving for sugary junk foods. It is better to keep these foods to a reasonable level, however, emphasizing fruits, vegetables, and complex starches such as those from grains and pasta, rather than loading up with refined sugar. Though athletes can do without added salt, people whose bodies are used to adding salt to their food will lose a lot of salt from sweating when cycling in hot weather and need to replace it at night. Soups and bouillon are good for replacing both the fluid and salt lost in perspiration. If you include a variety of fresh foods in your diet, you won't have any problems with vitamin deficiencies. And despite the old mythology of the football training table, people don't need extra protein simply because they are doing hard exercise. Most Americans, in fact, don't need nearly as much protein as they get.

Water

One disadvantage of makeshift campsites is that there is usually no water available, certainly no drinking water. It has to be assumed that any water close enough to the roads to be found at a bicyclist's camping place is contaminated. In the mountains, where you are camping above most of the polluters, you usually can assume that the water is contaminated only biologically and can be made safe by boiling or by chemical means. On most cycling trips, however, the water you come across is likely to be far enough downstream that you have to take into account the possibility of major agricultural or industrial pollution. Using such water can be very dangerous, with or without treatment, and it is better to carry your water to camp with you. If there is a stream, you can dip water out for washing clothes or your body. You can also use it for washing dishes as long as you rinse them afterward with safe water. You should not use water for drinking or cooking in places where it might contain fertilizers, pesticides, or industrial wastes. Carry any wash water well away from the stream or lake before using it so that you don't get soap and food particles into the source; don't be a polluter yourself.

Carrying water is a nuisance, of course, so look for a campsite that isn't too far from a water tap. In some cases you may want to find a campsite first and then have a couple of people ride into town to shop and pick up water. The advantage of this procedure is that it permits you to unpack first and to go for groceries and water with empty panniers. The disadvantage is that you won't want to travel too far to a store and water source unless you've had an easy day, since the riders going for food and water have to ride double the distance to these places after reaching camp. In most places, however, there are enough gas stations and farmhouses where you can obtain water so that finding some is not too much of a problem.

Sanitation

Washing in camp is no real problem. When supper is finished, perhaps after some hot drinks, heat a pot of water and wash the dishes. It is best to use an all-purpose soap that is easily biodegradable and to wash with it far from all water sources. Rinse the dishes well to remove all traces of soap. Grease and small fragments of food can be poured into a shallow hole and covered. Don't generate large amounts of garbage, though, since this attracts animals to dig it up. You can avoid the problem with careful planning; prepare only what you can eat. Carry all trash to the closest available receptacle. Don't litter or bury cans, jars, plastic, or foil. Never dump trash into outhouse holding tanks; it clogs pumping equipment.

Water also can be heated for personal washing and for clothes, if necessary, though it usually is easiest to stop occasionally at a laundromat to do your laundry. Commercially operated campgrounds and truck stops generally have showers that you can use for a modest fee.

If no toilets or outhouses are available where you camp, find a place that is well away from any water sources or spots that others might choose as campsites. Dig a hole between six and twelve inches deep (no more than six in the mountains) and bury your waste. Feces won't decompose as rapidly in deeper holes because bacteria are most active in the upper soil. Carry matches or a cigarette lighter with you to burn your toilet paper.

Insect Pests

Biting insects can make the camper's life miserable, though they are a lot easier to deal with than they used to be. When insects are particularly troublesome, put on your long clothing as soon as you stop for the night. Short, tight bicycle clothes leave far too much skin exposed.

Modern repellents work fairly well to discourage most biting bugs. Get one of the concentrated types with a large percentage of N, N-Diethyl-meta-toluamide, the most effective active ingredient. Smear repellent generously on exposed skin, avoiding your lips and eyes. Cyclists generally have fewer problems than other self-propelled travelers during the day because the breeze they generate while riding keeps most bugs away. Repellent can be used to deal with bothersome situations at other times.

If you have a tent with netting over the doors and vents or a bivy sack with netting over the face hole, they will provide adequate protection once you have finished cooking. If you are traveling in bad insect country with a shelter that has no netting, you can either rely on repellent to protect exposed skin or carry a mosquito bar, a large piece of netting you can use to cover the opening of your bag. Be sure to hold it away from your skin with a cord, pole, or pannier.

Close the netting or put on repellent before you go to sleep if the bugs are biting. When they are only moderately annoying, you sometimes can fool yourself into thinking there will be no problem, only to awake later covered with itching bites. By then your night's sleep may be ruined. Repellent only helps against the insects that haven't yet made a meal of you.

In the worst infestations, repellents and mosquito bars help, but only a philosophical attitude will help you come through the ordeal in marginally good humor.

Animal Hazards

Most animals larger than a horsefly cause little problem for the cyclist. Although you should be careful to look before reaching under rocks or logs in areas with poisonous snakes, both a snake's propensity to bite and the danger of bites to healthy adults are greatly exaggerated. Far more people die of bee stings every year in the United States than from the venom of poisonous snakes. The tarantulas found in this country are harmless. In the desert, I always follow the prescribed ritual of shaking out my clothes and shoes before putting them on in the morning, but I've never yet found a scorpion in them.

The only poisonous spiders found in the United States are the black widow, which has a shiny black and hairless body ¼ to ½ inch long and a red or orange mark on the bottom of its abdomen; and the brown recluse, about the same size. The brown recluse is shaped something like a violin, giving rise to another name, the "fiddleback." Its bite is less serious than that of the black widow, though a few children have died from it. Black widows are most frequently found in dark sheds, crawl spaces of houses, and rock crannies. They are timid and rarely bite if retreat is possible. Deaths are rare, but medical attention should be sought as soon as possible in the event of a bite. The victim should be kept quiet.

Some larger animals can be a nuisance, particularly in heavily used campgrounds. Food left out in such places is likely to become a meal for local rodents or raccoons. Bears are less common, but potentially more dangerous, scavengers, though they rarely are seen near roads in the lower forty-eight states, except in national parks. Bears in these parks can be dangerous because they are used to people and are not frightened of them. The only way for cyclists to foil them is to hang food from a length of strong cord tossed over a high tree branch. The bag must hang well below the branch, and in places like Yosemite and Yellowstone two separate lines should be used, since the bears have learned to break one.

Do not eat in your tent in bear country, and never store food in the tent at night. You should clean your equipment carefully if you spill food on it. A smelly tent or sleeping bag may attract bears, and a mouse is likely to eat away parts of a pannier on which butter has melted. Avoid smelly food and cosmetics in parks, such as Yellowstone, that are known for bears. Such foods as peanut butter, bacon, and sardines attract bears; if you carry them, at least hang the food away from camp at night.

Bears can be particularly dangerous when you are riding along the road. So many tourists have fed bears along some park roads that the bears aggressively demand handouts. Automobile drivers are not threatened by the begging bears, but such contact is altogether too intimate for cyclists. If you see a bear ahead on the road, wait for a car and ask the driver to run interference for you.

Be particularly careful in the northern parts of the United States, western Canada, and Alaska in parks where there are grizzly bears. Grizzlies are shier than the more common black bear, but they are far more aggressive and dangerous when they do encounter people. Keep food at least 100 feet from your tent in grizzly country, don't camp on game trails, and don't approach bears. Be particularly cautious of a sow with cubs. (There is always a sow near any cubs, whether you see her or not.)

Living Out of Your Panniers

Bicycle camping is a lot easier if you are as systematic as possible in packing your clothes and equipment. When all the cooking items are packed together it is much easier to start the meal. Knowing the exact location of the stakes for the tent is a definite advantage when you have to pitch camp in the rain, since you won't have to take out everything else in the downpour while you look for them. Develop a routine method of packing and stay with it. Segregating clothing and equipment in a number of plastic bags or stuffsacks helps to keep things dry and organized. You can color-code the bags or mark them with a permanent marker. It is best if the bags are made from a fairly lightweight fabric since the ounces can add up, but a few bags definitely are worth the weight.

It is important to keep everything as dry as possible so that you still have comfortable clothing and sleeping gear if you are caught in the rain. If you spend a wet night and have to pack up the next morning in a drizzle, get everything out and dry it at lunchtime if the weather becomes sunny. It may rain again that night, and it is worth the effort to make sure your equipment is dry. Especially avoid

getting your sleeping bag wet. If, despite your best
efforts, your gear does get sodden, you may want
to stop at a laundromat to dry everything. Even
down sleeping bags can be dried this way. Use the
low heat setting for any nylon gear and for sleeping
bags. Another solution is to spend the night in a
motel to get dried out and cleaned up. This is a
welcome relief after a couple of days of riding and
camping in the rain.

Be sure to put things away and tidy up before
going to bed at night. If it starts to rain in the
middle of the night, the clothing you left around
will be thoroughly soaked just when you need it. In
the rush to start off on a dreary morning it is easy
to lose small pieces of equipment that you left lying
around camp.

On cold nights use extra clothing to help you
keep warm. Ideally, everything you carry on a
bicycle camping trip should serve as many purposes as possible. One of the functions of an extra
sweater and a pile or down jacket is to add insulation to your bag on a cold night. Wrap a sweater
around your feet to help keep them warm, and wear
your hat to bed to reduce the large amount of heat
you can lose from your head.

Most of the tricks to bike camping are a
matter of common sense and practice. Since bicycle
camping is done on the periphery of civilization
rather than in the wilderness, it is an ideal way to
learn the techniques of lightweight camping. Most
important, however, it gives you the key to the most
interesting means of seeing the country and the
rest of the world. You can take your bike and
lightweight camping gear almost anywhere, from
Alaska's Panhandle to Central Park in New York,
or from the English lake country to rural Bulgaria.

The vehicle you ride permits you to have tremendous freedom of the roads, as well as providing an ideal means of breaking the ice in any country in the world. Good bicycling!

Appendices

Appendix I

Learning to Ride

IF YOU HAVE never ridden a bike at all, it is best to start without the additional complications posed by multiple gear-shift levers, toe clips, and the other paraphernalia of the touring bike. You should try to learn on a bicycle that is simpler and less vulnerable to abuse. An adult's one- or three-speed bike is fine, but many medium-to-large-sized children's bikes are even better. You probably can borrow or rent a suitable bike for a day or two. If not, chances are you can buy something secondhand for about fifteen dollars to serve your purpose. You should be able to ride before you shop for an expensive touring bike, both to aid in judging the bike's quality and to permit you to learn how to ride it without having a wreck in the process.

You should be able to straddle your learning bike easily, so a bike that is a little small for you is perfect. If possible, adjust the seat height so that you can sit on the bike with both feet on the ground (see Figure 48). Don't try to learn with a bike that is much too big—it's a long way down to the ground, farther than it is for a six-year-old. A girl's bike with no top tube is perfect, as are children's bikes with long enough seat posts and handlebar extensions so that you can raise them nearly to the

48. When learning to ride, use a bike on which you can adjust the seat low enough so that both your feet reach the ground.

height of your crotch. In a pinch, any bike can
do, providing you can straddle it and raise the seat
and handlebars enough so that your knees won't hit.
If you have to use a bike your own size, lower the
seat as far as it can go.

For your first practice rides, find a large
expanse of relatively empty pavement with a little
slope to it. Empty parking lots, schoolyards, and
streets with no traffic are best. After adjusting the
seat so that you can straddle it and still put both
feet on the ground, push off and coast slowly,
dragging your feet when you need to keep from
going too fast. It takes some practice to get the
knack of turning the handlebars and making
delicate balance adjustments to keep the vehicle
from falling over. Keep working at it until you can
keep your balance easily; then practice pedaling,
braking, and making turns. To progress further,
try to get hold of a bike that at least comes close to
fitting you, though it is not important what type of
bike it is.

Improving Your Riding Skills

Most riders, even those who bicycle fairly regularly,
can improve their skills significantly by spending
a few hours on a large expanse of traffic-free
pavement practicing maneuvering at various
speeds, braking, riding in a straight line, looking
around, and making hand signals without
deviating from the intended course. Paper or plastic
cups make good markers for obstacle courses.
Beginners should start with a bike that is easy to
handle. More experienced riders can use a touring
bike, complete with attached toe clips. After you
have acquired a ten-speed, return to your practice
area and go through the same routines, including
gear shifting and practicing with caliper brakes,
to familiarize yourself with the new bike.

Riding in an almost perfectly straight line is a basic cycling skill. There are many situations in which the rider has to keep the bicycle within a small lane at the side of the road for safety. Weaving can carry you into the path of a car that does not anticipate your swerving, so it is mandatory that you be able to keep your bike going straight. The same skill is important when drafting. Perhaps most important, the ability to maintain your course in this way is a good measure of your efficiency and control of the bicycle. To improve this skill, practice riding along painted shoulder lines on a road or on a line in a parking lot. You should be able to stay on a line that is only a few inches wide, even when you are shifting, braking, signaling with one hand, or looking over your shoulder momentarily.

Make obstacle courses to steer through and practice stopping at predetermined points from different speeds. If you have a friend who also is learning to ride or planning to start touring, practice following each other at close distances through obstacle courses and on straight roads. Riding in a group is much more efficient if the riders follow one another closely to reduce air drag. This can be done safely, however, only if the riders have the skill to follow each other closely without colliding, even in the event of an unexpected swerve or stop. Practice is important, so try a few exercises in which the lead rider brakes without warning to develop your ability to deal with unannounced stops.

Learning to Ride
a Touring Bike

If you have never ridden a derailleur-equipped bicycle with dropped handlebars, caliper hand brakes, and toe clips, you may find it unnerving at

first. Make sure that the bike you are learning on
fits you reasonably well, that the seat, brake
levers, and handlebars are in approximately the
right positions, and that brakes and gear controls
are correctly adjusted. If the bike is equipped with
toe clips, remove them until you are comfortable
with the rest of the equipment. Toe clips are an
extra complication you don't need at first. It is not
necessary to have a fancy touring machine to start
learning; if you can borrow or rent a cheap ten-
speed, it is adequate for your first few practice
sessions. Using one of these bikes also enables you
to appreciate a better-quality bike when you
experience it.

Before you ride the ten-speed, spend a little
time familiarizing yourself with it. Hang the bike
by its seat from some overhead support and turn
the pedals, working the gears until you understand
what they do. One of the gear-shift levers operates
the front derailleur, moving the chain back and
forth between the two large gears in front, which
are called the chainwheels. The larger front gear
pushes more links of the chain through for each
turn of the pedals, making the bike go faster but
requiring more effort—a higher gear.

The other lever operates the more complicated
derailleur at the rear of the bike, which functions
both to move the chain back and forth on the rear
cluster of gears and to take up the slack in the
chain that remains when the smaller gears are used.
The cluster of gears at the back of the bike is
attached to the rear wheel with a ratchet device
called the freewheel. The ratchet allows the wheel
to spin forward freely with a little clicking sound
(that's the ratchet) so that you can coast without
having to turn the pedals, but it catches when it is
turned the other way so that you can drive the

wheel forward with the pedals. The largest gear in
the back requires more chain—and therefore
more pedaling—to turn it and the attached wheel
around. It is therefore the lowest gear, just the
reverse of the chainwheel in front. The smallest gear
in the cluster, the one on the outside, is the high
gear.

Combinations of the two chainwheels and the
five gears in the cluster give a total of ten possible
gears, though usually not all of them are used.
With the proper choice of gears, the cyclist is able to
pedal the bike either at high speeds on the flats
and downhill or at low speeds up steep hills or
against the wind. The system is wonderfully
versatile once you learn how to use it.

When you shift the gears with the bike off the
floor, note which way the levers have to be moved to
shift up and down. The right-hand lever normally
controls the rear derailleur, and the forward
position usually allows the spring mechanism to
shift the chain to the highest gear. Different front
derailleurs work in opposite directions.

Since the shifting mechanism actually pushes
the chain from one gear to the next, the pedals
have to be moved forward to make the shift. They
should be turned lightly, without putting tension
on the chain. If you try to shift while pushing
forward hard on the pedals, as when you are
starting up from a traffic light, the entire drive train
grinds, skips, chatters, and generally sounds as if
it is about to self-destruct. Because the pedals have
to move without much tension in the chain in order
for the shift to be made correctly, you have to learn to
anticipate your gear changes. You must shift to a
lower gear before stopping at a light or slowing too
much on a steep hill, and you must learn to reduce
power momentarily as shifts are made. Conscious

coordination and forethought are required at first, but the process becomes natural after a while.

You will notice that there are no fixed positions of the levers corresponding to particular gears. Since the angle of the chain varies with different gear combinations, the proper positions of the two derailleur cages are interdependent. Therefore, if you shift up two or three gears on the rear cluster, the front derailleur may need a slight adjustment to stop it from rubbing against the chain. Once you have a good idea of the way the changers work, set the gears for a mid-range position, perhaps with the chain on the smaller chainwheel and the center gear of the rear cluster, and take the bike out to practice.

As with learning to balance a bike in the first place, a good place to practice with a ten-speed is in a large, traffic-free area with a slight slope to it. Straddle the bike and get the feel of the brake levers first. Note which lever operates the front brake and which one the rear. It usually is best to squeeze both levers at the same time. At high speeds most of the braking force comes from the front lever. Squeezing the rear one alone does not stop the bike very quickly and may cause the rear wheel to skid out from under you, while applying the front one alone may cause a skid or tend to make you and the bike pitch forward.

Ride the bike around your practice area, getting the feel of the handlebars and the brakes. Try different hand positions on the bars. One of the great advantages of properly shaped dropped handlebars is that they permit a wide variety of hand positions, reducing fatigue on long rides. Braking can be accomplished only from a couple of positions, however, and you have to get used to assuming them quickly when it is necessary to stop. For maximum force, usually needed only on steep descents with heavy loads or in wet weather, the brake levers are squeezed from a low position on the bars. Normally, however, they can be operated from above, with the hands resting on the upper portions of the brake-lever assemblies (the hoods). Brake lightly at first until you get a feel for the pressure required.

Once you have a basic feel for the bike's handling, it is time to learn to shift the gears. Get the bike moving at a comfortable speed, let up a little on the pedals while still turning them at the same speed, and pull the right-hand shift lever back. You will hear and feel the chain being pushed to a larger sprocket at the rear, resulting in a lower gear. Adjust the lever so that the chain isn't making any grinding or clicking noises; then pedal the bike forward again. Notice how much less effort is required to move the bike and how many more times around your feet revolve to travel each yard?

Let up on the pressure again and slowly push the right-hand lever all the way forward. The chain will shift to the smallest rear sprocket and you will be in a much higher gear. The bike then requires a lot more effort to pedal but goes much faster. Try shifting the front derailleur (the left-hand lever) and then work out the combinations between the front and the back. Avoid stopping the bike before the chain has shifted over, since you have to push hard on the pedals when starting up again at the same time that one of the derailleurs is pushing against the chain. This is hard on the bike. Also avoid the two gear combinations that require the chain to cross at the severest angles: the larger front chainwheel to the largest rear sprocket and the smaller front chainwheel to the smallest rear sprocket. The extreme angles are hard on the chain and the gears, and the ratios they provide frequently are duplicated by other combinations anyway (see Chapter 5).

Spend a fair amount of time learning to use the gears effectively. A section of road with hills and very little traffic is ideal. Try to anticipate the changes you need to make to lower gears so that you don't have to shift just as a hill is slowing you down. A good rider shifts gears quickly and exactly with almost no break in pedaling rhythm, but it takes time to develop this skill.

Adjusting the Bike

Though you can learn the basics of riding a ten-speed with virtually any derailleur bike that is not grossly misfitted, becoming a good rider requires that the bike fit you well and that the seat and handlebars are adjusted to match your body build. Details on proper fit are covered in Chapters 4 and 8, but rough approximations are sufficient here. You should be able to straddle the frame comfortably when you are standing on level ground; otherwise the frame is too big and is dangerous for you to ride. If you are using dropped handlebars the saddle should be fairly narrow to prevent chafing. A wider seat and upright bars are fine for a while, but they are not very suitable for riding long distances; if you have them, get them changed as soon as you feel comfortable enough on the bike to do so.

Adjust the seat so that the top is level, at least at the beginning. It should never slope backward and should tilt forward only slightly if you later find that to be a more comfortable position. Adjust the height of the seat so that when you are sitting evenly on it with one leg fully extended, your heel just rests on the pedal. When you pedal with the balls of your feet, as you should, this allows your knee to remain slightly flexed. Be sure that when this adjustment is made there are still *at least* 2½ inches of the seat post sticking into the seat tube. If you permit less overlap than this, there is a serious danger of seat-post breakage. If you cannot raise the seat high enough with the post you have, buy a longer one. If the seat does not go down far enough to allow you to get your heel flat on the pedal, the frame is too large, although if the fit is very close, a different seat or post might make a difference.

When you are beginning, adjust the handlebars so that the stem extension is level with the top of the seat. To loosen the stem so that you can move it up or down, loosen the bolt at the top of the stem several turns and then hit it with something soft enough not to make ugly dents, such as a mallet or a piece of wood struck with a hammer. The bolt is attached to a wedge at the bottom, and driving the bolt down loosens the wedge. Once you have determined the proper adjustment, make sure that *at least* 2½ inches of the stem will stick down into the headset. Having the stem break while you are speeding down a hill can cause a horrible crash. If need be, keep the handlebars lower than the seat rather than leaving less than 2½ inches in the headset.

The binder bolt farther forward on the stem extension obviously loosens the handlebars themselves. Adjust the bolt so that the lower grips tilt down just a bit, then move the brake levers if necessary so that you can lean forward comfortably with your thumbs hooked over the tops of the levers. Usually the levers are moved by loosening the cables, depressing the levers, and loosening screws placed just behind the tops of the levers. Later you may wish to make more subtle adjustments in the handlebar position, but this should give you an adequate fit to begin with.

Steering Positions

One of the primary advantages of well-designed dropped handlebars is that they permit a wide variety of positions for the hands, as well as different degrees of forward lean of the rider's torso. Variety is important to the cycle tourist for comfort, in order to relieve pressure on nerves in the hands and to allow the rider to stress different groups of muscles in the hands, wrists, arms, shoulders, and back. Some handlebar designs are better suited for these purposes than others, a topic discussed more thoroughly in Chapter 8. Any dropped handlebars are adequate at first, but designs intended primarily for racing are less comfortable. Racing-type designs frequently are found, oddly enough, on inexpensive ten-speeds.

Try riding with your hands in a number of positions: on top of the bar, thumbs pointed in; at the bends where the bars go forward, thumbs forward; leaning on the brake levers; and grasping the lower grips. All these positions and their variations have advantages. The lowest position, on the hooks, is the most powerful, enabling the cyclist to put the full strength of arms and torso into the pedaling action. It also is the most streamlined position, cutting wind resistance to a minimum. The tourist's favorite positions tend to be those on top of the bar.

Practice shifting, signaling, braking, and steering from all the handlebar positions so that you can use them comfortably and effectively. It is a good idea to have a friend call out signals for panic stops so that you become practiced at getting to the brakes quickly. As mentioned earlier, another good exercise once you are used to the brakes is to follow a riding companion closely and to have him or her make unexpected stops to hone your reaction time. The most common braking position is from the tops of the brake controls, though greater leverage is available when you brake from the lowest position on the bars.

Toe Clips

As soon as you feel comfortable riding a ten-speed bike, you should install toe clips on the pedals. Toe clips keep your feet properly centered in the correct pedaling position, prevent them from slipping off to one side, and allow power to be transmitted to the pedals during a larger portion of the rotation of the cranks. Proper fitting of toe clips is discussed in Chapter 8.

When you first start to ride with toe clips, you must get used to dealing with two minor problems. The first is getting the toe clips on. Since the clips are attached to the tops of the pedals (if they are the type that has a top and bottom), their weight turns the pedals down, and you have to get used to flipping the pedals right-side-up with your toes. Mount the bike in the usual way, either by swinging one leg over and placing that foot in the pedal first or by putting the near-side foot in the pedal, pushing the bike off, and swinging your other foot over. The second pedal is the tricky one, since the bike will be moving. First pedal a bit with your foot on the underside of the second pedal until the bike picks up speed; then concentrate on flipping the pedal up with a flick of your toe. Slick-soled shoes, including some leather-soled cycling shoes, don't give much traction on some pedals, so you may want to put pieces of tape on the soles to ensure a better grip. Friction tape or some other rough-surface tape works best.

The second problem with toe clips is one of habit rather than facility. You must remember to pull your foot backward from the clip as you come to a stop and lower one foot to the ground. The common habit of cyclists unused to riding with toe clips is to try and slide a foot off to the side of the pedal and place it on the ground just as the bike comes to a stop. I still remember vividly the day that I first started pedaling with toe clips. I came whizzing down the street and stopped smartly at a red light, and as I feeblemindedly tried to slide my foot off the pedal, I toppled majestically off to one side onto the pavement, still mounted and strapped to the pedals. In this respect the novice rider without firmly established habits may be better off than the long-time rider who is just beginning to use the clips. In any case, it is worthwhile making a number of practice stops in your familiar empty parking lot to get used to pulling your foot out of the clip and getting it back in as you start up again.

Appendix II

Building a Wheel

THERE ARE A number of methods of wheel building, but this one is fairly straightforward. The directions that follow are for building a cross-three wheel, the most common type. A high-flange hub is shown for clarity, though I recommend using a low-flange one. Make sure your rims and hubs have the same number of holes, usually thirty-six for touring purposes. The spoke holes in the hub may be countersunk on both sides, or each hole may be countersunk on only one side. Note that the countersinking is not for the head of the spoke, as you might assume, but for the bend, so that it does not pass over a sharp edge. When you buy your spokes, the bike shop should have a reference manual showing the proper lengths. Take your hubs and rims along.

Determine whether you have a left-handed (more common) or right-handed rim. To do this, hold the rim in your hands and rotate it until you are looking at the valve hole from the outside of the rim. Note that the spoke ferrules are staggered, first to one side and then to the other. If you hold the rim up and down as though you were looking at the wheel from behind the bike, the ferrule above the valve hole will be to the left on a left-handed rim and to the right on a right-handed rim. The illustrations depict a left-handed rim.

Get all your materials together before you start. When building a rear wheel, it is preferable to use spokes a couple of millimeters shorter for the freewheel side, though this is not essential. If you do, be sure to lay the shorter spokes to one side and the longer ones to the other. You also should have a can of oil, a rag, a spoke wrench, the hub, the rim, and a screwdriver that fits the slots in the nipples.

49. LACING A WHEEL.

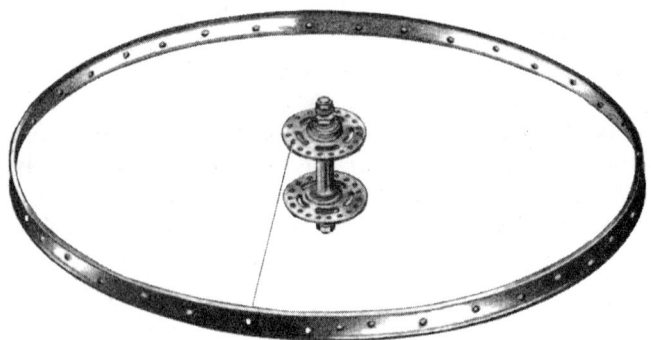

A. Set the rim and the hub in front of you with the valve hole toward you. If you are building a rear wheel, start with

*the freewheel side of the hub (with the threads) facing
up. This upper side will be the right side of the wheel, and
the first nine spokes inserted will be the trailing spokes on
the right side, the ones that pull the wheel around when you
are pedaling. Insert one spoke up through a hole in the
top flange, making sure that it is countersunk on the upper
side. The spoke is head down, bend up. Put the end
through the first upper ferrule to the left of the valve hole.
On a left-handed rim, as shown, this is the second ferrule
over, and on a right-handed rim it is the first ferrule over.
Put a drop of oil in a nipple and screw it on two turns only.*

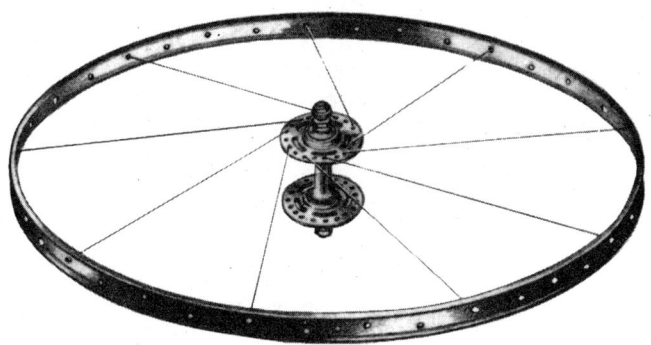

*B. Insert another spoke up through the second hole
clockwise around the upper flange from the first, put the
end through the fourth ferrule clockwise from the first, oil
a nipple, and screw on the nipple just two turns. The hole in
the flange should be countersunk on the upper side, and
the ferrule should be on the upper side of the rim. Repeat
this operation all the way around the rim, using a total of
nine spokes in a 36-hole wheel; these will be the right-hand
trailing, or pulling, spokes. If you are lacing a rear wheel
and have a shorter set of spokes for the freewheel side,
these nine spokes should be short ones.*

C. Turn the rim and the hub in opposite directions so that the nine trailing spokes are pulled tight. Count three spokes counterclockwise from the valve hole and locate the first unused hole in the upper flange of the hub counterclockwise past the third spoke. Insert a spoke down through this hole (head up, bend down) and bring it through the first upper ferrule counterclockwise from the valve hole. Oil a nipple and screw it on two turns. This is the first right-hand leading spoke. As you bring the spoke across the three trailing spokes it crosses, pass it below the first two, but lift it above the third; the two will rest against one another.

D. Continue around the wheel counterclockwise, inserting each of the right-hand leading spokes on the upper side of the wheel the same way, running to the upper ferrules and passing each spoke under the first two crossing spokes and over the third. Again, these spokes should be *short ones if you are using two lengths for a rear wheel. All the spokes on the right side of the wheel are now in place.*

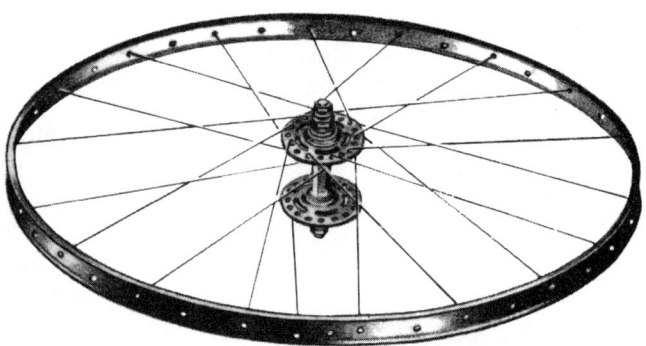

E. Leave the wheel lying the same way, with the valve hole facing you, and find the first spoke to the left of the valve hole (the first one you put in). Kneel above the wheel so that you can look straight down on the hub and then, from the hole this first spoke goes through, sight down to the lower flange. The holes in the lower flange are offset from those in the upper one. Locate the first hole in the lower flange counterclockwise from the one occupied by your first spoke. (If you have a right-handed rim instead of a left-handed rim, locate the first hole clockwise instead.)

Run a spoke down through this hole so that it emerges head up (inside) and bend down (outside). Check to make sure that the hole in the hub is countersunk on the outside. Normally it is, but if yours isn't, you will have to chamfer it yourself or run the bend on the inside instead, which is not desirable. Bring this spoke through the first lower ferrule clockwise from the valve hole, oil a nipple, and screw it on two turns. On a left-handed rim this ferrule will be next to the valve hole; on a right-handed rim it will be one ferrule over. Note that the spokes on either side of the valve hole run away from it, so that the space is clear for pumping a tire. It is possible, but wrong, to lace the wheel so that the spokes cross adjacent to the valve hole.

Continue clockwise, running a spoke down through every other hole in the lower flange and bringing it through every fourth ferrule in the rim. These spokes should be *long ones if you are using two lengths for a rear wheel. They are the left-hand trailing, or pulling, spokes. There should be a total of nine.*

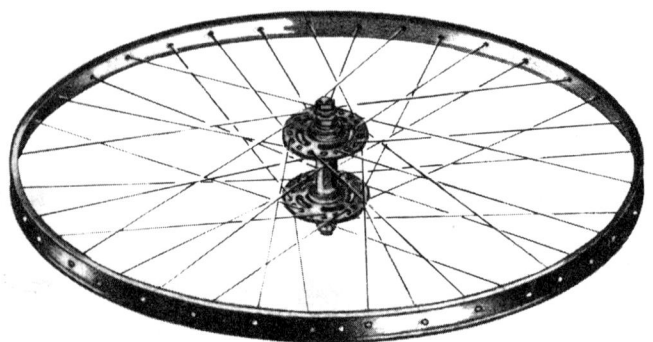

F. Lace the left-hand leading spokes just as you did the right-hand ones. With the wheel in the same position, run them up through the hub holes (heads outside, bends inside) and lace them so that they stay on the inside of the first two trailing spokes and run outside of the third. Oil the nipples and screw them on just two turns. The wheel is completely laced.

Truing the Wheel

The final procedure consists of tightening all the spokes equally to produce a round, perfectly aligned wheel, the main art of wheel building. The most important ingredient is patience. Work slowly, tightening each spoke a little at a time. The best way to achieve a perfect wheel is to maintain the circular shape of the rim, rather than tightening one section too rapidly, distorting the circle, and then trying to compensate.

The first step is to take the slack out of the wheel, not trying to put any tension on the spokes, but simply bringing the nipples up against the ferrules. Go around the wheel turning each nipple one turn at a time until the slack is out, skipping any that are starting to get tight. Next you need to mount the wheel in some sort of truing jig. It is best to use a regular truing stand since it makes the job easier and faster, but you can true the wheels using the brakes on your bike as indicators. Mount the wheel in the appropriate fork and adjust the brakes so that they are equidistant on both sides and so that the tops of the blocks are just above the rim. Set some sort of straightedge across the top as a roundness indicator. As you proceed, adjust your guides to closer tolerances.

The main principles of truing are to keep working all the way around the wheel, tightening each spoke just a little at a time and trying to keep the tension on all the spokes equal. (The right side of the rear wheel will be tighter than the left, but the spokes within either side should be at the same tension.) Work out each small irregularity as it appears, making corrections with groups of spokes rather than with single ones. Wobbles from side to side are easy to correct once you understand the principle. If the wheel has a wobble to the left, you tighten the spokes in that area that pull from the right flange. The most important adjustments, however, are in the roundness of the wheel, and roundness is harder to achieve. When you find a flat spot starting to develop, slack off on the group of spokes in that area.

Because of the dish in the rear wheel, once the slack is out you usually should start off by tightening all the way around on the right side. Remember to tighten each nipple a little at a time. Once the wheel is centered, start tightening both sides equally.

You should end up with a wheel that has tight spokes. A group of four spokes should feel springy and equally tensioned when you squeeze it. You want all the nipples to be tight, but not so tight that they are starting to pull the ferrules out of the rim. Once the wheel seems true and tight, take it out of the jig, put it flat on the floor so that it rests on one end of the hub, and push on opposite sides of the rim. Turn it around, stressing it at 4-inch intervals all the way around. Turn the wheel over and repeat this procedure on the other side. The wheel should feel strong, but have a little give. You will hear lots of twangings as various spokes relieve rotational stresses that have been left in the wheel. Put the wheel back in the jig and retrue it. Repeat the procedure until the wheel stays true; this stressing process is the key to having a wheel remain true after a couple of weeks of riding.

Once you have finished building the wheel, put it on your bike and go for a ride. There is a special satisfaction in speeding down a steep grade and watching the wheel you've built yourself spin perfectly true, without a hint of a wobble. You also won't have any problem truing a wheel in the field once you have built your own.

Appendix III

Equipment Suppliers

THERE ARE THOUSANDS of fine bicycle shops across the United States, and there are many good reasons, already mentioned, for buying bicycles and equipment at a local shop. However, lower prices, greater selection, distance from local shops, and other factors often make it worthwhile to buy some items from mail-order houses. This is particularly true when buying many specialized components and touring gear, which can be quite hard to obtain locally, particularly at shops catering to racers rather than tourists.

The precautions you must take when purchasing components by mail have been covered thoroughly in the text. If you have any doubt as to fit, it is better to write to a supplier in advance than to order a part and hope that you will get the right size. In general, a catalogue that is specific about sizes and compatibility indicates that the mail-order house is more conscientious about such matters. After you have received a part, be careful to check its fit before trying to mount it on your bike. If you damage any threads, score a stem or seat post, or otherwise mar a part, you are not likely to get a refund or a replacement, even if the company made the mistake. Check all sew-ups before gluing them.

The following list of suppliers is bound to be somewhat arbitrary, particularly with regard to small companies doing a fine job of distributing specialized products. I have tried to include all the major mail-order houses which distribute reasonably complete catalogues. Some smaller companies that I know provide good service or a unique selection of gear also are included, as are a few suppliers of camping equipment that either make gear of particular interest to cyclists or offer an extremely wide selection. All the companies listed are mail-order establishments. I have not included manufacturers who do not sell directly to the public nor shops that do not sell through catalogues. Comments regarding service are nec-essarily incomplete, since I have had to rely on my own experience and that of friends. Readers also should understand that the information here is bound to become dated; prices rise, new companies enter the market while old ones fold, and service over the years can improve or decline.

American Youth Hostels, Metropolitan Council, 132 Spring Street, New York, NY 10012, runs a 'hostel store.' The organization markets a variety of packs and camping equipment, most of which are reasonably priced and on the heavy side.

Bikecology, P.O. Box 1880, Santa Monica, CA
90406, is one of the largest mail-order houses
in the United States handling quality bicycle
equipment, particularly the latest Japanese
components. Its catalogue is informative and
well worth the $1 charge. Generally the firm's
prices are the lowest available. The catalog
includes weights for most items.

Bike Warehouse, 215 Main Street, New
Middletown, OH 44442, will send four catalogs
a year for $1.25. Prices are competitive, but
reports of service are mixed.

Branford Bike Shop, 202 Main St., Branford, CT
06405, is a small mail-order operation with a
free catalogue and flyers. The company tries
hard and offers some very good prices. The
catalogue includes weights for most items.

Cannondale, 35 Pulaski St., Stamford, CT 06902,
is primarily a manufacturer but also handles
mail orders through a catalogue. The company
makes the only generally available bike trailer
with decent bearings and wheels, which is
worth considering if you want to take kids on
tours as passengers or have some other reason
to haul ridiculously large loads. The trailer
weighs as much as a bike. Cannondale also
makes panniers and other touring bags as well
as some camping gear.

Cycle Goods, 17710 Leeman Dr., Minnetonka,
MN 55343, publishes a $3 catalogue that in-
cludes directions for servicing some models
of derailleurs and three-speed hubs. The company concentrates on older components and
parts for inexpensive bikes, but also sells some
useful tools and parts for a number of standard,
older components. The catalogue generally
does not include weights. Slow service.

Early Winters, 110 Prefontaine Pl. S., Seattle,

WA 98104, manufactures high-quality, innovative camping equipment, usually lightweight. The firm also sells other good-quality lightweight items for cycle camping, such as Lexan utensils. Good service.

EMS, Vose Farm Rd., Peterborough, NH 03458, offers one of the most complete catalogues of lightweight camping gear, including a few bicycle packs. The catalogue currently is free, though the company has charged for it in the past, and includes some useful information and comparison charts. Generally good-quality equipment.

Flying Dutchman, 155 Elm, Denver, CO 80220, publishes a $2 catalogue that includes many standard, high-quality brands of bikes and components. Of special interest to short riders is a line of stock frames proportioned for small riders. The catalogue lists some weights.

Frostline, Frostline Circle, Denver, CO 80241, markets kits for making lightweight camping equipment, including bicycle panniers. The catalogue is free.

Holubar, P.O. Box 7, Boulder, CO 80306, publishes a free catalogue of quality lightweight camping equipment, including a few bicycle packs.

Kettering Bike Shop, 3120 Wilmington Pike, Dayton, OH 45429, publishes an excellent $1 catalogue that includes most weights. You must ask permission to return items, which is a nuisance, but the company responds quickly. The catalogue is particularly useful for ordering frame-building materials.

Lickton's Cycle City, 310 Lake St., Oak Park, IL 60302, sells its catalogue for $1, which is refundable with an order of $20 or more. The company offers a good selection of quality components but accepts only phone orders with payment by credit card, COD, certified check, or money order. The catalogue lists most weights.

Marmot Mountain Works, 331 S. 13th St., Grand Junction, CO 81501, publishes a free catalogue of excellent and innovative lightweight camping gear. The firm's prices are high.

Moor and Mountain, 63 Park St., Andover, MA 01810, offers a free catalogue of lightweight camping gear, including some items for cycle touring. Unlike most backpacking suppliers, the company has a selection of gear that reflects an understanding of the needs of bicycle tourists.

Mountain Safety Research, 631 S. 96th St., Seattle, WA 98108, publishes a $1 catalogue of equipment primarily intended for climbers. MSR carries a variety of camping gear but is of interest to cyclists mainly for its helmets, stoves, and headlamps.

Palo Alto Bicycles, P.O. Box 1276, Palo Alto, CA 94302, publishes a carefully thought out, free catalogue. The firm's prices are competitive, and service is good. Although the catalogue is not as complete as Bikecology's, all the components offered are of very high quality. Most weights are listed, and many are tabulated in weight comparison charts.

Recreational Equipment, Inc., P.O. Box C-88125, Seattle, WA 98140, is a cooperative that publishes a free catalogue but requires a one-time $2 membership fee, entitling you to year-end rebates of approximately 10 percent. REI's catalogue offers one of the most complete selections of lightweight camping gear available

and includes some bike bags. Although the
co-op advertises a catalogue of bicycles and
accessories, I have never been able to obtain
one. REI has excellent buys on some items, but
its down gear is not up to par.

Rosewood Cycle Supply, P.O. Box 3163, Cama-
rillo, CA 93010, sends out a small catalogue
and special flyers free of charge. The company
offers good buys on some items.

Ski Hut, P.O. Box 309, Berkeley, CA 94701, makers
of Trailwise gear, publishes a free catalogue of
lightweight camping equipment. The company's
down gear is excellent.

Synergy Works, 255 4th St., Oakland, CA 94607,
publishes a free catalogue of its carefully
designed outdoor clothing.

Touring Cyclist Shop, P.O. Box 4009, Boulder,
CO 80302, offers a small, free catalogue of the
cycling luggage it manufactures and other
items to meet the needs of bicycle tourists. The
firm created the designs used in most modern
panniers, and workmanship is always superb.
Good service.

Warmlite, RFD 4, Box 398, Gilford, NH 03246,
publishes a free catalogue of its *lightweight*
camping gear that includes some of the
best thought-out—and most opinionated—
discussions of equipment design you can find.
Jack Stephenson is responsible for a great
number of the new designs in lightweight
equipment that have appeared in the last
fifteen years. Good service.

Wilshire West Bicycles, 11841 Wilshire Blvd.,
Los Angeles, CA 90405, publishes an informative, free catalogue of well-chosen items;
all weights are listed, including weights
for tools.

Appendix IV

Organizations

BY NATURE, TOURING is an anarchical sport, and most touring cyclists prefer things that way. Remember, however, that roads in the United Stated originally were paved as a result of organized pressure by bicyclists. Nowadays, cyclists lack political clout when highways and intersections are designed and built and when traffic laws are formulated and enforced. The cyclist, who ought to be a social hero in a society facing a severe energy crisis, is considered to be a nuisance or a pariah instead. Bicycling organizations can help correct this situation and also sponsor group tours, which are fun.

Local bike clubs are too numerous and change too quickly to list here. *Bicycling* magazine periodically publishes a list of local groups, and the **Bicycle Institute of America,** a trade organization, will send you a free copy of its directory of bicycle clubs if you write to them at 122 E. 42nd St., New York, NY 10017.

The oldest bicycle club in America deserves special mention. The **League of American Wheelmen,** which welcomes wheelwomen as well, dates back to 1880 and has been revived during the last few years both as a club and as an advocacy group for cyclists. The $14 membership fee entitles you to a subscription to the *L.A.W. Bulletin.* The organization is interested in all forms of touring, commuting, and other cycling activities aside from racing. The club's address is 19 S. Bothwell, Palatine, IL 60067.

Bikecentennial is an organization of cyclists interested in the development and promotion of long-distance touring routes. It was founded in a successful effort to research and mark a scenic, low-traffic transcontinental bike route in celebration of the United States Bicentennial. The group continues to work on other long-distance bike routes, including one in the Rockies (the Great Parks Route) and one paralleling the Mississippi River (the Great River Route). Bikecentennial publishes guides to its trails, brochures with touring advice, and a bimonthly newsletter, as well as offering group tours. The membership fee is $12 for an individual and $17 for a family. The organization's mailing address is P.O. Box 8308, Missoula, MT 59807.

American Youth Hostels is the American affiliate of the international organization of youth hostels. The group organizes trips and coordinates hostels located in the United States. The $14 membership fee entitles you to a membership card that permits you to stay (for a fee) at both American hostels and any other hostels listed in the *International Youth Hostel Handbook.* The handbook consists of separate volumes covering different parts of the world. Memberships and handbooks can be obtained from the American Youth Hostels National Campus, Delaplane, VA 22025, or from any affiliated local hostel.

The **International Bicycle Touring Society** is a group that organizes bike tours in other countries. Membership entitles you to the schedule and the privilege of participating in the tours. The touring style is moderate, with nights spent in hotels, pensions, or bed and breakfast places. Sag-wagons frequently are used. The club's address is 846 Prospect St., La Jolla, CA 92037.

The **Cyclists' Touring Club** is a British club dedicated to touring both in the British Isles and in the rest of Europe. Its handbook of bed and breakfast establishments in Great Britain is very helpful, and the club arranges tours, distributes maps, and operates a travel service. Membership is about $12 at the time this is written. The club's address is Cotterell House, 69 Meadrow, Goldalming, Surrey, England GU7 3HS.

Appendix V

Additional Reading and Resources

THERE ARE NUMEROUS approaches to both
bicycling and bicycle touring. This book em-
phasizes one particular style—the use of very
lightweight equipment and a responsive bike
designed for good roads. For differing points of view
on cycling, I suggest that you read through some
back issues of the two major bicycling magazines:
Bicycling (33 E. Minor St., Emmaus, PA 18049)
and *Bike World* (Box 366, Mountain View, CA
94040). Some excellent publications are available
to cyclists who become members of cycling organizations, particularly the League of American
Wheelmen and the Cyclists' Touring Club (see
Appendix IV for addresses). Local publications
often prove more valuable than national ones,

but their life spans tend to be short, and quality is likely to vary from issue to issue.

Cycling and Touring

One of the most delightful general books about touring and bicycling in general is Tom Cuthbertson's *Bike Tripping* (Berkeley, Calif.: Ten Speed Press, 1972), which includes a final chapter on frames written by the fine builder Albert Eisentraut. For a compendium of accurate technical information and strong opinions about cycling that are the product of many years on the roads, I suggest *Delong's Guide to Bicycles and Bicycling* (Philadelphia: Chilton, 1978), written by long-time cyclist Fred Delong. Also worthwhile is *Richard's Bicycle Book,* by Richard Ballantine (New York: Ballantine, 1978).

Bike-building, Design, and Repair Manuals

The books mentioned above also provide a reasonable amount of information and personal opinion on frames and equipment. New products are reviewed regularly in cycling magazines and in mail-order catalogues. Those interested in the details of frame design may want to start by reading Delong's book, the Eisentraut chapter in Cuthbertson, and Joe Kossack's *Bicycle Frames* booklet (Mountain View, Calif.: World Publications, 1975). For a complete treatment, read the *Proteus Frame Building Handbook,* edited by Barry Konig (College Park, Md.: Proteus, 1976). It can be obtained from the Kettering Bike Shop, listed in Appendix III.

The best basic book on bicycle repair is *Anybody's Bike Book,* by Tom Cuthbertson (Berkeley, Calif.: Ten Speed Press, 1971). The Ballantine and Delong books listed earlier also provide useful information. Another worthwhile book for beginners is Xyzyx Information Corporation's *How To Maintain and Repair Your 5, 10 & 15-Speed Bicycle* (New York: McGraw-Hill, 1978). For thorough coverage, many people have found *Glenn's Complete Bicycle Manual,* by Clarence Coles and Harold Glenn (New York: Crown, 1973), to be useful, but I have not. The authors spend a lot of time telling you how to take bearings out of a Sting-Ray and very little time on the sticky problems you might need help with and would expect a large, complete manual to cover. The definitive book on threads, compatibility of components, spoke length, and the like is Howard Sutherland's *Handbook for Bicycle Mechanics* (Berkeley, Calif.: Sutherland Publications, 1977), which can be ordered from a number of the mail-order houses listed in Appendix III.

The best publication on bicycle wheels is Robert Wright's booklet *Building Bicycle Wheels* (Mountain View, Calif.: World Publications, 1976).

Books on Camping

Bicycle campers often encounter articles and books that either recommend equipment that is altogether too heavy or advocate wrapping a plastic sheet around your body and sleeping in the bushes, guaranteeing an early start the next morning. My *Freewheeling: The Bicycle Camping Book* (Harrisburg, Pa.: Stackpole, 1974) presents a somewhat heavier and slower style of touring than the one advocated here. A lot of good information can be culled from books about backpacking, including Colin Fletcher's *The New Complete Walker* (New York: Knopf, 1974) and my *America's*

Backpacking Book (New York: Scribner's, 1981).
Also excellent is John Hart's *Walking Softly in the
Wilderness: The Sierra Club Guide to Backpacking*
(San Francisco: Sierra Club Books, 1977).

Touring Guides

There are many guides to local cycling tours
available, primarily in neighborhood bike shops,
bookstores, and outdoor specialty shops. Little
has been written for American cyclists traveling
abroad, however, where the need is greater. Most
of the guidebooks that do exist deal more with
elementary cycling technique than with touring in
other countries. Karen and Gary Hawkins' *Bicycle
Touring in Europe* (New York: Pantheon, 1973)
offers some good information and suggests a
number of interesting trips. Good general information on costs and strategies for obtaining accommodations can be found in Arthur Frommer's
Europe on $10 a Day (New York, Arthur Frommer,
Inc., revised annually) and in the other Frommer
guides, though these books tend to focus on large
cities. The *CTC Handbook* published annually by
the Cyclists' Touring Club (see Appendix IV for
address) includes a useful listing of bed and
breakfast establishments in Great Britain that
welcome cyclists and charge reasonable rates.

Campground Directories

The standard directory is Rand McNally's
Campground and Trailer Park Guide, published in
separate editions for the eastern and western
United States and updated annually. AAA has a
useful series of booklet-sized directories, covering
about a half-dozen regions of the United States;
these are free to members.

Maps

See Chapter 15 for general information, recommendations, and cautions about maps. Topographic maps can be obtained from the United
States Geological Survey (the address east of the
Mississippi is Washington, DC 20242; for the
western states it is Denver, CO 80225). Some
regional USGS offices also stock maps. For trips
abroad, a catalogue of road maps for many
countries is available from the American Map
Company, 1926 Broadway, New York, NY 10023.

Checklist for Bicycle Tours

Asterisks indicate items most likely to be carried by the lightweight tourist. *Take only what you need.*

Special Items

* panniers and
    other packs
* stuff sacks or
    plastic bags
* water bottles
* map(s)
  compass
  guidebook
  map measurer
* first-aid kit
* money
* travelers checks
  credit cards
  locking device

* leg light or
    Belt Beacon
  spare bulb
    and batteries
* passport or
    other identification
* watch

To Wear While Riding

* helmet
* sunglasses
* rearview mirror
* cycling jersey or
    other shirt
* cycling gloves

To Wear While Riding (con't)

* cycling shorts
* socks
* cycling shoes
    with cleats
  underwear

Clothing for Changing Weather

* arm warmers
* leg warmers
  cycling tights or
    warm-up pants
  long-sleeved jersey
* sweater, vest,
    or pile jacket
  windbreaker (if rain
    suit does not double)
* wool hat
  sun hat
  warm mittens
* rain suit
* booties for
    rain or cold

Clothing to Wear Off the Bike

* shoes for walking
* long pants
  skirt
  sport jacket
  dressy shirt or blouse
  down jacket
* underwear
* bathing suit

Spare Clothing

* cycling shorts
* jersey or tee-shirt
* underwear
* socks

Miscellaneous Personal Gear

  glasses or contact
    lenses and spares
* pocket knife (with can
    opener, corkscrew,
    awl, bottle opener,
    and screwdrivers)
* toilet paper
* sunscreen
* hand cleaner
* all-purpose, biode-
    gradable liquid soap
* small towel
  bandana
* tooth brush
* tooth powder
* dental floss
* comb or brush
* nail clippers
  razor
  mirror
  feminine napkins
    or tampons
  other toilet and
    grooming items
* petroleum jelly
* book

Camping Gear

*tent or other shelter
 ground cloth or
  bivouac sack
*sleeping bag
*pad or air mattress
*stove
*fuel
*pots
 frying pan
*utensils
*cup
*bowl
*headlamp or flashlight
 spare batteries
*spare bulb
*butane lighter or
  matches in
  waterproof case
*water carrier, one
  gallon collapsible
 water purification
  tablets or solution
*pot scrubber in film can
*insect repellent

*condiments and
  beverage mixes
 extra food

Repair Items and Spares

*repair kit (see page 228)
*pump
*tape
*parachute cord
 spare tire(s)
 spare tube
*sewing kit
 pedal strap
*spokes

Hobby Items

camera, film, film
  mailers,
   photographic gear
binoculars
nature or cultural
  guides
fishing gear
writing materials

Index